International Series in Operations Research & Management Science

Volume 288

More information about this series at http://www.springer.com/series/6161

Marcus Matthias Keupp
Editor

The Security of Critical Infrastructures

Risk, Resilience and Defense

Springer

Editor
Marcus Matthias Keupp
Department of Defense Economics
Military Academy at the Swiss Federal
Institute of Technology Zurich
Birmensdorf, Switzerland

ISSN 0884-8289 ISSN 2214-7934 (electronic)
International Series in Operations Research & Management Science
ISBN 978-3-030-41825-0 ISBN 978-3-030-41826-7 (eBook)
https://doi.org/10.1007/978-3-030-41826-7

This Springer imprint is published by the registered company Springer Nature Switzerland AG.
The registered company address is: Gewerbestrasse 11, 6330 Cham, Switzerland

Preface

Itaque si qui voluerit ex his commentariis animadvertere et eligere genus structurae, perpetuitatis poterit rationem habere.
—Vitruvius, *De architectura*, liber secundus, VIII(8)

Critical infrastructures are now a target for intentional attacks. This volume responds to this challenge. It analyzes the risk structure of such attacks, the resilience with which critical infrastructures may withstand them, and the defenses available to fight them.

This volume represents 5 years of work. Many experts from reputed institutions have contributed chapters. Six among them served in the militia system of the Swiss Armed Forces, combining and leveraging their civilian and military expertise. All authors have delivered contributions that are of interest to national defense, homeland security, academic research, and practical infrastructure operations.

It is always a challenge to find a balance between specialization and generalization. As the editor of this volume, my approach was to interpret Switzerland as a densely populated model economy, both regarding human beings and complex critical infrastructure networks. This environment provides excellent conditions for scenario modeling and simulation. I sincerely hope that the solutions this volume offers will be transferable and applicable to many other economies. Many authors have provided generally applicable models and code, and I invite future research to expand and build on the contributions presented here.

While editing the volume I could always rely on the support of my team of assistants, and it is to them that I express my gratitude. Dimitri Percia David, Kilian Cuche, Adrien Coste, and Sébastien Gillard have all contributed significantly to the coordination of a complex LaTeX template and production schedule. Finally, I thank my executive editor at Springer Nature, Dr. Christian Rauscher, who always supported the work and positioned it in the renowned *International Series in Operations Research & Management Science*.

The challenge to defend infrastructure against intentional attack is certainly an architectural one. As historically grown amalgams of infrastructures are replaced, a systematic and defense-oriented approach to the construction of novel generations should be considered after much careful scenario analysis. Now the readers must judge whether or not these notes are productive for this purpose, and I hope they live up to Vitruvius' immortal words: Choose your structure pondering these notes, and you will have something that will last.

Birmensdorf ZH, Switzerland Marcus Matthias Keupp
April 2020

Contents

About the Authors

Donnino Anderhalden received a Doctorate in Theoretical Physics from the University of Zurich, Switzerland, in 2013. Since then, he has been working in the reinsurance industry, first as a pricing actuary and currently as a risk management actuary. His main interests involve various aspects of quantitative and qualitative risk management, in particular assessments of emerging risks such as cyber and terrorism, as well as insurability analysis.

Philipp Baumann received his BSc, MSc, and PhD in Business Administration from the University of Bern (Switzerland) in 2007, 2009, and 2013, respectively. He did his postdoc at the Department of Industrial Engineering and Operations Research at the University of California, Berkeley. Currently, he is associate professor at the Department of Business Administration at the University of Bern. His research interests include optimization in finance, project management and project scheduling, production planning and control, machine learning, and network-based optimization. He has published in European Journal of Operational Research, Flexible Services and Manufacturing Journal, IEEE Transactions on Big Data, International Journal of Production Research, Journal of Scheduling, and Mathematical Methods of Operations Research.

Reinhard Bürgy received a Doctorate in Economics and Social Sciences from the University of Fribourg, Switzerland, in 2014. After spending about 3 years at Polytechnique Montréal and GERAD, Canada, from 2015 to 2018, he returned to the University of Fribourg where he is currently a senior researcher and lecturer. Reinhard's main research interests are in the development of optimization models and methods for solving practically relevant planning, routing, and scheduling problems. In particular, he has been developing generic combinatorial optimization algorithms for solving job-shop scheduling problems with complex process characteristics and complicated objective functions. His algorithms are, for example, applied to (re-)schedule trains in large rail networks and to schedule robots, machines, and automated guided vehicles in flexible manufacturing systems.

Furthermore, Reinhard is broadly interested in combinatorial optimization, network flow theory and applications, operations and service management, and revenue management.

Eoghan Casey is professor at the School of Criminal Justice and a partner of Digital Forensics Solutions, where he performs R&D related to digital forensics and cybersecurity. Previously, as Chief Scientist of the Defense Cyber Crime Center (DC3), he prioritized research and development across multiple organizational units and provided strategic and technical guidance to navigate evolving challenges in digital forensic science and data breach investigation. He has consulted on a wide range of digital investigations, including network intrusions with an international scope. He has delivered expert testimony in civil and criminal cases and has submitted expert reports and prepared trial exhibits for computer forensic and cybercrime cases. He wrote the foundational book Digital Evidence and Computer Crime, now in its third edition, and he created the advanced smartphone forensics courses taught worldwide. He has also coauthored several advanced technical books including Malware Forensics and the Handbook of Digital Forensics and Investigation. Since 2004, he has been Editor in Chief of Digital Investigation: The International Journal of Digital Forensics & Incident Response, publishing cutting edge work by and for practitioners and researchers. He was nominated as CASE Presiding Director to lead development of an international standard for sharing cyber-investigation information. He serves on the Digital Forensic Research Workshop (DFRWS) Board of Directors and helps organize digital forensic research conferences in the EU, US, and APAC. He also contributes to forensic science definitions, guidelines, and standards as Executive Secretary of the Digital/Multimedia Scientific Area Committee (DMSAC) of the Organization of Scientific Area Committees (OSAC).

Carlo Ghezzi is an emeritus professor at Politecnico di Milano, Italy, where he has been Professor and Chair of Software Engineering, Department Chair, Rector's delegate for research, and member of the Academic Senate and of the Board of Governors. He has been President of Informatics Europe. He is ACM Fellow, IEEE Fellow, Member of Academia Europaea, and Member of the Italian Academy of Sciences (Istituto Lombardo). He has been awarded the ACM SIGSOFT Outstanding Research Award (2015) and the Distinguished Service Award (2006). He has been on the evaluation board of several international research projects and institutions in Europe, Japan, and the USA. He has been a regular member of the program committee of important conferences in the software engineering field, such as the ICSE and ESEC/FSE, for which he also served as Program and General Chair. He gave keynotes at several international conferences, including ESEC/FSE and ICSE. He has been the Editor in Chief of the ACM Transactions on Software Engineering and Methodology and associate editor of Communications of the ACM, IEEE Transactions on Software Engineering, and Science of Computer Programming. His research has been focusing on software engineering and programming languages. He has been especially interested in methods and tools to improve the dependability of adaptable and evolvable distributed applications, such as service-oriented architectures and ubiquitous/pervasive computer applications. He coauthored more than 200 papers and 8 books. He coordinated several national and international (EU funded) research projects and has been awarded an Advanced Grant from the European Research Council.

Sébastien Gillard received a Master of Science in Physics from the University of Fribourg, Switzerland, in 2016. He specializes in computational physics and statistics, in particular, data analysis and applied modeling with various software applications, and analytical and numerical resolution methods for differential equations. His master thesis focused on recommender systems; results from this thesis were published (with colleagues) in Physica A. His current research interest is the application of insights from recommender systems to critical infrastructure defense, including the development of code that can power deep learning algorithms.

Timo Kehrer is a professor at Humboldt-Universität zu Berlin, heading the Model-Driven Software Engineering Group at the Department of Computer Science. He received diplomas in Computer Engineering and Computer Science in 2007 and 2011, respectively, and a PhD in Computer Science from the Faculty of Natural Sciences and Technology at the University of Siegen in 2015. He worked as a research assistant in the Software Engineering and Database Systems Group at University of Siegen from 2011 to 2015, as a postdoctoral research fellow in the Dependable Evolvable Pervasive Software Engineering Group at Politecnico di Milano from 2015 to 2016, and as a visiting researcher at the Department of Computer Science at University of Leicester in 2016. He has active research interests in various fields of model-driven and model-based software and systems engineering, with a particular focus on various phenomena of software and system evolution.

Marcus Matthias Keupp is the editor of this volume. He chairs the Department of Defense Economics at the Military Academy of the Swiss Federal Institute of Technology, Zurich. He was educated at the University of Mannheim (Germany) and Warwick Business School, and he obtained his PhD from the University of St. Gallen (Switzerland). He has authored, coauthored, and edited eight books and more than 30 peer-reviewed journal articles and received numerous awards for his academic achievements. His interdisciplinary work concentrates on strategic, organizational, and innovation management, with a strong focus on econometric and psychometric methods. This book is the result of a 5-year research project he created and led.

Vincent Lenders is the director of the Cyber-Defence Campus and of the C4I division at armasuisse Science and Technology. He is also the cofounder and chairman of the executive boards of the OpenSky Network and Electrosense associations. He graduated with an MSc and PhD degree in Electrical Engineering and Information

Technology from ETH Zurich and was also postdoctoral researcher at Princeton University. He has served for 8 years as a research director on "Cyberspace and Information" for armasuisse Science and Technology and he was industrial director of the Zurich Information Security and Privacy Center (ZISC) at ETH Zurich from 2012 to 2016. His research work has appeared in more than 120 publications at peer-reviewed international conferences and journals and has received various best paper awards.

Jonas I. Liechti graduated as a physicist (dipl. phys. EPFL, MSc) in 2012 from the Ecole Polytechnique Fédérale de Lausanne and obtained a PhD from ETH Zurich in 2019. His research interests focus on the structural description of complex systems and the effect of structure and its dynamics on propagation processes, such as the spread of information or disease. Research projects comprise theoretical work in clustering—a field in unsupervised learning, a machine learning domain—simulation and data-driven studies in the field of epidemiology and contributions in the field of animal social societies, in particular social insects and rodents.

Ivan Martinovic is a professor at the Department of Computer Science, University of Oxford. His research focuses on designing, measuring, and evaluating the security of distributed systems. He currently focusses on authentication and intrusion detection, mobile security, and the analysis of trade-offs between security and system's performance. Ivan Martinovic has published more than 70 papers in these areas and he serves as a steering committee member of the ACM Conference on Security and Privacy in Wireless and Mobile Networks. For his research on the security and privacy of wireless data-links used in aviation, Ivan Martinovic received the MPLS Impact Award 2017. Before coming to Oxford, he worked at the Security Research Lab, UC Berkeley and at the Secure Computing and Networking Center, UC Irvine. He obtained his PhD from TU Kaiserslautern and MSc from TU Darmstadt, Germany. His PhD thesis on wireless security was awarded the Best Computer Science Dissertation Award by the German Association for Data Protection and Data Security (GDD).

Jean-Claude Metzger holds both an MSc and PhD in Mechanical Engineering from ETH Zurich. During his undergraduate studies, he focused on robotics, systems, and control and conducted his master thesis at the Massachusetts Institute of Technology (MIT) in Cambridge, USA. His doctoral thesis focused on the development and clinical evaluation of a hand rehabilitation device for stroke patients. Jean-Claude started his professional career in 2014 as a project and team leader with Roche Diagnostics where he was responsible for the hardware development of a post-analytics device for in vitro diagnostics heading a team of six engineers. In December 2017, Jean-Claude has joined the medical device start-up company hemotune and is leading there the development of hemotune's blood purification device.

Eva Morstein received her Bachelor's and Master's degree in Business Administration from the University of Bern in 2017 and 2019, respectively, majoring in Financial Management. She currently works as a data scientist, analyzing personalized marketing, customer segmentation, and text mining.

Bruce Nikkel is the director of Cybercrime Intelligence & Forensic Investigation at UBS. He has worked for the bank's security and risk departments since 1997. He is also a professor at the Bern University of Applied Sciences where he teaches digital forensics and is the director of the Masters in Digital Forensics & Cyber Investigation. Bruce is an editor for FSI's Digital Investigation Journal and on the organizing committee for DFRWS Europe. He holds a PhD in network forensics and is the author of the book *Practical Forensic Imaging*.

Sasa Parad studied Mathematics at ETH Zurich and was a research assistant at the Chair of Natural and Social Science Interface at the Department of Environmental System Sciences at ETH Zurich 2009–2011. He was involved in the project "Vulnerability and Potential Analysis of the Swiss Energy System," which was carried out jointly with the Swiss Federal Office of Energy (SFOE). He currently works as Actuarial and Pension Consultant at Valucor Group AG and Valucor (FL) AG. He completed his certification as an Actuary SAA in May 2019.

Stephan Ravizza holds a PhD in operations research and data mining from the University of Nottingham and a Master of Science with distinction in Mathematics from the ETH Zurich. He is the author of multiple publications including a recent publication in Nature Medicine. Stefan Ravizza won one of the largest competitions in the history of IBM with the idea of automating the writing of meeting minutes. He has been distinguishing himself as a thought leader by leading first-of-a-kind projects with AI, filing more than a dozen cognitive patents, and winning further innovation challenges. He is currently leading the Swiss Cognitive Business Decision Support unit within IBM's consulting unit.

Martin Strohmeier is a scientific project manager at the Cyber-Defence Campus in Zurich and a junior research fellow of Kellogg College, University of Oxford. His main research interests are in the area of network security, including wireless sensor networks and critical infrastructure protection. During his PhD at Oxford, he extensively analyzed the security and privacy of wireless aviation technologies of this generation and the next. His work predominantly focuses on developing cyber-physical approaches which can improve the security of air traffic control quickly and efficiently. He is also a cofounder of the aviation research network OpenSky. Before coming to Oxford in 2012, he received his MSc degree from TU Kaiserslautern, Germany and joined Lancaster University's InfoLab21 and Lufthansa AG as a visiting researcher. His work on aviation security received several awards from the aviation and computer security communities, including the EPSRC Doctoral Prize Fellowship. His dissertation was further highly commended by the British Computer Society.

Christos Tsigkanos is Lise Meitner fellow at TU Vienna (Austria). Formerly, he was postdoctoral researcher at the Distributed Systems Group at TU Vienna and previously at Politecnico di Milano (Italy), where he received (2017) his PhD defending a thesis entitled "Modeling and Verification of Evolving Cyber-Physical Spaces." He holds a BSc degree in computer science from University of Athens (Greece) and an MSc degree in software engineering from University of Amsterdam (the Netherlands). His research interests lie in the intersection of dependable systems and software engineering and include security and privacy in distributed, self-adaptive, and cyber-physical systems, requirements engineering, and formal verification.

The Security of Critical Infrastructures: Introduction and Overview

Marcus Matthias Keupp

1 The Vulnerability of Critical Infrastructures

Human life and economic organization in urban areas must fundamentally rely on essential systems that provide water, health services, electricity, supply, mobility, and communication to the population. Any temporary or permanent disruption of these critical infrastructures has severe negative consequences that range from reduced economic productivity to the loss of human life.

Much work has described erratic failures of critical infrastructure as a result of weather-related incidents (e.g., [23, 46]). Severe natural disasters such as the 2005 hurricane *Katrina* can put complete critical infrastructure systems out of operation, and heatwaves as well as heavy snowfall can disrupt transportation and communication networks. Further, the urbanization of the human population increases. While as of 1950, only 30% of the world's population lived in cities, the United Nations expect that rate to grow to 68% by 2050 [53]. Since increased power demand induced by population growth already causes power outages [6], future generations of infrastructure will face an intensifying challenge to respond to this demand [26].

While this book does not dispute the relevance of such weather- and demand-related factors, it points to another, non-erratic risk which all critical infrastructure operators must face, namely, intentional attack. Three major reasons motivate this analytical focus.

First, the analysis of natural hazards and demand fluctuation fundamentally differs from the analysis of intentional attacks since probabilistic risk analysis is

M. M. Keupp (✉)
Department of Defense Economics, Military Academy at the Swiss Federal Institute of Technology Zurich, Birmensdorf, Switzerland
e-mail: mkeupp@ethz.ch

M. M. Keupp (ed.), *The Security of Critical Infrastructures*, International Series in Operations Research & Management Science 288,
https://doi.org/10.1007/978-3-030-41826-7_1

inappropriate if risk is induced by an intelligent adversary [7, 8, 11, 12, 20, 37, 40]. As a result, forecasting models that assume a random occurrence of disruptive events are not applicable to a scenario of intentional attack.

Second, any particular infrastructure can be thought of as a cyber-physical system in which three layers are intertwined: the physical infrastructure, i.e. mechanical and electric components, operating systems (OS) that steer and control these components, and information systems (IS) that connect and remote-control OS. Industrial control systems on the OS layer which control physical components are designed for failsafe and stable operations. Originally, these systems were relatively isolated and maintained locally, remote access being the exception rather than the norm. However, today they are linked and remote-controlled by software applications on the IS layer, many of which are connected to the internet and therefore exposed to the cybersphere [2, 59]. As a result, access paths to OS can be identified by specialized search engines such as `shodan.io`, and weaknesses in their protocols can be exploited [55]. It goes without saying that if this exploitation is done with an intention to disrupt or demolish system components, significant damage to the OS layer can be inflicted. The `dragonfly` attacks of 2014 and 2015 that targeted critical infrastructures in many countries exemplify this problem [18]. This exposure is intensified by an increasing integration of third-party supplier systems that interact with the operator's proprietary architecture. OS components such as metering devices or sensors often come without a graphical user interface, and they have weak or no password protection [26]. As services are outsourced to third-party suppliers, dependabilities and vulnerabilities are also created. For example, in the `dragonfly` case, infrastructure operators were lured to doppelganger update servers from which they downloaded the code, assuming it would be a regular vendor update [50]. Using the same method, an attacker could first infiltrate a supplier and then exploit links between supplier and infrastructure operator.

Third, such intentional damage is worst when it is inflicted by terrorist and state actors, and there is growing evidence that critical infrastructures have become a target for both groups. Terrorist attacks intend to physically demolish system components and therefore do not require technological knowledge about the system. As a result, the operative cost of such attacks is negligible. For example, the cost of the 2005 London attacks which targeted mass transit infrastructure is estimated at a mere eight thousand British pounds [52]. It is therefore not surprising that organized terrorism is targeting critical infrastructures. In particular, EIAD data suggest that energy infrastructures have become a significant target for terrorist attacks in many countries [30]. Ever since the Iraq War began in 2003, attacks on energy and oil transport infrastructure in the Middle East continue [51]. The universal feasibility of such attacks is exemplified by the recent drone attacks on oil refineries in Saudi Arabia [15].

In stark contrast to organized terrorism, state actors do not (or not yet) intend to demolish infrastructure, but rather to study and eventually control systems on the OS layer, such that they can credibly threaten to demolish or deactivate infrastructures. In principle, state actors attempt to obtain access to the OS layer by exploiting weaknesses in the IS layer. Recent press coverage suggests that state actors are attempting to realize such access. Russia is purported to have infiltrated the national power grid of the USA [48, 49], Northern Ireland [44], and Ukraine [57], and the USA seem to have signaled that they are capable of attacking the Russian energy grid [45]. Such intentional attacks are unlikely to disappear soon. One might argue that Articles 22 and 23 of the 1907 Hague Convention should provide a backstop against critical infrastructure becoming a war target since they restrict belligerents' rights to choose methods or means of warfare, forbid action that causes suffering and destruction, and restrict the destruction of opponent property. However, the application of these articles requires attribution, and it is questionable whether or not a state actor who intentionally targets critical infrastructure would be willing to assume responsibility under international law. If an intentional attack is executed remotely by the cybersphere, attribution may be impossible to establish. Moreover, the convention only applies after a state of war has been explicitly declared, and hence it cannot consider de facto and hybrid warfare scenarios.

2 Contributions and Structure

This edited volume focuses on intentional attacks on critical infrastructure. It thus complements the vast contextual work that has studied quantitative analytical methods [39], sustainability and resiliency of operations [21, 42], interdependencies between infrastructures [24], engineering and industry-specific challenges [16, 43, 56], and technical standards [28].

However, the book also attempts to develop this literature by focusing on intentional attack as the very reason why sustainability, interdependency, and technical construction should be reconsidered in our time. Much of the above work has concentrated on static vulnerability analyses that identify weak spots in a network of system components (e.g., [29, 35]). In contrast, this book offers more complex attacker-defender scenarios, and it derives architectural implications for next-generation infrastructure. This choice is not only one of scope, but it also predisposes the methodological approach since the analysis of nonprobabilistic risk requires scenario-based setups, dynamic modeling, and numerical solution. The reader can reproduce the computation of these solutions since many authors share the original code they developed for this purpose.[1]

This scenario modeling unfolds in an interdisciplinary way. The authors in this volume have extensive backgrounds in economics, operations research, engineering, science, and computer science. Each author adds to the analysis from their disciplines' backgrounds, which yields a multifaceted, comprehensive work. The book therefore deploys a multi-method approach; it features graph analysis,

[1] Authorized readers can obtain the respective electronic supplementary material from the publisher's website.

linear programming, compartmentalized models, friction time analysis, and applied mathematical and statistical modeling.

All simulation and computation presented here was designed such as to maximize generalizability. While in many chapters, real supply and demand data from Switzerland is used to illustrate the analytical power of the models, their contribution is not limited to this context. Instead, the analytical procedures offered here can be globally applied to any infrastructure network in any country or economy. The book therefore addresses a global audience of both infrastructure operators, homeland security officials, and academic researchers.

The volume begins with the analysis of the risk implied by intentional attacks. This risk can be interpreted as a transitory or permanent imbalance between supply and demand once particular system components are demolished. As a result of such imbalances, the network may destabilize topologically. *Bürgy* explores such scenarios, using graph theory to formulate a generalizable operator model. He analyzes different attack strategies, the feasibility of which is contingent on the attacker's budget. Further, he calculates a complex illustration, using data from the Anytown model. His findings not only confirm that operator models can reveal vulnerabilities in the system. They also corroborate prior research that found that network elements cannot be prioritized by criticality [3].

Since such priority setting may be flawed, and since an all-hazard approach that would maximize the resilience of each and every element likely requires excessive investment, operators may choose to not invest at all and hedge the risk by buying insurance. Therefore, *Gillard* and *Anderhalden* analyze whether or not commercial insurers would be willing to offer such insurance. They estimate alphas required to calculate risk premiums, fitting a Pareto distribution to a sample of damages caused by terrorist attacks against critical infrastructure. Their analysis not only suggests that such risk premiums would be substantially larger than in the case of natural disaster. It also shows that the insurer would face an essentially unpredictable risk of bankruptcy. They conclude it is highly unlikely that any private firm would offer any insurance. They finally argue that substitutes such as the public sector or the capital market are unlikely to resolve this problem, confirming prior reserved assessments [54].

Both chapters demonstrate that any risk analysis of uncertain hazards, such as weather-related failure, is fundamentally different from a risk analysis of intelligent adversaries [40]. Still, industry groups and government officials worldwide continue to produce flawed probabilistic risk analysis and priority lists (e.g., [10, 13, 38, 47]). The contributions in the second part of this volume suggest that dynamic simulation and scenario evaluation is a much more productive approach when weaknesses and resilience are to be evaluated. Rather than debating the relevance of particular elements, these contributions look at the system as a whole, assuming that infrastructure operators are left to their own devices when it comes to protecting their systems. In particular, the analyses in this second section produce generalizable results that are applicable irrespective of the idiosyncratic setup of any particular network.

Liechti considers the fundamental requirement for human life: freshwater. He analyzes the consequences of a deliberate demolition of pipes that carry freshwater from reservoirs to urban areas as well as the utilization of such pipes to transmit organisms or substances which harm human health. He specifies a compartmentalized model that captures interactions between the attacker and the affected population, captures these interactions by a set of differential equations, and provides numerical solutions. His analysis clearly signals the benefits of dynamic scenario simulation that captures interactions instead of assigning static risk scores.

Human life is also at risk once intentional attacks on critical infrastructure have produced a mass casualty incident that strains the nation's medical treatment capacity. *Metzger* and *Keupp* consider such a case, using friction time analysis to estimate both recovery time and the capacity of the medical system to organize appropriate resources for timely treatment. Parametrizing their model with data from three model economies, they also show that a focus on restoring economic productivity may require preferential treatment and thus induce ethical dilemma.

Moreover, human life in urban areas must rely on a continuous and reliable supply of energy that not only provides heating and lighting but also powers all other critical infrastructure. Since that energy is typically transmitted from distant production sites to urban areas by the maximum voltage power grid, a disruption of this grid may cut off power supply. *Metzger*, *Parađ*, *Ravizza* and *Keupp* consider such a scenario. They use graph theory to specify a network interdiction model and apply this model to the case of Switzerland by using real topological, supply, and demand data. Specifying six different attack strategies by which nodes and edges are sequentially removed from the network, they analyze the resulting uncovered demand. They thus deepen prior approaches to dynamic analysis that recommend to delete nodes or arcs and reroute network flow over remaining network elements (e.g., [27, 34]). Their findings suggest that a blackout scenario is unlikely, whereas supply gaps are likely to persist for a long time, implying that power supply will have to be rationed. Their chapter does not only relativize populist and speculative scenarios by which the dire consequences of a total blackout are portrayed, but they also contribute to making networks more robust in a topological sense.

Human life in urban areas also depends on a continuous supply of goods required for food, consumption and production. Therefore, *Morstein* extends a network flow model designed by prior research, applying it to the level of a complex economy with multiple import routes and stockpiling. She then simulates the consequences of blocked import routes for both supply and stockpiling. Her results emphasize that significant cost savings can be achieved if disruption risk is assessed properly. The supply of such goods requires physical traffic, and in modern economies and urban areas, it is roads on which the majority of this traffic flows. Hence *Baumann* and *Keupp* provide a highly granular analysis of Switzerland's complete road network, using graph theory and supercomputing analysis to identify both topological weaknesses and consequences of traffic flow disruptions within and across urban areas. While the analysis of railway systems is beyond their scope, they nevertheless predict their model is transferable to such networks.

Finally, economic exchange and organization requires communication, and intentional attacks may target communication systems in order to disrupt or falsify any flow of information. *Strohmeier*, *Martinovic* and *Lender*s study such a scenario in the context of air traffic control. They provide a deep review of the extant literature, elaborating both an overview of extant technological vulnerabilities and an agenda of how future research should contribute to isolating communication systems against outside interference. This contribution can be extended to any type of information exchange once one considers that physical elements within critical infrastructures are controlled by OS that continuously exchange information with each other and interact with these physical elements (e.g., ETCS transponders control train movements, radio communication steers shipping traffic, etc.). Once such communication is distorted of falsified, physical damage may ensue, and hence there is a strong need for encryption whenever system elements exchange information.

The identification of vulnerabilities and topological weaknesses is useful when it comes to increasing the resilience of any critical infrastructure to intentional attack. However, the options available to operators are not limited to passive measures that focus on maximizing resilience. On the contrary, there are many ways by which infrastructure can be actively defended. Therefore, the three chapters in the third part of this volume discuss the extent to which such defense is feasible, and they show how systems can be designed to implement such defense.

Appropriate systems architecture is a prerequisite for effective defense. This is why *Kehrer*, *Tsigkanos*, and *Ghezzi* propose to conceive of critical infrastructures as cyber-physical systems that connect elements from the physical and the virtual world. Their formal and hence generalizable approach is rooted in bi-graph analysis. They develop a model that defines dependability requirements and proposes verification techniques which ensure that the system complies with the requirements, even in the presence of changes and unforeseen system evolution. This integrative approach is highly productive since it opens up a structured path to identifying integrative solutions.

Further, a crucial step to guarantee the security of a cyber-physical system is the detection and neutralization of unauthorized access, as well as the insulation of the system against future intrusions. *Casey* and *Nikkel* propose that digital forensics can realize these goals. Illustrating their approach with case vignettes from documented incidents, they explain how organizations can deploy forensic intelligence in order to improve their defense capabilities. They also provide counter-intuitive advice, indicating that it can be productive to quietly observe attackers that have infiltrated the infrastructure in order to study their behavior, rather than to eliminate the attack immediately. As organizations are attacked repeatedly and forensic insight from prior attacks accumulates over time, an iterative learning cycle is triggered whereby operators' responses to attacks become more and more effective.

Gillard essentially pursues the same motive, arguing that the analysis of past attacks is crucial to develop defense options that can neutralize subsequent attacks. However, he discusses this idea in the context of machine learning and automated defense. Using prior research on recommender systems, he develops a generalizable model that adapts its response function to past attackers' actions. He demonstrates that such attacker-defender interaction is comparable to a multi-period game during which the specification of the response function continuously adapts and becomes the more effective the more rounds are played. While such dynamic adaptation is superior to a static rule-based approach, it requires a high incidence rate of attacks if quick learning is desired.

3 Building Better Infrastructure

The physical and virtual topology of a critical infrastructure, the human beings intentionally attacking it, and other human beings defending it constitute an ecosystem in which all of these elements continuously co-evolve. This is why any critical infrastructure should be perceived as a dynamic system that requires continuous architectural adaptation as novel generations of infrastructures are to replace extant systems.

Most fundamentally, the construction of such novel generations should not be prejudiced by extant architectures. The contemporary topology and control of any system always constitutes an artifact that must be judged by its historical context. There is hence no coercing necessity that extant architectures should be replicated as next-generation systems are built. Today's physical infrastructures vital for human life and productivity, such as dams, water power plants and the national power grid, were constructed in the first three quarters of the twentieth century, i.e. at a time when deliberate attacks on this infrastructure by exploiting weak spots in the OS or IS layer were technologically infeasible or quite simply unimaginable. Hence, the planning of future generations of infrastructure should adopt a perspective of total analytical deconstruction.

Operators and researchers alike should confront themselves with the question how they would build a replacement infrastructure from scratch if the current system was rendered completely inoperative as a result of intentional attack. Thus, creative thought not prejudiced by the existence of today's physical structures would emerge. For example, when designing railway systems, operators often take the historically grown network of tracks as a given and try to optimize secure flow subject to this constraint. However, an efficient design should first consider which flow originates from where with which destination and then build tracks and security infrastructure that can satisfy this demand. This approach may entail deconstructing extant tracks and control systems as well as reconsidering geospatial planning.[2]

Until such novel generations of infrastructure are built, operators face the challenge of making extant infrastructures resilient not only to the weather, but also to intentional attack. Insulating infrastructure against the probabilistic risk

[2]The author thanks Thomas Süssli and Martin Ball for sharing these ideas and for some inspiring discussion.

of random failure is not equivalent to neutralizing the nonprobabilistic risk of intentional attack. Therefore, infrastructures designed to be resilient to weather-inflicted damage are not automatically protected from such attacks. There need not be any positive spillover effect whereby investments or insurance against random failure would also neutralize nonprobabilistic risk. In fact, investment models used to date might have to be reconsidered since the extant generation of physical infrastructure components was not designed to withstand intentional attacks. As a result, every architectural option which increases physical resilience to intentional attack requires significant investments.

The most radical way to produce such resilience is to minimize the exposure of physical infrastructure by moving it underground. Consider the case of alternating current power grids. While moving such grids underground is feasible for low- and medium-voltage local power lines, the case is different for high-voltage architectures, both because the air can no longer be used for insulation, and because high-voltage earth cables have lower transmission capacity due to reactive current and thermic loss. As a result, such cables require cooling and compensators every ten miles or so, moreover, they are difficult to inspect and maintain and more susceptible to failure than overhead lines. The only option would be a radical change of the complete grid architecture to a direct current design whose cables can span large distances underground even at high voltages (e.g., in underwater sea cables). However, in both cases, protecting power lines is not enough; transformer stations and rectifiers would have to be moved underground too. While the associated investment cost is probably excessive for a developed economy with a grown infrastructure, developing economies which build novel grids from scratch may consider such options.

However, rebuilding structures underground is not a panacea. Consider the sewage system, i.e. an infrastructure built underground by design. The structure is both critical for population health in urban areas and it is exposed to intentional attack. In contrast to the water supply system, sewage canals are not pressurized, hence they provide an open and easily accessible physical pathway to virtually every installation in an urban infrastructure. Since the system is designed to withstand extreme water flow caused by thunderstorms or flooding, the diameter of its pipes exceeds the diameter required for ordinary operation by a factor of 100. As a result, main sewage pipes have diameters of several yards but carry but a trickle of wastewater most of the time. This architecture makes the system eligible as a carrier structure for intentional attacks.[3] In this case, minimizing exposure requires sealing off all access points in streets and buildings, and introducing physical blocking, degassing, or purification devices. The associated investment cost is certainly significant.

Since physical network elements cannot be prioritized by criticality, investment in the robustness of particular components is arbitrary and hence does not necessarily provide security. Still, operators are advised to build redundant

[3]The author is grateful to Jonas I. Liechti for developing and sharing these points.

architectures, i.e. to replicate several instances of components or subsystems (e.g., [5, 36]). Such blanket advice is questionable. For example, recommendations to always store at least one replica of complex components made to specification and difficult to replace at short notice (e.g., large transformers in power stations) comes at significant investment cost but ignores network topology and connectivity. Whenever the robustness of a complete network to intentional attack is to be maximized, its topological structure should be considered first. For example, scale-free networks are highly robust to random failure of elements, but not to intentional attack.

Inhomogeneous networks characterized by few but highly connected nodes have a significantly lower attack survivability; they break into many isolated fragments when the most connected nodes are targeted [1]. Since many critical infrastructures are scale-free networks (e.g., communication, power distribution), investments in redundancy must be subject to prior connectivity analysis. Such investments are also inversely related to the substitutability of any capacity between any two nodes. If a particular arc is intentionally attacked but network flow can be rerouted at low cost while the network stays connected, there is no need for additional redundancy, and vice versa. This relationship is nicely illustrated by the Rastatt incident. While not an intentional attack, it provides an ideal case study of what a lack of substitutability implies should such an attack occur.

In summer 2017, in the vicinity of the German city of Rastatt, tracks that route significant European north- and southbound railway freight traffic were disrupted for several weeks due to unintentional subsidence of the ground as a result of tunnel work (see [9] for extensive background documentation). Due to construction works, underutilization, and technical incompatibility on neighboring routes, this traffic could only be rerouted partially, and costly substitutes had to be improvised. Total loss to manufacturing, logistics, and operator companies is estimated at two billion Euros [25]. Since the European railway network is not a designed infrastructure, but rather an historically grown amalgam of very different technologies and standards, network redundancy is significantly limited as long as the interoperability of national subsystems is not improved or novel harmonized infrastructure built.

By contrast, the drone attacks on oil refineries in Saudi Arabia in September 2019 had no such long-term effect. Although global supply was reduced by 6% in a single day as a consequence of the attack, the network had both excess capacity and technological homogeneity that provided a high degree of substitutability. About 40% of the supply gap was compensated after 2 days, while full capacity was restored after several weeks [15].

Decentralization of network components does not only remove high-value targets such as power parks, thus raising both the transaction and the opportunity cost of terrorist attacks [17]. It also increases network reliability since centralized elements typically have greater connectivity. As future generations of physical infrastructures are built, decentralizing these by design may prove to be more effective than increasing the robustness of centralized networks. For example, today's power systems are essentially characterized by spatially separated supply (plants) and demand (urban areas) which are connected through a centralized maximum voltage transfer network. This grid must therefore fulfil three tasks at the same time: equalize supply and demand network-wide to keep frequencies stable, trade energy internationally, and provide supply to urban areas.

The development of decentral microgrid architectures may reduce the importance of the latter task. Already today, energy-producing infrastructure can restart itself after an outage if kinetic energy from local primary reserves is available to power a black start and provide voltage stability [14]. As the efficiency of renewable energy sources, batteries and hydrogen tanks improves, urban areas may soon be able to provide a basic autonomous supply of power for themselves even in the case of main grid failure [32, 41]. Depending on the infrastructure in question and local geography, such autonomy could be designed at low cost. For example, if natural freshwater supplies are adjacent to urban areas, equipping the population with nanofiltration tubes that use physical membranes for universal water purification may provide an affordable, autonomous, individual-level fresh water supply if the main supply network is interrupted or contaminated.

While redundancy and decentralization may be effective, they only address the physical, but not virtual aspect of the architecture. Since cybersecurity is paramount to provide protection against intentional attacks on critical infrastructure [4, 33], measures on the OS and IS layers must complement efforts to strengthen the physical resilience of infrastructures. The challenge here is to shut off the system against unauthorized intrusion while maintaining connectedness with customers and suppliers. One way to address this challenge is the construction of 'onion models'. In such a model, the IT landscape is partitioned by design into three security zones.

The inner zone comprises critical OS that control electrical or mechanical parts the mishandling of which carries significant security concern (e.g., machinery that controls the immersion of fuel rods in the cooling water in a nuclear power plant). Such OS must be fully isolated from any other IT system; ideally, any manipulation of the system should require the cooperation of at least two certified individuals. Suppliers and any other third parties should not be granted access to this zone.

The medium zone comprises less critical local OS that is to be remote-controlled by higher-level OS. All such intra-OS layer communication should be strongly encrypted, and all communication should be logged and monitored in real time. Ideally, the controlling OS application could be programmed as a closed system with firmware authentication procedures, such that it would refuse to execute non-proprietary code. Operators should also welcome novel point-to-point communication architectures that raise the technological barrier for outside intrusion. For example, the SCION architecture strives to remains highly available even in the presence of distributed adversaries that attempt to reroute traffic through self-created corrupted paths [58].

Finally, the outer zone isolates supplier and customer interaction on the IS layer, hence, there must be strong barriers to the medium zone. Suppliers should not be allowed to interact with or maintain OS systems unless they are closely surveilled in real time. This may both entail deconstructing remote-controlled and supplier-controlled architectures to some extent as well as reintroducing personalized control of equipment which is currently operated remotely.

Lastly, these protective measures should not deter operators from planning more proactive measures of defense. Besides strengthening the resilience of the physical, OS and IS layers, the system may also defend itself autonomously once intrusions are detected. Threat reconnaissance systems should continuously scan the environment for intentional attacks on both the OS, the IS, and the physical layer. Such systems may then launch a tailored response (e.g., erect magnetic fields to restrict drone operability once flight movements are detected) and learn from the attack, improving such response over time. The contributions by *Casey* and *Nikkel* and *Gillard* in this volume have demonstrated that such iterative learning cycles are productive, and automating such learning processes in machine learning procedures or AI algorithms seems a promising step. While such measures can require human authorization on the physical level, they can be fully automated on the IS and OS level, in order to shorten the cyber kill chain as much as possible, ideally, to zero days.

As such solutions and architectural changes are implemented in the context of national security, there are significant policy issues both within and beyond the organization that operates critical infrastructure. For the operator organization, appropriate investment planning does not only entail confronting the problem that systems and software on the IS layer obsolesces fast, whereas OS applications are operative for years and the physical infrastructure for decades until replacement investments are made. Given the disruptive effect of intentional attacks for the operation of critical infrastructure, operators should revise static investment models, such as [22]. Further, behavioral operations research postulates that human behavior is associated with the efficiency of systems operation and hence defense [19]. Since formal analytical models—including those deployed in this volume—explicitly or implicitly assume that human agents behave rationally, relaxing this assumption may lead to a better understanding of both intentional attacks and their defense. Further, operators should understand the contingencies that govern other operators' willingness to share or not share information about intentional attacks they have experienced [31].

National security policies may also have to be revised as novel generations of critical infrastructure are built. As long as government officials continue to produce probabilistic risk analysis and priority checklists, their work is of little use to operators who face intentional attacks. 'Spending down' such flawed priority lists until budgets are exhausted will do little, if anything, to improve security. Instead, governments should promote institutional innovation that can motivate operators to provide for the necessary security measures themselves. Since the architectural options discussed in this chapter require significant investment, operators might face the moral hazard of not investing enough in security measures since such investments reduce profitability. To alleviate this problem, the government should create a national supervisory authority that supervises operators and demands proof of effective security measures, but leaves the implementation of such measures and the associated investment planning to them.

Moreover, government should consider how to prepare its armed forces for a scenario of intentional attacks on critical infrastructure. In the absence of a highly qualified engineer corps, the armed forces could probably help to mitigate the consequences of such attacks (e.g., public unrest, looting, mass casualty treatment), but they could not prevent the attack from happening in the first place. Therefore, cooperation between the armed forces and critical infrastructure operators, with the goal of developing effective defense capabilities, is certainly desirable.

The authors in this volume have used publicly available data to simulate intentional attacks on critical infrastructure, and there is no reason to believe that attackers could not do the same. Critical infrastructure operators cannot prevent intentional attacks from happening, but they can do much to strengthen the resilience of their infrastructures, and they can equip them with measures and procedures for automated defense. The contributions in this volume provide much useful material that helps to simulate and implement such solutions. The high degree of generalizability of these contributions makes them applicable on a global scale. Operators can and should use them to build defensible architectures that provide secure supply to future generations of urban populations.

References

1. Albert, R., Jeong, H., Barabasi, A.L.: Error and attack tolerance of complex networks. Nature **406**, 378–382 (2000)
2. Alcaraz, C., Zeadally, S.: Critical infrastructure protection: requirements and challenges for the 21st century. Int. J. Crit. Infrastruct. Prot. **8**, 53–66 (2015)
3. Alderson, D., Brown, G., Carlyle, M., Cox, L.: Sometimes there is no 'most-vital' arc: assessing and improving the operational resilience of systems. Mil. Oper. Res. **18**(1), 21–37 (2013)
4. Anderson, R., Fuloria, S.: Security economics and critical national infrastructure. In: Moore, T., Pym, D., Ioannidis, C. (eds.) Economics of Information Security and Privacy, pp. 55–66. Springer, Boston (2010)
5. Bauer, E., Adams, R., Eustace, D.: Beyond Redundancy: How Geographic Redundancy Can Improve Service Availability and Reliability of Computer-Based Systems. John Wiley & Sons, Hoboken (2011)
6. Benna, U., Benna, I. (eds.): Urbanization and Its Impact on Socio-Economic Growth in Developing Regions. IGI Global, Hershey (2018)
7. Brown, G., Cox, L.: How probabilistic risk assessment can mislead terrorism risk analysts. Risk Anal. **31**, 196–204 (2011)
8. Brown, G., Cox, L.: Making terrorism risk analysis less harmful and more useful: another try. Risk Anal. **31**(2), 193–195 (2011)
9. Büchel, B., Partl, T., Corman, F.: The disruption at Rastatt and its effects on the Swiss railway system. In: Proceedings of the 8th International Conference on Railway Operations Modelling and Analysis (ICROMA), Norrköping, pp. 201–218 (2019)
10. Council of the European Union: Directive 2008/114/EC on the identification and designation of European critical infrastructures and the assessment of the need to improve their protection. Council of the European Union, Brussels (2008)
11. Cox, L.: Some limitations of "Risk = Threat x Vulnerability x Consequence" for risk analysis of terrorist attacks. Risk Anal. **28**, 1749–1761 (2008)
12. Cox, L.: Improving risk-based decision making for terrorism applications. Risk Anal. **29**, 336–341 (2009)

13. Department of Homeland Security: National infrastructure protection plan. Washington DC (2013)
14. Ekman, C., Jensen, S.: Prospects for large scale electricity storage in Denmark. Energy Convers. Manag. **51**(6), 1140–1147 (2010)
15. Energy Intelligence Group: Market forces: Saudi recovery. Report. Energy Compass (2019). http://www.energyintel.com/pages/login.aspx?fid=art&DocId=1051919
16. Ericsson, G.: Cyber security and power system communication-essential parts of a smart grid infrastructure. IEEE Trans. Power Delivery **25**(3), 1501–1507 (2010)
17. Frey, B., Luechinger, S.: Decentralization as a disincentive for terror. Eur. J. Polit. Econ. **20**, 509–515 (2004)
18. Genge, B., Kiss, I., Piroska, H.: A system dynamics approach for assessing the impact of cyber attacks on critical infrastructures. Int. J. Crit. Infrastruct. Prot. **10**, 3–17 (2015)
19. Gino, F., Pisano, G.: Toward a theory of behavioral operations. Manuf. Serv. Oper. Manag. **10**(4), 676–691 (2008)
20. Golany, B., Kaplan, E., Marmur, A., Rothblum, U.: Nature plays with dice-Terrorists do not: allocating resources to counter strategic versus probabilistic risks. Eur. J. Oper. Res. **192**, 198–208 (2009)
21. Gopalakrishnan, K., Peeta, S. (eds.): Sustainable and Resilient Critical Infrastructure Systems. Springer, Berlin (2010)
22. Gordon, L., Loeb, M.: The economics of information security investment. ACM Trans. Inf. Syst. Secur. **5**, 438–457 (2002)
23. Guikema, S.D.: Natural disaster risk analysis for critical infrastructure systems: an approach based on statistical learning theory. Reliab. Eng. Syst. Saf. **94**(4), 855–860 (2009)
24. Hall, J., et al. (eds.): The Future of National Infrastructure: A System-of-Systems Approach. Cambridge University Press, Cambridge (2016)
25. Hanseatic Transport Consultancy: Estimation of the economic damage of the Rastatt interruption from a rail logistics perspective. Hamburg (2018). http://www.hupac.ch/EN/Study-Rastatt-disruption-b26dcc00
26. Huq, N., Hilt, S., Hellberg, N.: US cities exposed: industries and ICS. A shodan-based security study of exposed systems and infrastructure in the US (2017)
27. Kinney, R., Crucitti, P., Albert, R., Latora, V.: Modeling cascading failures in the North American power grid. Eur. Phys. J. B **46**(1), 101–107 (2005)
28. Knapp, E., Langill, J.: Industrial Network Security, 2nd edn. Elsevier, Amsterdam (2014)
29. Lopez, J., Setola, R., Wolthusen, S. (eds.): Advances in Critical Infrastructure Protection: Information Infrastructure Models, Analysis, and Defense. Springer, Berlin (2012)
30. Melkunaite, L., Giroux, J., Burgherr, P.: Research note on the energy infrastructure attack database (EIAD). Perspect. Terrorism **7**(6), 113–125 (2013)
31. Mermoud, A., Keupp, M., Huguenin, K., Palmié, M., Percia David, D.: To share or not to share: a behavioral perspective on human participation in security information sharing. J. Cybersecurity **5**(1), tyz006 (2019)
32. Mohammed, O., Youssef, T., Cintuglu, M., Elsayed, A.T.: Design and simulation issues for secure power networks as resilient smart grid infrastructure. Smart Energy Grid Engineering, pp. 245–342. Academic Press, Cambridge (2017)
33. Moore, T.: The economics of cybersecurity: principles and policy options. Int. J. Crit. Infrastruct. Prot. **3**, 103–117 (2010)
34. Motter, A., Lai, Y.C.: Cascade-based attacks on complex networks. Phys. Rev. E Stat. Nonlinear Soft Matter Phys. **66**(6), 065102 (2002)
35. Murray, A., Grubesic, T.: Critical Infrastructure: Reliability and Vulnerability. Springer Advances in Spatial Science, Berlin (2007)
36. National Infrastructure Advisory Council: A Framework for Establishing Critical Infrastructure Resilience Goals. Department of Homeland Security, Washington DC (2010)
37. National Research Council: Review of the Department of Homeland Security's Approach to Risk Analysis. The National Academy of Sciences, Washington, DC (2010)
38. Olsson, S. (ed.): Crisis Management in the European Union. Springer, Berlin (2009)

39. Ouyang, M.: Review on modeling and simulation of interdependent critical infrastructure systems. Reliab. Eng. Syst. Saf. **121**, 43–60 (2014)
40. Parnell, G., Smith, C., Moxley, F.: Intelligent adversary risk analysis: a bioterrorism risk management model. Risk Anal. **30**(1), 32–48 (2009)
41. Patrao, I., Figueres, E., Garcera, G., González-Medina, R.: Microgrid architectures for low voltage distributed generation. Renew. Sust. Energ. Rev. **43**, 415–424 (2015)
42. Petit, F., et al.: Resilience Measurement Index: An Indicator of Critical Infrastructure Resilience. Argonne National Lab. (ANL), Argonne (2013)
43. Rinaldi, S.: Modeling and simulating critical infrastructures and their interdependencies. In: Proceedings of the 37th Annual Hawaii International Conference on System Sciences (HICSS'04) (2004)
44. Rogan, A., Bridge, M.: Russia-Backed Hackers Try to Hijack Britain's Power Supply. The Times, London (2017)
45. Sanger, D., Perlroth, N.: U.S. Escalates Online Attacks on Russia's Power Grid. The New York Times (2019)
46. Sarker, P., Lester, H.D.: Post-disaster recovery associations of power systems dependent critical infrastructures. Infrastructures **4**(2), 30 (2019)
47. Singh, A., Gupta, M., Ojha, A.: Identifying critical infrastructure sectors and their dependencies: an Indian scenario. Int. J. Crit. Infrastruct. Prot. **7**, 71–85 (2014)
48. Smith, R.: Russian Hackers Reach U.S. Utility Control Rooms, Homeland Security Officials Say. The Wall Street Journal (2018)
49. Smith, R., Barry, R.: America's Electric Grid has a Vulnerable Back Door-and Russia Walked Through It. The Wall Street Journal (2019)
50. Symantec Corporation: Dragonfly: Western energy sector targeted by sophisticated attack group. Outlook Series (2017). https://www.symantec.com/blogs/threat-intelligence/dragonfly-energy-sector-cyber-attacks
51. Tichý, L.: Energy infrastructure as a target of terrorist attacks from the Islamic State in Iraq and Syria. Int. J. Crit. Infrastruct. Prot. **25**, 1–13 (2019)
52. United Kingdom Home Office : Report of the Official Account of the Bombings in London on 7th July 2005. United Kingdom Home Office, London (2006)
53. United Nations: World Urbanization Prospects: The 2018 Revision. United Nations: Department of Economics and Social Affairs, Population Division (2018)
54. United States Department of Energy: Insurance as a risk management instrument for energy infrastructure security and resilience. U.S. Department of Energy, Washington DC (2013)
55. Xu, W., Tao, Y., Guan, X.: The landscape of industrial control systems (ICS) devices on the internet. International Conference on Cyber Situational Awareness, Data Analytics and Assessment, Glasgow (2018)
56. Yusta, J., Correa-Henao, G., Lacal Arantegui, R.: Methodologies and applications for critical infrastructure protection: state-of-the-art. Energy Policy **39**, 6100–6119 (2011)
57. Zetter, K.: Inside the Cunning, Unprecedented Hack of Ukraine's Power Grid. Wired (2016)
58. Zhang, X., Hsiao, H.C., Hasker, G., Chan, H., Perrig, A., Andersen, D.: SCION: Scalability, control, and isolation on next-generation networks. In: Proceedings – IEEE Symposium on Security and Privacy, pp. 212–227 (2011)
59. Zhu, B., Joseph, A., Sastry, S.: A taxonomy of cyber attacks on SCADA systems. In: Proceedings of the 2011 International Conference on Internet of Things and 4th International Conference on Cyber, Physical and Social Computing, pp. 380–388. IEEE Computer Society, Washington (2011)

Part I
Risk

Networks of Critical Infrastructures: Cost Estimation and Defense of Attacks

Reinhard Bürgy

1 Introduction

Critical infrastructures (CIs) are systems that provide vital services to society, such as the supply of drinking water, electricity, or transportation. Any significant disruption of these services directly threatens the security and the economic system of a society, public health and safety, or any combination of the above [5]. Even small disruptions and component failures can strongly reduce performance and cause major economic damage. Hence, a physical or cyber-attack on a CI generates massive negative externalities, especially because of the increasing interdependency and technical interconnectedness of different CIs. Particularly, the cascading effect of failures among CIs could pose a serious threat to society [2, 10]. Therefore, CIs are an ideal target for terrorist, politically motivated, or criminal attacks.

Such attacks constitute the most dangerous asymmetric threat CIs have to face today and in the future [5]. Hence, there is the need to develop applied models that can evaluate the costs and consequences of intentional attacks on CIs. In this work, infrastructure networks are investigated, and a specific method for evaluating the cost of attacks on CIs is presented. A generic theoretical model is suggested that can account for different network types and attack patterns. The practical application of the model allows the reader to identify weak spots within the network.

R. Bürgy (✉)
Department of Informatics, University of Fribourg, Fribourg, Switzerland
e-mail: reinhard.buergy@unifr.ch

M. M. Keupp (ed.), *The Security of Critical Infrastructures*, International Series in Operations Research & Management Science 288,
https://doi.org/10.1007/978-3-030-41826-7_2

2 Background

The model is grounded in solid scientific work from the operations research domain. The model builds on prior work by Brown et al. [6], Golany et al. [9], and Alderson et al. [3] who have all modeled and evaluated attacks on CIs. It employs linear programming and network flow theory [1, 8] and applies prior research on network interdiction [7]. To date, this research resonates little in the communities of experts responsible for CI protection. Attempts to prioritize efforts for critical infrastructure protection typically produce descriptive lists and planning instruments. For instance, both the Swiss Federal Office for Civil Protection, the U.S. Department of Defense, and the U.S. Department of Homeland Security have all prioritized critical infrastructure elements in an attempt to produce comprehensive protection. However, this practice is questionable from a scientific perspective since particular components cannot be prioritized by criticality [2]. The model in this chapter is proposed as an alternative.

3 Methods

3.1 Operator Model

The model assumes that a homogeneous good or service is transported across a network. The network contains supply nodes that provide the good or service, demand nodes that consume it, and transit nodes that transfer it to other nodes.

In order to graphically represent the model, a simple directed graph $G = (V, E)$ is given, where V represents a set of nodes (the circles in Fig. 1 and all following figures), and E a set of arcs (the arrows in Fig. 1 and all following figures). The set of nodes is partitioned into $V = V_A \cup V_N \cup V_T$, where V_A is the set of "supply nodes", V_N the set of "demand nodes" and V_T the set of "transit nodes". The set of

Fig. 1 A small operator network with five nodes

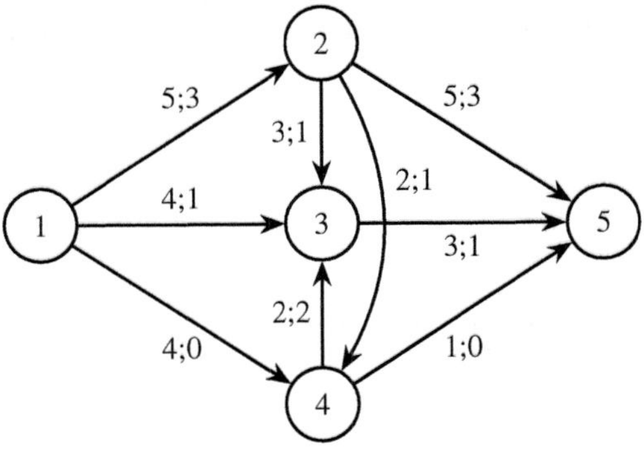

arcs E represents the connections between the objects. In this paper, an arc $e \in E$ is either indicated as e or by its end nodes $e = (v, w)$.

For each node $v \in V$, if $v \in V_A$, it can provide a (non-negative) supply a_v, and if $v \in V_N$, it has a (non-negative) demand n_v. Each arc $e \in E$ has an arc capacity u_e, which is the maximal flow of a good or service through the arc (for a given time span), and cost c_e for each unit of the good or service transported by this arc.

Figure 1 illustrates this setting for a system with five nodes. In this specific example, node 1 is a supply node with a supply of $a_v = 7$ and node 5 is a demand node with a demand of $n_v = 5$. All other nodes are transit nodes. Each arc $e \in E$ is represented by an arrow and a pair of numbers $u_e; c_e$ which indicate the capacity and the unit cost of the arc.

A solution is sought for a feasible flow $x \in \mathbb{R}^E$ that minimizes total cost (a so-called cost-optimal flow). Thus, a respective flow x_e has to be found for every arc $e \in E$. For a given node $v \in V$ the net inflow $f_x(v)$ is defined as total inflow less total outflow, formally:

$$f_x(v) = \sum_{w:(w,v)\in E} x_{wv} - \sum_{w:(v,w)\in E} x_{vw}$$

A flow is feasible if the flow constraints as well as the capacity constraints are satisfied. The flow constraints state that a supply node cannot provide more than its supply, a demand node must satisfy demand, and a transit node has to relay the flow without losses:

$$f_x(v) \leq a_v \text{ for all } v \in V_A,$$
$$f_x(v) = n_v \text{ for all } v \in V_N,$$
$$f_x(v) = 0 \text{ for all } v \in V_T.$$

The capacity constraints guarantee that the capacity of the arcs is not exceeded:

$$0 \leq x_e \leq u_e \text{ for all } e \in E.$$

Among all feasible flows, we seek to find a minimum-cost flow x, i.e. $\sum_{e\in E} c_e x_e$. Together, these conditions yield the following minimum-cost flow problem (P1):

$$\min \sum_{e\in E} c_e x_e$$

subject to:

$$f_x(v) \leq a_v \text{ for all } v \in V_A, \tag{P1}$$
$$f_x(v) = n_v \text{ for all } v \in V_N,$$
$$f_x(v) = 0 \text{ for all } v \in V_T,$$
$$0 \leq x_e \leq u_e \text{ for all } e \in E.$$

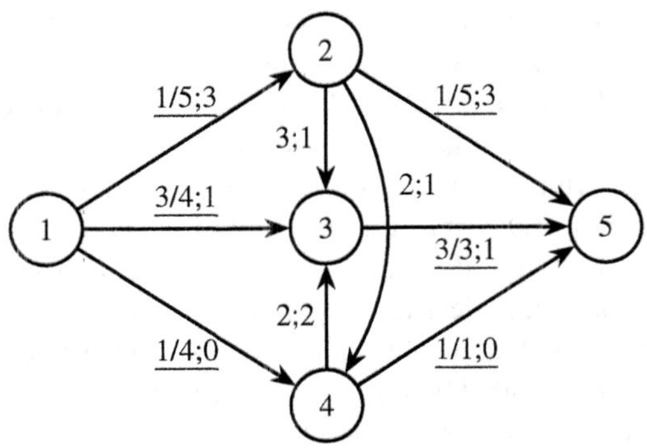

Fig. 2 Cost optimal flow for the network given by Fig. 1

Figure 2 gives an optimal solution for the example specified by Fig. 1. For each arc with a positive flow, the calculated flow value is given next to the arc and before the slash. For example, the flow from node 1 to node 2 equals $x_{12} = 1$. In this example, the total cost of this optimal solution is 12.

3.2 Inclusion of Shortage and Formulation in Standard Form

The above model is now extended and applied to a situation where the network cannot or not completely satisfy all demands. This is done by assigning a penalty cost p_v to each demand node $v \in V$. Additionally, all flow constraints are now described by equations in order to formulate the problem in a standard form. Hence, the following elements are added to graph $G = (V, E)$:

(a) A pseudo supply node v_a with supply $a_{v_a} = \sum_{v \in V_N} n_v$
(b) For every demand node $v \in V_N$, an arc (v_a, v) with cost p_v and capacity n_v
(c) A pseudo demand node v_n with demand $n_{v_n} = \sum_{v \in V_A} a_v$
(d) For every supply node $v \in V_A \cup \{v_a\}$, an arc (v, v_n) with zero cost and capacity a_v

The pseudo supply node can deliver missing units to demand nodes at penalty cost p_v. The resulting graph is denoted by $G' = (V', E')$. For every node $v' \in V'$ the demand b_v is defined as:

$$b_v = \begin{cases} -a_v & \text{if } v \in V_A \cup \{v_a\} \\ n_v & \text{if } v \in V_N \cup \{v_n\} \\ 0 & \text{else.} \end{cases}$$

Figure 3 illustrates these modifications for a unit penalty cost of 100.
This extended problem can now be described as follows in $G' = (V', E')$:

$$z = min \sum_{e \in E'} c_e x_e$$

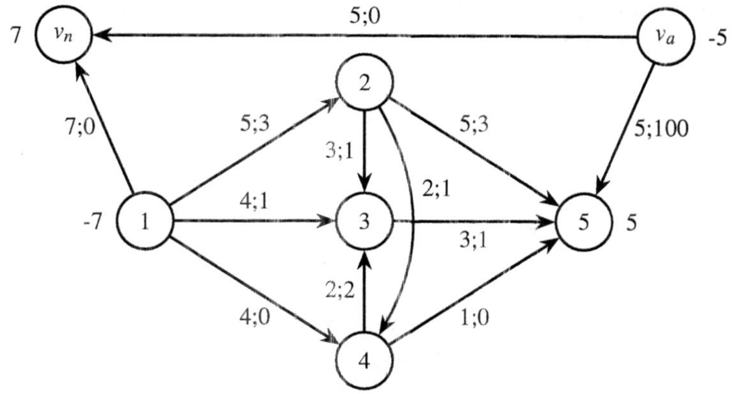

Fig. 3 Modified model in standard form

subject to:

$$f_x(v) = b_v \text{ for all } v \in V', \tag{P2}$$
$$0 \leq x_e \leq u_e \text{ for all } e \in E'.$$

It is assumed that the operator runs the network at optimal cost. In this case the value of the optimized solution of the following model simply indicates the "regular" operating costs.

3.3 Modeling an Attack Scenario

It is assumed that an attack on a network can target both nodes and arcs. If an arc is attacked, it becomes inoperative, i.e. its capacity is reduced to zero. If a node is attacked, it cannot deliver supply nor serve as a transit node, but its demand remains unchanged. This situation is modeled by reducing the capacity of all arcs interrupted as a consequence of the attack to zero.

An attack scenario $U = (V_u, E_u)$ is defined by the sets of attacked nodes $V_u \subseteq V$ and arcs $E_u \subseteq E$. Pseudo nodes and pseudo arcs cannot be attacked. A valid solution for this attack scenario must satisfy the following constraints:

$$x_e = 0 \text{ for all } e \in E_u,$$
$$x_{vw} = 0 \text{ for all } v \in V_u,$$
$$x_{vw} = 0 \text{ for all } w \in V_u.$$

Once these constraints are added to the model, a given attack scenario $U = (V_u, E_u)$ can be described as:

$$z_U = min \sum_{e \in E'} c_e x_e$$

subject to:

$$f_x(v) = b_v \text{ for all } v \in V', \tag{P3}$$
$$0 \leq x_e \leq u_e \text{ for all } e \in E',$$
$$x_e = 0 \text{ for all } e \in E_u,$$
$$x_{vw} = 0 \text{ for all } v \in V_u,$$
$$x_{vw} = 0 \text{ for all } w \in V_u.$$

If $V_u = \varnothing$ and $E_u = \varnothing$ then (P3) is equivalent to (P2). Problem (P3) is also a minimum cost flow problem, implying that it can be solved efficiently and that integer input vectors b and u yield integer solutions. This is an important characteristic of network flow problems.

Again, it is assumed that the network is run at optimal cost after an attack. Hence, the target variable z_U of an optimal solution of (P3) indicates the operating cost after an attack $U = (V_u, E_u)$. For every attack U the costs K_U are defined as:

$$K_U = z_u - z.$$

Hence, the operating costs after an attack exceed those of normal operations, i.e. $z_U \geq z$ and hence $K_U \geq 0$ for any attack U. Figure 4 illustrates an attack scenario $U = (V_u, E_u)$ with $V_u = \{4\}$ and $E_u = \{(1, 3)\}$. Only graph G instead of G' is shown. Dashed arcs are unavailable after the attack. Arcs with a positive flow are underlined. The demand of node 5 can still be met. Total operating cost after the attack is 27, implying the cost K_U of the attack is $K_U = 27 - 12 = 15$.

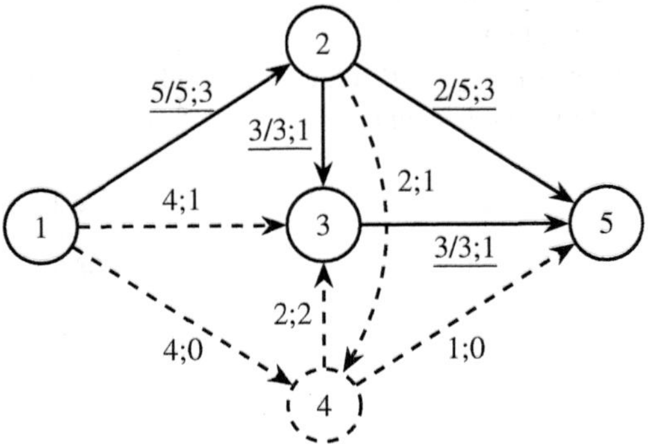

Fig. 4 Modified model with an attack on node 4

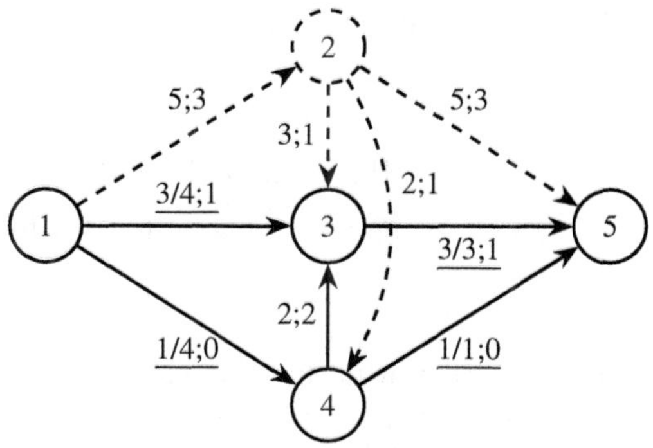

Fig. 5 Modified model with an attack on node 2

Figure 5 illustrates an attack scenario where only node 2 is attacked, i.e. $U_2 = (V_{u_2}, E_{u_2})$ with $V_{u_2} = \{2\}$ and $E_{u_2} = \varnothing$:

The demand at node 5 cannot be fully satisfied. One unit cannot be delivered, implying a penalty cost of 100. The total operating cost of the network is now 106, such that attack has caused a damage of $106 - 12 = 94$ monetary units.

3.4 *The Attacker-Defender Model*

While the CI operators may not know how exactly the network will be attacked in the future, they can assume that a well-informed attacker will likely attempt to maximize any damage. i.e. to maximize the network's total operating cost. In the following, the model is modified further to reflect this intention. An attacker has a given budget B. Every element of the network has a certain strength, which represents the resources an attacker must invest to disable this element. Specifically, the attacker incurs a cost of p_v units for an attack on any node $v \in V$, and a cost of p_e units for an attack on any arc $e \in E$. The following decision variables are introduced to model the attack decision:

y_e for all $e \in E$: y_e is 1 if arc e is attacked and 0 otherwise,

y_v for all $v \in V$: y_v is 1 if node v is attacked and 0 otherwise.

Further, the attacker is subject to the budget constraint:

$$\sum_{e \in E} p_e y_e + \sum_{v \in V} p_v y_v \leq B.$$

In a first step, the attack is modeled by adjusting the arc capacities:

$$0 \le x_e \le u_e \text{ for all } e \in E' - E,$$
$$0 \le x_e \le u_e (1 - y_e) \text{ for all } e \in E,$$
$$0 \le x_{vw} \le u_{vw} (1 - y_v) \text{ for all } (v, w) \in E,$$
$$0 \le x_{vw} \le u_{vw} (1 - y_w) \text{ for all } (v, w) \in E.$$

The constraints in the first line address those pseudo arcs whose capacities remain unchanged. For an arc $e = (v, w) \in E$, the capacity is u_e unless either arc e or node v or w are attacked. In any of these cases, the constraints in lines 2 to 4 specify that the capacity of any such node or arc is reduced to zero. Hence, the following model results:

$$\max_y \min_x \sum_{e \in E'} c_e x_e$$

subject to:

$$\begin{aligned} & f_x(v) = b_v \text{ for all } v \in V', \\ & 0 \le x_e \le u_e \text{ for all } e \in E' - E, \\ & 0 \le x_e \le u_e (1 - y_e) \text{ for all } e \in E, \\ & 0 \le x_{vw} \le u_{vw} (1 - y_v) \text{ for all } (v, w) \in E, \\ & 0 \le x_{vw} \le u_{vw} (1 - y_w) \text{ for all } (v, w) \in E, \\ & \sum_{e \in E} p_e y_e + \sum_{v \in V} p_v y_v \le B, \\ & y_e \in \{0, 1\} \text{ for all } e \in E, \\ & y_v \in \{0, 1\} \text{ for all } v \in V. \end{aligned} \tag{P4}$$

Problem (P4) is a bi-level optimization problem to which standard mathematical solvers such as CPLEX or Gurobi cannot be applied directly. To transform this bi-level into a single-level optimization problem, (P4) is reformulated by following the approach described in Brown et al. [6]. Flows over attacked arcs are penalized, letting M denote a sufficiently high penalty cost. Hence, (P4) can be rewritten as:

$$\max_y \min_x \sum_{e \in E' - E} c_e x_e + \sum_{e = (v, w) \in E} (c_e + M (y_e + y_v + y_w)) x_e$$

subject to:

$$\begin{aligned}
& f_x(v) = b_v \text{ for all } v \in V', \\
& 0 \leq x_e \leq u_e \text{ for all } e \in E', \\
& \sum_{e \in E} p_e y_e + \sum_{v \in V} p_v y_v \leq B, \\
& y_e \in \{0, 1\} \text{ for all } e \in E \\
& y_v \in \{0, 1\} \text{ for all } v \in V.
\end{aligned} \tag{P5}$$

The solution spaces of (P4) and (P5) are not identical but if M is chosen correctly, the optimal solutions and the optimal objective values are the same in both problems. (P5) is still a bi-level optimization problem, but the inner optimization problem can be transformed using duality theory [8]. Informally speaking, the inner optimization problem (P5) is transformed into a maximization problem while the value of the optimal solution stays the same. Two types of dual variables are introduced: α_v for each flow constraint of node $v \in V'$ in (P5) and β_{vw} for each capacity constraint of arc $(v, w) \in E'$ in (P5). Developing the corresponding dual constraints for all primal variables and the dual objective function, the following dual problem is obtained:

$$\max \sum_{v \in V'} b_v \alpha_v - \sum_{e \in E'} u_e \beta_e$$

subject to:

$$\begin{aligned}
\alpha_w - \alpha_v + \beta_{vw} &\leq c_{vw} \text{ for all } (v, w) \in E' - E, \\
\alpha_w - \alpha_v + \beta_{vw} &\leq c_{vw} + M\,(y_e + y_v + y_w) \text{ for all } e = (v, w) \in E, \\
\beta_e &\geq 0 \text{ for all } e \in E'.
\end{aligned} \tag{P6}$$

The inner optimization problem of (P5) always has a solution and the optimum is limited since all cost factors c_e are positive. In this case, the objective value of the optimal solution of (P6) equals the objective value of (P5). Hence, the inner optimization problem (P5) can be replaced by (P6), which yields the following reformulation of (P5):

$$\max \sum_{v \in V'} b_v \alpha_v - \sum_{e \in E'} u_e \beta_e$$

subject to:

$$\alpha_w - \alpha_v + \beta_{vw} \leq c_{vw} \text{ for all } (v, w) \in E' - E, \tag{P7}$$

$$\alpha_w - \alpha_v + \beta_{vw} \leq c_{vw} + M\,(y_e + y_v + y_w) \text{ for all } e = (v, w) \in E,$$

$$\beta_e \geq 0 \text{ for all } e \in E',$$

$$\sum_{e \in E} p_e y_e + \sum_{v \in V} p_v y_v \leq B,$$

$$y_e \in \{0, 1\} \text{ for all } e \in E,$$

$$y_v \in \{0, 1\} \text{ for all } v \in V.$$

Problem (P7) is a mixed-integer linear program. While we specify this problem here, we also note that current optimization solvers, such as CPLEX and GUROBI, are not able to find optimal solutions for large-size instances of this problem in acceptable computation time. Future research may focus on improving the numerical analysis and compatibility of this linear program.

3.5 *Application to a Small Example*

The attacker-defender model is now applied to the operator network example. The strength p_e of each arc $e \in E$ is indicated at the third position of the respective data lines next to the arcs. Nodes are considered infinitely resilient, i.e. $p_v = \infty$ for all $v \in V$:

Table 1 below gives optimal attack strategies for different attack budgets B. It demonstrates that there is no straightforward correlation between the attack budget and the number of attacked arcs.

To illustrate this fact, Figs. 6, 7 and 8 give the respective graphs for attack budgets of $B = 1$ and $B = 13$. Although the cost of the attack increases by a factor of more than 81 in the latter scenario, only two more arcs are attacked.

Table 1 Optimal attacks and cost of these attacks for all attack budgets

Attack budget B	Optimal attack	Cost of attack
$B = 1$	(4,5)	$6 = (18 - 12)$
$B = 2$	(3,5)	$6 = (18 - 12)$
$3 \leq B \leq 9$	(3,5),(4,5)	$18 = (30 - 12)$
$B = 10$	(2,5)	$94 = (106 - 12)$
$B = 11$	(2,5),(4,5)	$194 = (206 - 12)$
$B = 12$	(2,5),(3,5)	$388 = (400 - 12)$
$B \geq 13$	(1,2),(1,4),(3,5)	$488 = (500 - 12)$

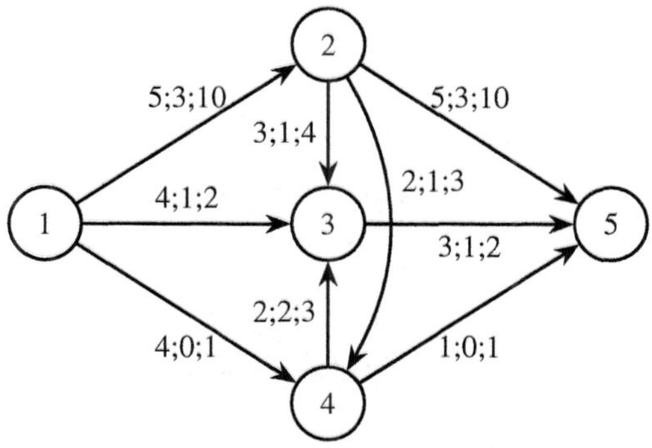

Fig. 6 Application of the model to an attack on arcs

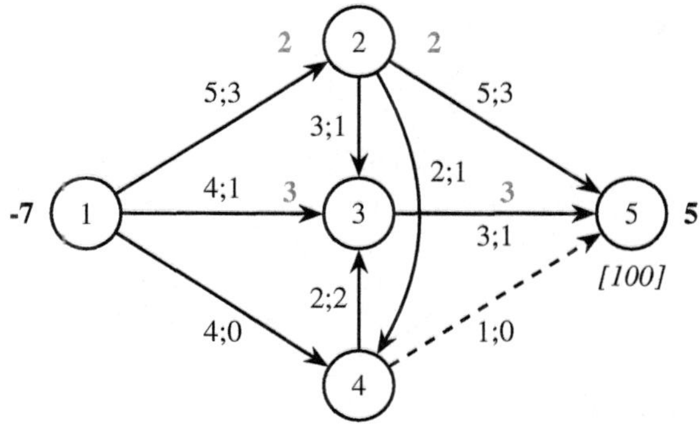

Fig. 7 Optimal attack strategy for $B = 1$

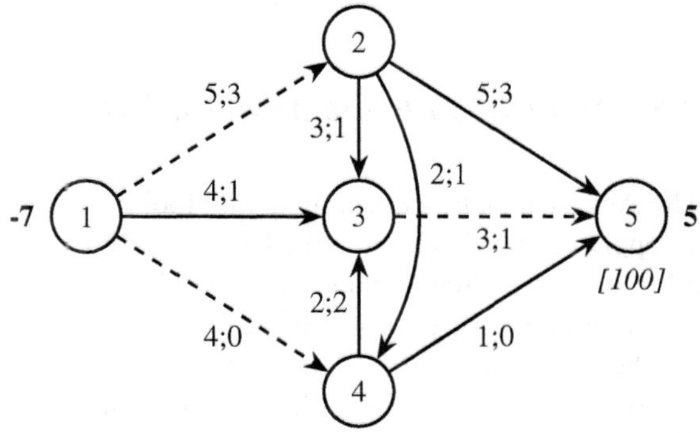

Fig. 8 Optimal attack strategy for $B = 13$

Further, a particular arc need not constitute an attractive target in an optimal strategy anymore as the attack budget increases. This effect shows as B is increased from 1 to 2 and from 9 to 10. Hence, optimal attacking strategies are not nested with respect to an increase in B. This implies that network elements cannot be prioritized by criticality, which confirms the initial criticism of [3].

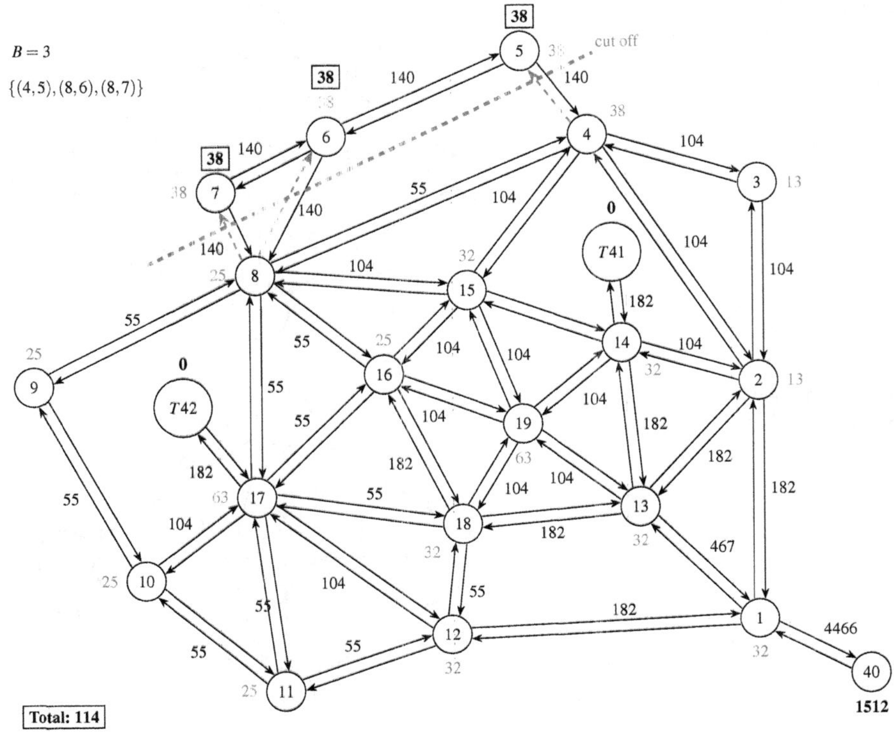

Fig. 9 Attack on the Anytown network for $B = 3$

3.6 Application to the Anytown Network

The Anytown Network is a modeling tool for diverse problems in network design. To apply it, I used data from the University of Exeter Centre for Water Systems.[1] In all following diagrams, nodes T41 and T42 are water reservoirs whose analysis is not required for the purposes of our model.

The model allows for bidirectional flows and hence specifies bidirectional arcs whose capacity is identical. All arcs have unit cost 1 and the penalty cost for all demand nodes is 1000 per missing unit. It is assumed that all nodes and arcs incident to node 1 cannot be attacked, while all other arcs have a strength of 1. We calculated models and generated their corresponding graphs for all attack budgets. For reasons of space only a selection of the results is discussed here. The full set of graphs is available on request.

[1] http://emps.exeter.ac.uk/engineering/research/cws/.

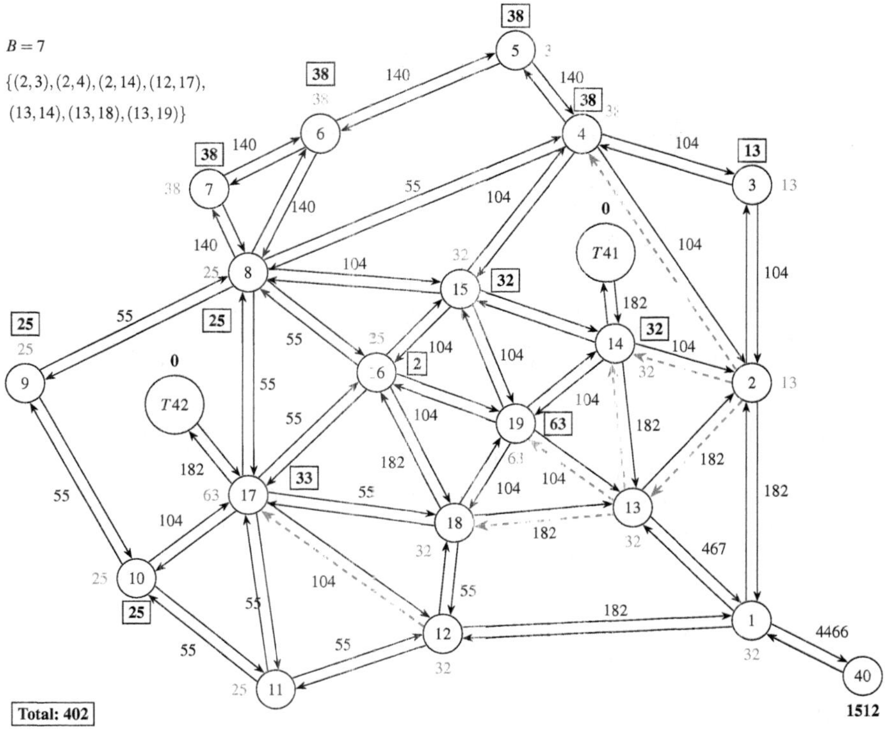

Fig. 10 Attack on the Anytown network for $B = 7$

Figure 9 shows the results of an attack on the network for $B = 3$. A subsection of the graph (nodes 5, 6 and 7) is cut off from both the remaining nodes and from the source, as illustrated by the bold dashed line.

Figure 10 illustrates an attack for $B = 7$. While the graph remains strongly-connected, several central elements are attacked, and bidirectional flow is significantly reduced, implying a significant increase in operating cost.

Figure 11 shows the results for an attack budget of $B = 9$. The graph is split into two sub-graphs, and no other nodes than those directly linked to node 1 can be operated.

4 Conclusion and Outlook

In this chapter, the cost of an attack on critical infrastructure networks was assessed with a generic model. This model was implemented as a mixed-integer linear program and applied to several small-scale examples. Future work could use this operationalization to analyze actual infrastructures, such as energy or drinking water

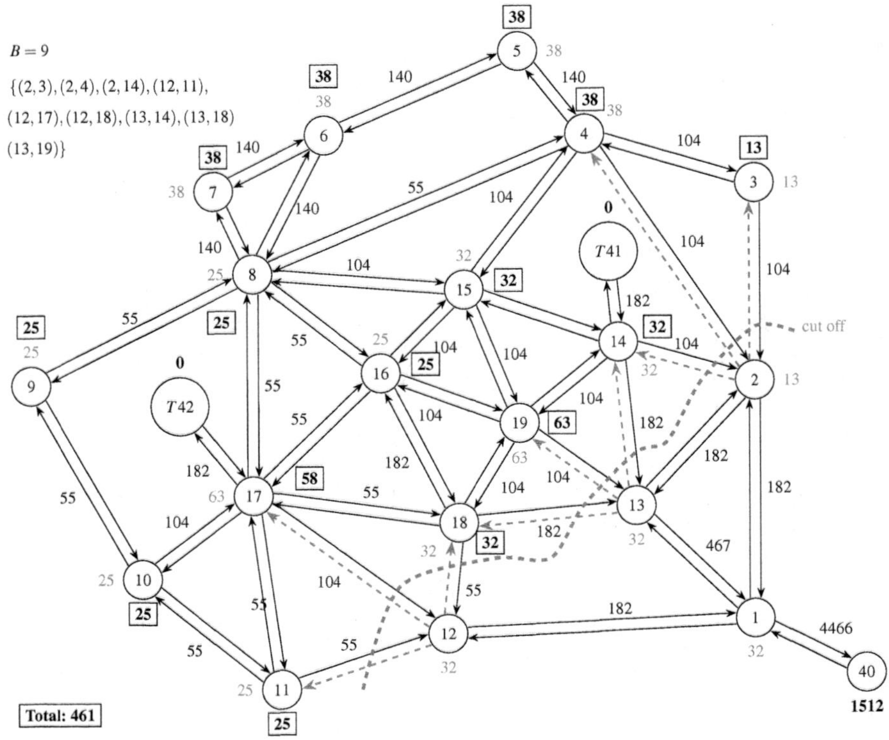

Fig. 11 Attack on the Anytown network for $B = 9$

networks. While the challenges of modeling such real networks are anything but trivial, related work may draw on some of the ideas presented here.

Further, the attacker-defender model considered here could be extended to scenarios where the operator attempts to protect the infrastructure in question by investing into the strength of the network. Such an operator would use a particular defence budget to invest in measures that minimize the maximum costs of an attack (e.g., by increasing the robustness or redundancy of critical components). Future work may analyze optimal investment strategies for this defence budget. While the analysis of such defender-attacker-defender models [4, 6] builds on the basic scenarios we have illustrated here, it is significantly more complex.

References

1. Ahuja, R.K., Magnanti, T.L., Orlin, J.B.: Network Flows: Theory, Algorithms and Applications. Prentice Hall, Englewood Cliffs (1993)
2. Alcaraz, C., Lopez, J.: Wide-area situational awareness for critical infrastructure protection. Computer **46**(4), 30–37 (2013)

3. Alderson, D.L., Brown, G.G., Carlyle, W.M., Cox Jr, L.A.: Sometimes there is no "most-vital" arc: assessing and improving the operational resilience of systems. Mil. Oper. Res. **18**(1), 21–37 (2013)
4. Alderson, D.L., Brown, G.G., Carlyle, W.M., Wood, R.K.: Solving defender-attacker-defender models for infrastructure defense. Technical Report, Naval Postgraduate School Monterey CA Department of Operations Research (2011)
5. Anderson, R., Fuloria, S.: Security economics and critical national infrastructure. In: Economics of Information Security and Privacy, pp. 55–66. Springer, Berlin (2010)
6. Brown, G., Carlyle, M., Salmerón, J., Wood, K.: Defending critical infrastructure. Interfaces **36**(6), 530–544 (2006)
7. Collado, R.A., Papp, D.: Network Interdiction–Models, Applications, Unexplored Directions. Rutcor Res Rep, RRR4, Rutgers University, New Brunswick (2012)
8. Frederick, S., Hillier, L., Gerald, J.: Introduction to Operations Research. McGraw-Hill Education, New York (2014)
9. Golany, B., Kaplan, E.H., Marmur, A., Rothblum, U.G.: Nature plays with dice–terrorists do not: allocating resources to counter strategic versus probabilistic risks. Eur. J. Oper. Res. **192**(1), 198–208 (2009)
10. Gordon, L.A., Loeb, M.P., Lucyshyn, W., Zhou, L.: Externalities and the magnitude of cyber security underinvestment by private sector firms: a modification of the Gordon-Loeb model. J. Inf. Secur. **6**(1), 24 (2015)

Insurability of Critical Infrastructures

Sébastien Gillard and Donnino Anderhalden

1 Introduction

The business model of an insurance company is centered around the idea of risk assessment and control. Insurance is a mechanism that transfers risk from the policy holder to the insurance company for the cost of a predefined premium [16]. The firm must minimize any volatility that comes with this risk in order to minimize the probability of bankruptcy. If the risk event can be observed often, the firm can use the law of large numbers to achieve this goal. This statistical theorem states that the average outcome of large numbers of independent trials is close to the expected value [4]. Therefore, by holding a large number of individual and independent policies of the same line of business (e.g. motor and life insurance) in a portfolio, the insurance company can reduce volatility and does, on average, not expect any large deviations from the calculated mean [16, 21].

Specialized work in extremal risk and damage management illustrates that coverage can be provided as long as the risk is observable and occurs at random [7, 10]. Therefore, insurance for large-scale weather-related damage and even natural disaster exists, as exemplified by Table 1 [29]. The capability of an insurance

Electronic Supplementary Material The online version of this chapter (https://doi.org/10.1007/978-3-030-41826-7_3) contains supplementary material, which is available to authorized users.

S. Gillard (✉)
Military Academy at the Swiss Federal Institute of Technology Zurich, Birmensdorf, Switzerland
e-mail: sebastien.gillard@milak.ethz.ch

D. Anderhalden
Capital & Risk, PartnerRe Europe Ltd., Zurich, Switzerland

M. M. Keupp (ed.), *The Security of Critical Infrastructures*, International Series in Operations Research & Management Science 288,
https://doi.org/10.1007/978-3-030-41826-7_3

Table 1 Examples of insurance coverage for extreme events

Year	Major disaster	Insured loss [m USD]	Total loss [m USD]
1992	Hurricane Andrew (US)	51,875.1	105,310.4
1994	Northridge Earthquake (US)	45,083.6	159,894.7
1999	Winter Storm Lothar (EU)	51,929.8	165,498.7
2001	9/11 Attacks (US)	53,369.5	200,043.0
2005	Hurricane Katrina, Rita, Wilma (US)	139,741.1	313,045.9
2010	Chile & New Zealand Earthquakes	58,640.6	263,860.5
2011	Japan & New Zealand Earthquakes, Thailand flood	142,728.4	454,402.0
2012	Hurricane Sandy (US)	78,748.3	200,382.3
2015	Earthquake in Nepal (NP)	39,437.9	99,317.7
2017	Hurricanes Harvey, Irma, Maria (US)	150,089.9	349,580.5
2018	Camp Fire (US), Typhoon Jebi (JP)	84,669.9	164,986.1

firm to sustain such large payouts for extremal damage is further strengthened by geographic or business segment diversification [14] and reinsurance. While the expected payout is identical whether or not the firm purchases reinsurance, volatility is significantly reduced as the risk is partially transferred to the reinsurer. This effect also reduces the insolvency risk of the firm [6, 9].

However, natural disaster risk is essentially probabilistic, i.e. such disasters occur at random, and they can be predicted from past observed events.

Weather-related and seismic movements are monitored by many institutions on a global scale. The data and predictions these researchers generate are not publicly available, but they also inform the catastrophe modeling software that is widely used in the insurance industry.

However, information about intentional attacks on infrastructure is often kept secret or only shared in non-public industry expert groups. This implies it is difficult to specify a probability distribution of extreme events because the low number of observations biases estimators. Most importantly, intentional attacks do not change at random like the weather does, on the contrary, their strength and effectiveness grows as attackers learn about the architecture of the infrastructure. The attack pattern may also change as the attacker's resource endowment changes. As a result, intentional attacks are essentially random, such that it is almost impossible to build a probabilistic model for intentional attacks.

Our analysis begins with a sample of documented intentional attacks on infrastructures and the financial damage inflicted by these attacks [3]. Table 2, documents the 20 most costly terrorist acts of the past decades. We fit a Pareto distribution to these data, proposing a method to generate unbiased estimators for its auxiliary parameters (Sect. 2). In a second step, we adapt a compartmentalized model to our context, infusing it with the above estimators to simulate a private insurance firm's accumulated net profit and loss over time (Sect. 3). Our results suggest that it is highly unlikely that such a firm would ever offer coverage for intentional attacks on infrastructure, and we provide some discussion of potential alternatives (Sect. 4).

Table 2 The 20 worst terrorist acts—insured property loss in 2017 USD

Event	Date	Location	Insured property loss [m USD]	Fatalities
9/11 Attacks	09.11.2001	New York, Washington DC	26,215	2982
Bomb in financial district	24.04.1993	London	1276	1
IRA bombing	15.06.1996	Manchester	1038	0
Bomb in financial district	10.04.1992	London	937	3
Bomb in World Trade Center	26.02.1996	New York	872	6
Rebels destroy military and civilian aircrafts	24.07.2001	Colombo	555	20
IRA bombing	09.02.1996	London	361	2
Bombing on board of a 747	23.06.1985	North Atlantic	227	329
Truck bomb	19.04.1995	Oklahoma City	203	166
Hijacked Swissair/BOAC dynamited on ground	12.09.1970	Jordan	178	0
Hijacked PanAm dynamited on ground	06.09.1970	Cairo	154	0
Bomb in financial district	12.04.1992	London	134	0
Attack on two hotels	26.11.2008	Mumbai	117	172
Bomb attack on a prison	27.03.1993	Weiterstadt	99	0
Bomb at Barajas airport	30.12.2006	Madrid	82	2
Bomb on board of a PanAm	21.12.1988	Lockerbie	80	270
Riot	25.07.1983	Sri Lanka	65	0
Bombing in a tube and a bus	07.07.2005	London	65	52
Hijacked airplane ditched at sea	23.11.1996	Indian Ocean	62	127
Bomb attack on Israel's embassy	17.03.1992	Buenos Aires	53	24

2 Pareto Estimation of Risk Premiums

Using a Pareto distribution (*PA*) is advantageous whenever a limited sample of observations on extreme events is to be analyzed [17]. Specified by a scale parameter ($x_0 > 0$) that captures minimum loss and a shape parameter ($\alpha > 0$) that determines curvature and tails, its distribution function for a continuous random variable X is given by Quandt [24].

$$F_X(x, \alpha) = \mathbb{P}(X \leq x) = \begin{cases} 1 - \left(\frac{x_0}{x}\right)^{\alpha} & \text{if } x \geq x_0 \\ 0 & \text{else} \end{cases} \tag{1}$$

Since we are using the discrete sample data in Table 2 to estimate x_0 and α, we can exploit the fact that the distribution functioncan be rewritten as follows for a discrete random variable X, where n corresponds to the number of observations in the dataset [28]:

$$F_n(x) = \frac{1}{n} \sum_{i=1}^{n} \mathbf{1}_{X_i \leq x} \text{ with } \mathbf{1}_{X_i \leq x} = \begin{cases} 1 \text{ if } X_i \leq x \\ 0 \text{ else} \end{cases} \tag{2}$$

Applying (2) to the observations in Table 2, $F_n(x)$ can be determined and plotted once maximum likelihood estimators for x_0 and α are available. Since the losses in Table 2 are numerically large, the estimator for x_0 is simply given by

$$\hat{x_0} = \min_{i \in [1,n]} X_i \tag{3}$$

Hence, $\hat{x_0} = 53$ m USD. The specification of an estimator for α is more complex since it requires a likelihood function [24, 27] which we specify as

$$\mathfrak{L}(X_i, \alpha) = \prod_{i=1}^{n} \frac{\alpha^n x_0^{\alpha n}}{X_i^{(1+\alpha)}} \tag{4}$$

Logging this function and calculating partial derivatives yields

$$\frac{\partial \ln(\mathfrak{L}(X_i, \alpha))}{\partial \alpha} = \frac{n}{\alpha} + n \ln(x_0) - \sum_{i=1}^{n} \ln(X_i) = 0 \tag{5}$$

which, after isolation of α, gives the estimator

$$\hat{\alpha} = \frac{n}{\sum_{i=1}^{n} \ln\left(\frac{X_i}{x_0}\right)} \tag{6}$$

$\hat{\alpha}$ is a biased estimator that requires transformation such that a minimum-variance consistent unbiased estimator can be obtained. Since $\ln\left(\frac{X_i}{x_0}\right)$ follows an exponential distribution, the consistent estimator $\tilde{\alpha}$ is

$$\tilde{\alpha} = \frac{n-1}{\sum_{i=1}^{n} \ln\left(\frac{X_i}{x_0}\right)} \tag{7}$$

Now that we have obtained estimators for both the scale and the shape parameter, the Pareto distribution specified by these is fitted to the data in Table 2. We obtained an initial estimate of $\tilde{\alpha} = 0.6143$. To improve the accuracy of $\tilde{\alpha}$, following [15] we used the method of least squares to minimize the deviation between measured and predicted values $S(\alpha)$:

$$S(\alpha) = \sum_{i=1}^{n} (F_n(X_i) - F(X_i, \alpha))^2 \tag{8}$$

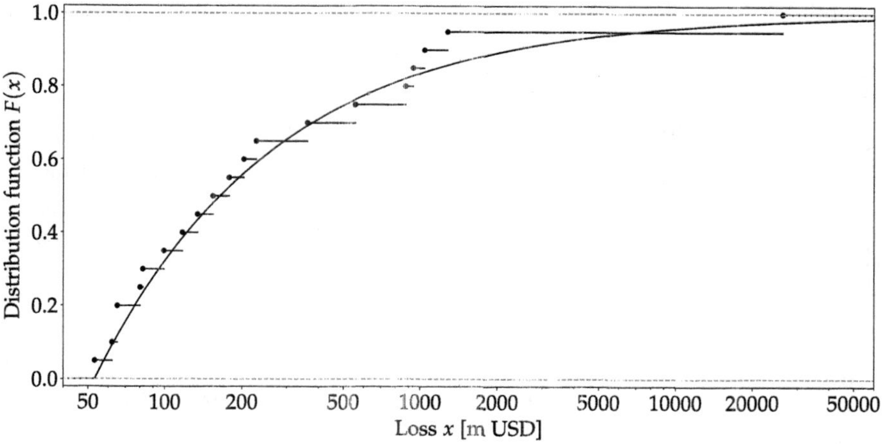

Fig. 1 Fitted Pareto distribution function

This procedure was implemented by iteratively deploying the Python function `scipy.stats.pareto.fit()` [12]. It converged on an optimal estimator $\tilde{\alpha}_f = 0.6405$.

Figure 1 plots the fitted Pareto distribution as specified by x_0 and $\tilde{\alpha}_f$. The empirical distribution function $F_n(x)$ is indicated by black dots, and the fitted distribution function is shown as a solid black curve. As the distribution function $F_X(x, \alpha)$ converges to 1 the faster the more α increases, predicted loss increases as α decreases.

The numerical magnitude of α therefore reflects the firms' loss expectation. To calculate risk premiums for natural disasters, firms in the commercial reinsurance industry use α's between 1.5 and 1.8 for fire, between 0.8 and 1.3 for windstorm, and between 0.6 and 1.0 for earthquake peril [20]. These values far exceed our estimate for $\tilde{\alpha}_f = 0.6405$. Figure 2 plots these differences, suggesting that the risk premium for insurance against intentional attacks will far exceed the premium paid for insurance against natural disasters.

This risk premium can be specified as

$$\mathfrak{R} = \text{VaR}_\beta + C_f + C_v + B, \text{ for } \{C_f, C_v, B\} \in \mathbb{R}_{\geq 0} \tag{9}$$

where C_f represents the fixed costs, C_v the variable costs, B the profit and $\text{VaR}_\beta(X)$ is the value at risk (VaR). This probabilistic term captures the risk of loss or impairment of any insured assets subject to an event threshold β. Its value approximately corresponds to the premium the infrastructure operator must pay to receive coverage. Exploiting the fact that this risk can be captured by a Pareto distribution function when extreme events are considered [23], VaR simply corresponds to the minimum value of x for which the distribution function $F_X(x, \alpha)$

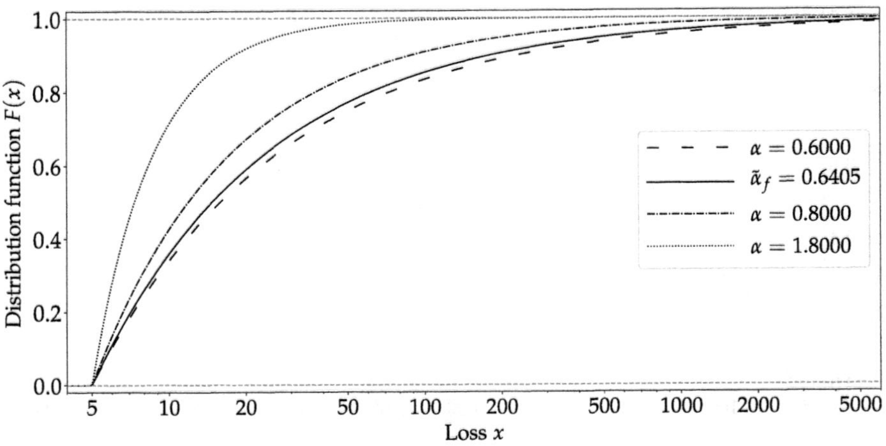

Fig. 2 Convergence of the Pareto distribution as a function of α

equals the event threshold β, formally:

$$\text{VaR}_\beta(X) = F_X{}^{-1}(x, \alpha) = \min(x : F_X(x, \alpha) \geq \beta) \tag{10}$$

Then, integrating (1) in (10) yields

$$\text{VaR}_\beta(X) = \frac{x_0}{\sqrt[\alpha]{1-\beta}} \tag{11}$$

Finally, VaR calculation requires a specification of return time, i.e. the period between any given occurrence of an extreme event and the next occurrence of such an event. Considering (1), this return time T can be specified as a function of beta [5]:

$$T = \frac{1}{1-\beta} \tag{12}$$

Using (11) and (12) with the data in Table 2, we can now calculate VaR as a function of β. Table 3 provides results for selected β values. Considering that the commercial insurance industry uses a standard level of $\beta = 0.95$, an insurance firm can expect a minimum loss of USD 5696 million once every 20 years.

Moreover, the values in Table 3 represent but a lower bound of expected loss, i.e. they give the minimum risk cover that any insurer would have to provide. As according to (9), the fixed and variable cost of operation have to be considered also, actual risk premiums are likely higher. Finally, Table 3 suggests that expected loss grows exponentially as β increases, implying that the firm faces a high risk of bankruptcy even if the extreme event occurs only rarely.

Table 3 VaR for different event thresholds β

β	$\mathrm{VaR}_\beta(X)$ [m USD]	T [years]
50.0%	157	2
90.0%	1930	10
95.0%	5696	20
99.0%	70,270	100
99.6%	293,800	250
99.9%	2,558,672	1000

3 Simulation of Bankruptcy Risk

To simulate the economic situation of the insurance firm, particularly, its risk of going out of business as a result of an extreme event occurring, we use an adapted SIR model. Often used in epidemiology, the standard SIR model tracks a population as an infection spreads, grouping individuals into a susceptible (S), infected (I), and recovered (R) compartment. The dynamic spread is captured by an incidence rate γ and a recovery rate λ [13].

We suggest that can be adapted to our setting. The compartment S can be reinterpreted as the insurer's cumulative net profit. As our simulation begins at $t = 0$, S starts at zero, hence $S(t = 0) = 0$. Accumulation of this profit over time crucially depends on whether or not an extreme event occurs. If it does, the insurance firm incurs a loss since high damage-related payouts far exceed the risk premiums paid by operators. Otherwise, it makes a profit as it avoids such payouts but still earns risk premiums. The insurance firm has an incentive to accumulate profits in eventless periods in order to finance payouts in periods when an event occurs. Thus, the compartment R can be reinterpreted as the 'recovery contribution' to accumulated net profit, such that this profit increases whenever an extreme event does not occur ($R > 0$) and vice versa ($R \leq 0$). Hence, accumulated net profit can be written as:

$$S_{t+1} = S_t + R_t \tag{13}$$

Finally, the compartment I can be reinterpreted as an 'infected' asset (i.e. one that is covered by insurance and damaged or destroyed by an intentional attack). Hence, the recovery contribution R_t can be calculated as the difference between VaR and the loss the insurance suffers at time t, formally:

$$R_t = \mathrm{VaR}_\beta - I_t \tag{14}$$

For the sake of simplicity, fixed and variable costs are omitted in this calculation. Since we use a Pareto distribution function to model the occurrence of extreme events, I_t has a Pareto distribution:

$$I_t \sim PA(x_0, \alpha) \tag{15}$$

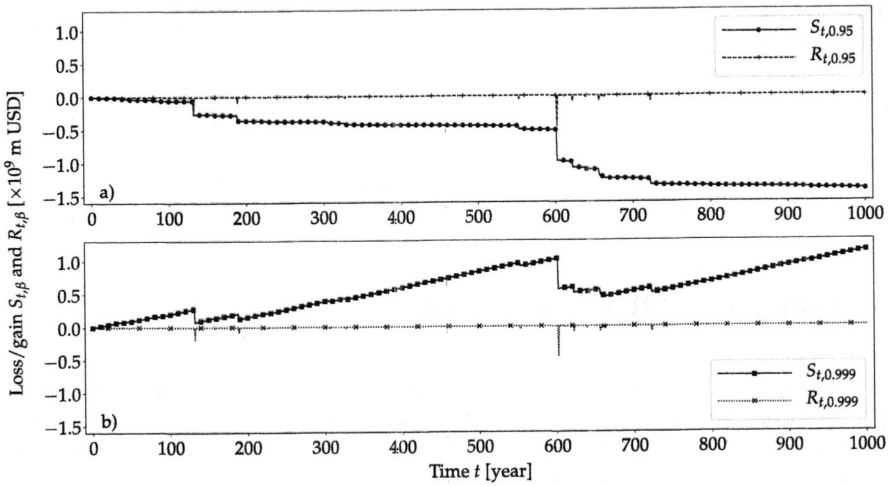

Fig. 3 Accumulated net profit for extreme event occurring late

Our setting considers discrete events that appear in an unpredictable sequence over time. Hence, rather than following the original SIR model which specifies fixed parameters for incident and recovery rates, we use a Pareto randomization process by deploying the Python function `scipy.stats.pareto.rvs()` [12] to produce numeric values for I_t based on the estimators for x_0 and $\tilde{\alpha}_f$ we found in the preceding section. Each randomization round is based on a time interval of $T = 1000$ years. The randomization process comprises 10,000 rounds.

Figure 3 shows a simulation where an extreme event occurs after $t = 602$ years of operations, i.e. relatively late. The upper panel uses $\beta = 0.95$ for VaR calculation, and the lower panel uses $\beta = 0.999$.

The firm has accumulated profits over the first 601 periods of its operations. However, for the case of $\beta = 0.95$ even these significant savings cannot offset the loss inflicted by the extreme event. Over the complete timespan, the accumulated loss amounts to 1.4244 billion USD. It is not until β is increased to 0.999 that an accumulated profit of 1.1311 billion USD results. Hence, even in the case that the extreme event occurs relatively late, insurance companies would have to charge very high risk premiums.

Figure 4 details the case that the extreme event occurs after only $t = 55$ years, i.e. very early. Both panels use the same VaR specifications as in Fig. 3. They suggest that the firm can never recover from the accumulated net loss even if operations are continued for the remaining 945 years, and it can never reestablish profitability. For $\beta = 0.95$ (0.999), accumulated loss is 18.35 (16.379) billion USD at $T = 1000$.

Since there is an infinite number of possibilities for both the time at which the extreme event occurs and the magnitude of the damage it inflicts, the firm can neither generate reliable pricing information for risk premiums, nor can it predict

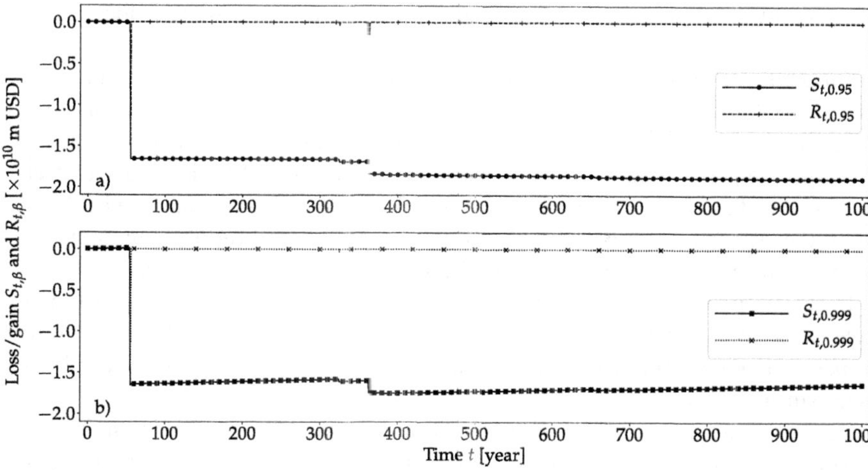

Fig. 4 Accumulated net profit for extreme event occurring early

the probability with which it may go out of business. Hence, the fate of an insurance company is essentially left to chance once it offers insurance for non-probabilistic extreme events.

4 Conclusion

Probabilistic events that occur at random, such as weather-related damage, can be captured and predicted by stochastic models [22]. As a result, insurance firms can offer coverage for such events since they can measure the variability of past events and compare expected losses to the mean or the median of past losses in order to calculate a risk premium.

By contrast, the analysis of non-probabilistic events such as intentional attacks require a deterministic approach that must make qualitative assumptions about possible worst-case scenarios. The results of such models hence crucially depend on the assumptions made and the corresponding risk scenarios. Our approach to risk modeling featured in this chapter illustrates this fundamental problem. The way we determine the scale and shape parameters of our Pareto distribution is deterministic. In particular, we assume that data on past observed events are representative of future damage. However, there is no other way to assess risks that have not yet been observed. The challenge is hence to develop an extensive catalogue of extreme events and to reliably estimate the business risk if they occur. As long as such predictions cannot be made, an insurance firm is highly unlikely to offer any coverage, and any reinsurer would most probably refuse to underwrite such risk. It should be noted that our estimates merely constitute lower boundaries of the actual damage, since the failure of key infrastructure, such as electricity or drinking water supply, may cause secondary damage in other sectors of the economy [1, 2, 8, 11, 25, 26, 30].

Since private firms are unlikely to offer insurance for intentional attacks, are there any alternatives operators could turn to? There have been proposals to use the capital market—and, in particular, private risk-taking investment—to provide coverage [18]. For example, insurance-linked securities (ILS) have been created to raise funding for coverage in the capital markets. Such 'catastrophe bonds' allow the issuer to share peak catastrophe risks with institutional investors who are disconnected from reinsurance markets [17]. It may hence be possible to issue 'infrastructure terror bonds', although, to the best of our knowledge, no such bonds have been issued in the industry. Further, since publicly issued bonds require a proper evaluation from a rating agency, the issuers would have to rely on third-party terrorism risk models.

Public-private initiatives have proposed 'terrorism pools' as a solution. The idea is to create a national fund, backed by state-level guarantees, that could collect enough financial means to provide coverage for intentional attacks.

Although these initiatives differ, they share a similar operational structure [19]. Private insurance companies provide a basic retention D. Over and above this amount, up to a pre-defined aggregate limit C, excess coverage is provided by the reinsurance market. If the aggregated loss L should exceed the sum of D and C, the government would cover the difference. While the idea seems appealing, only about one third of all OECD member countries offer such a national terrorism risk insurance program. Further, given the extreme losses inflicted by intentional damage of infrastructure, it remains questionable for how long the government can afford to compensate the loss not covered by private insurers and reinsurers. Operators should therefore expect that neither private industry nor the government are willing or able to provide insurance for intentional attacks on critical infrastructure.

References

1. Alcaraz, C., Lopez, J.: Analysis of requirements for critical control systems. Int. J. Crit. Infrastruct. Prot. **5**(3–4), 137–145 (2012)
2. Alcaraz, C., Zeadally, S.: Critical control system protection in the 21st century. Computer **46**(10), 74–83 (2013)
3. Background on: Terrorism risk and insurance. Technical Report. Insurance Information Institute (2019). https://www.iii.org/article/background-on-terrorism-risk-and-insurance
4. Bernoulli, J.: Ars conjectandi: Usum & applicationem praecedentis doctrinae in civilibus, moralibus & oeconomicis, chap. 4. Turneysen Brothers, Basel (1713). Translated into English by Oscar Sheynin
5. Cornell, C.A.: Engineering seismic risk analysis. Bull. Seismol. Soc. Am. **58**(5), 1583–1606 (1968)
6. Cummins, J.D., Trainar, P.: Securitization, insurance, and reinsurance. J. Risk Insur. **76**(3), 463–492 (2009)
7. Embrechts, P., Schmidli, H.: Modelling of extremal events in insurance and finance. Z. Oper. Res. **39**(1), 1–34 (1994)

8. Gordon, L.A., Loeb, M.P., Lucyshyn, W., Zhou, L.: Externalities and the magnitude of cyber security underinvestment by private sector firms: a modification of the Gordon-Loeb model. J. Inf. Secur. **6**(1), 24 (2015)
9. Gurenko, E.N.: Catastrophe Risk and Reinsurance: A Country Risk Management Perspective. The World Bank, Washington, DC (2004)
10. Harrington, S.: Market discipline in insurance and reinsurance. Market Discipline Across Countries and Industries **1**, 159–173 (2004)
11. Harrison, K., White, G.: A taxonomy of cyber events affecting communities. In: 44th Hawaii International Conference on System Sciences, pp. 1–9. Institute of Electrical and Electronics Engineers (IEEE), Piscataway (2011)
12. Jones, E., Oliphant, T., Peterson, P.: SciPy: Open source scientific tools for Python (2001)
13. Kermack, W.O., McKendrick, A.G.: A contribution to the mathematical theory of epidemics. Proc. R. Soc. London, Ser. A Math. Phys. Charact. **115**(772), 700–721 (1927)
14. Liebenberg, A.P., Sommer, D.W.: Effects of corporate diversification: evidence from the property–liability insurance industry. J. Risk Insur. **75**(4), 893–919 (2008)
15. Marquardt, D.W.: An algorithm for least-squares estimation of nonlinear parameters. J. Soc. Ind. Appl. Math. **11**(2), 431–441 (1963)
16. Marshall, C.L., Marshall, D.C.: Measuring and Managing Operational Risks in Financial Institutions: Tools, Techniques, and Other Resources. John Wiley, Hoboken (2001)
17. McNeil, A.J., Frey, R., Embrechts, P.: Quantitative Risk Management: Concepts, Techniques and Tools-Revised Edition. Princeton University Press, Princeton (2015)
18. Michel-Kerjan, E., Morlaye, F.: Extreme events, global warming, and insurance-linked securities: how to trigger the "tipping point". Geneva Pap. Risk Insur. – Issues Pract. **33**(1), 153–176 (2008). https://EconPapers.repec.org/RePEc:pal:gpprii:v:33:y:2008:i:1:p:153-176
19. Michel-Kerjan, E., Pedell, B.: Terrorism risk coverage in the post-9/11 era: a comparison of new public–private partnerships in France, Germany and the US. Geneva Pap. Risk Insur. – Issues Pract. **30**(1), 144–170 (2005)
20. Mitchell-Wallace, K., Foote, M., Hillier, J., Jones, M.: Natural Catastrophe Risk Management and Modelling: A Practitioner's Guide. John Wiley & Sons, Hoboken (2017)
21. Mutenga, S., Staikouras, S.K.: The theory of catastrophe risk financing: a look at the instruments that might transform the insurance industry. Geneva Pap. Risk Insur. – Issues Pract. **32**(2), 222–245 (2007)
22. Pawlak, Z., Wong, S., Ziarko, W.: Rough sets: probabilistic versus deterministic approach. Int. J. Man Mach. Stud. **29**, 81–95 (1988)
23. Pflug, G.C.: Some remarks on the value-at-risk and the conditional value-at-risk. In: Probabilistic Constrained Optimization, pp. 272–281. Springer, Berlin (2000)
24. Quandt, R.E.: Old and new methods of estimation and the Pareto distribution. Metrika **10**(1), 55–82 (1966)
25. Rinaldi, S.M.: Modeling and simulating critical infrastructures and their interdependencies. In: Proceedings of the 37th Hawaii International Conference on System Sciences. Institute of Electrical and Electronics Engineers (IEEE), Piscataway (2004)
26. Rinaldi, S.M., Peerenboom, J.P., Kelly, T.K.: Identifying, understanding, and analyzing critical infrastructure interdependencies. IEEE Control. Syst. Mag. **21**(6), 11–25 (2001)
27. Rytgaard, M.: Estimation in the Pareto distribution. ASTIN Bull. J. IAA **20**(2), 201–216 (1990)
28. Shorack, G.R., Wellner, J.A.: Empirical Processes with Applications to Statistics. SIAM, Philadelphia (2009)
29. SwissRe: sigma 2/2019: Secondary natural catastrophe risks on the front line. https://www.swissre.com/institute/research/sigma-research/sigma-2019-02.html
30. Yusta, J.M., Correa, G.J., Lacal-Arántegui, R.: Methodologies and applications for critical infrastructure protection: state-of-the-art. Energy Policy **39**(10), 6100–6119 (2011)

Part II
Resilience

Deliberate Attacks on Freshwater Supply Systems: A Compartmentalized Model for Damage Assessment

Jonas I. Liechti

1 Introduction

Water is a non-substitutable resource for human health and survival [1, 6]. Humans in urban areas must therefore rely on a functioning infrastructure that collects, purifies and distributes freshwater from natural sites to the urban population [2, 4].

Water supply systems in urban areas are tailored to local geospatial and climatic conditions, hence, they are virtually unique [3, 5]. Nevertheless, these systems share the generic design categories *sources*, *facilities*, and *distribution* (viz. Fig. 1).

Sources are natural sites that collect and hold raw water by drainage basins, seep areas, or direct extraction from lakes, rivers, and groundwater.[1] Facilities are industrial architectures that purify raw into drinking water (purification), store water supply in cisterns, water towers, and industrial facilities (storage), and manage flows to urban areas for distribution (control). Control facilities can both exist as physical (manned) sites and as remote-controlled or virtual systems. Manned sites typically have access restrictions, whereas the level of IT security for remote-

Electronic Supplementary Material The online version of this article (https://doi.org/10.1007/978-3-030-41826-7_4) contains supplementary material, which is available to authorized users.

[1] A notable exemption are catchment lakes which are not considered for the purposes of this model.

J. I. Liechti (✉)
Swiss Federal Institute of Technology Zurich, Institute for Integrative Biology, Zurich, Switzerland

M. M. Keupp (ed.), *The Security of Critical Infrastructures*, International Series in Operations Research & Management Science 288,
https://doi.org/10.1007/978-3-030-41826-7_4

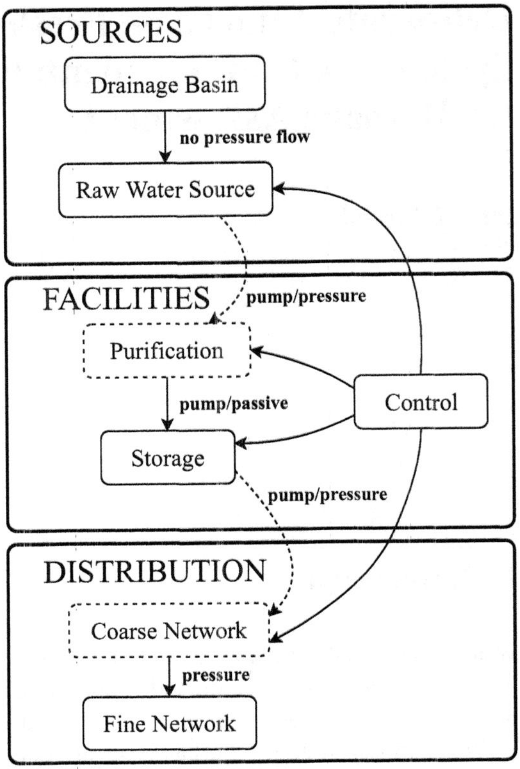

Fig. 1 Schematic representation of an urban drinking water supply system

controlled and virtual installations may vary. Finally, distribution elements organize water distribution from the storage facilities to the urban population. The coarse distribution network conveys large quantities of water by main distribution pipes.[2] The fine distribution network further partitions these quantities and directs them to individual homes by smaller pipes. Both systems are pressurized, although the pressure in the fine distribution network is significantly lower.

Irrespective of how these generic elements are combined for the construction of any specific water supply system, they are prone to two attack vectors. First, an attack may physically damage a specific element or any combination of elements to interrupt water supply (destruction). Second, it may contaminate the water supply by infiltrating a nuclear, biological or chemical agent that causes illness or death among the population that drinks from such contaminated water (pollution). Hence, by the first vector, attackers intend to physically damage or destroy the infrastructure as such, whereas by the second vector they use this very infrastructure as a carrier for the attack. However, not all elements of a water supply system are equally exposed to both vectors.

[2]However, not all water supply systems have a coarse distribution network since storage facilities are sometimes located within urban areas.

The risk of physical damage is highest for large and publicly accessible intake sites. As raw water sources are generally accessible, so is the extraction equipment. While physical damage to this equipment can be repaired, mechanical damage to raw water intake (e.g., by demolishing or blocking intake sockets) can temporarily disconnect the raw water source from the supply system. This disruption risk is significant if supply must depend on few or even a single water intake(s).

While purification facilities are not as easily accessible as raw water intake sites, physical damage to these elements is costly and repairs take a long time. Since such facilities play a central role as a gateway for subsequent distribution, physical interruption is a significant risk. Technologically advanced societies may supply the population with nanofiltration devices for individual purification, but the organization of such workaround solutions comes at a significant cost. Further, physical damage to storage facilities—in particular, to water towers—interrupts supply whenever natural geographical conditions are unable to generate sufficient pressure to self-pressurize the distribution system.

Physical damage may also be inflicted by the attacker damaging or taking over a control facility. In the first case, the system is denied functionality by shutting down its power supply, cutting cables, or organizing DDoS attacks. In the second case, the attacker attempts to intrude into the facility's IT systems and gain control. If successful, the attacker can then inflict damage by intentionally mishandling technical components.

Finally, physical damage to the distribution system can be caused if the kinetic energy resulting from its pressurization is exploited maliciously. For example, the abrupt shutting of a valve in the distribution network causes the water flow to suddenly stop, such that the kinetic energy of flowing water is unleashed onto the carrier pipes and valves, causing them to burst. The repair or replacement of such elements is expensive and may require shutting down the distribution system partially or completely.

While drainage basins are almost immune to physical damage, any pollution renders them unusable for raw water collection. As such basins typically expand over substantial areas, effective pollution requires significant quantities of any pollutant. Still, cleaning such large sites to remove the pollutant can be difficult, particularly so for seep areas, even if the polluting substance should be easily separable from water. Drainage basins collect raw water at a slow pace, such that fresh water may take days or weeks to diffuse from the drainage basin into the associated raw water source. Hence, if the pollutant cannot be removed, large quantities of water will remain contaminated for a long time.

Storage facilities are even more vulnerable to pollution since they are both centralized and the water supply they carry is not yet pressurized. An attacker may therefore choose to insert the harmful agent into a storage facility to circumvent dilution at the purification stage and then use the pressurized distribution system to contaminate the water as it is being supplied to the population. By contrast, the insertion of a harmful agent at the distribution stage is likely less effective. As the distribution network is pressurized, contamination is only possible if the pressure differential can be overcome. While this differential is large in coarse distribution networks, finer networks operate at lower pressures and are also more accessible. Such networks can be polluted at a lower cost, but the effects would be limited to local areas.

The damage caused to the population by both attack vectors can be analytically partitioned into direct and indirect (ramification) damage. Direct damage then comprises all costs the population must incur for the repair of damaged physical and IT systems (paid for by higher taxes, fees, or water prices) and to secure alternative freshwater supply (e.g., by buying bottled water, carrying water from cisterns, or installing filtration devices). Indirect (ramification) damage captures all indirect costs caused as the population becomes aware the water supply system is attacked. As the water supply is cut off or contaminated, the population's health and life expectancy decreases, implying higher medical expenditure and reduced workforce productivity and political stability.

2 Model Compartments and Parameters

A compartmentalized model is proposed to simulate the effect propagation of a single, discrete attack on a freshwater supply system. It is constructed from the viewpoint of an external observer who wants to quantify the effect of an attack. The purpose of the model is to provide an estimate rather than an exact prediction of this damage. The model uses a limited set of elements, and it does not require extensive information about the behavior of either attacker or defender. It is assumed that the observer has limited knowledge both about the specific course of an attack and the specific layout of the water supply system.

The model is visualized in Fig. 2. It comprises four interacting compartments. The variable *population* partitions the population into a fraction H of consumers

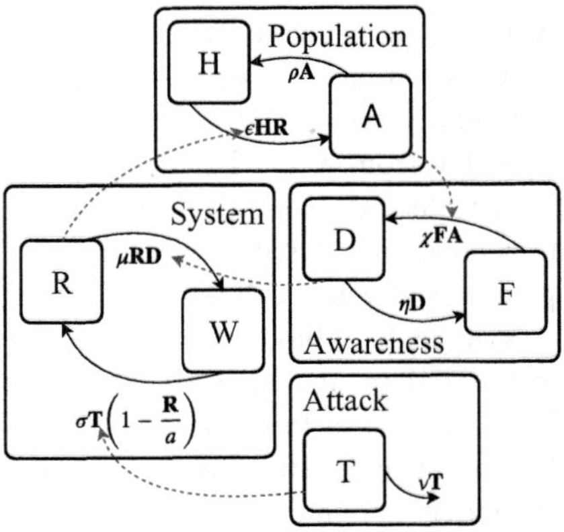

Fig. 2 Model for effect propagation

that remain healthy during the attack, and a fraction A whose health suffers as a result of the attack. The variable *system* partitions the water supply system into a working fraction W and a fraction R that is in need of repair. The variable *awareness* partitions the population into a fraction D that is aware of the attack, and a fraction F that is unaware. Finally, *attack* is a variable that captures an attack of intensity T.

The effect propagation following an attack is modeled by flows that occur within and between these compartments. The strengths and directions of these flows are specified by the following ten parameters. For all of these parameters, it is rather their relative size than their absolute value that influences model dynamics. Note that the model considers a singular attack and thus the *attack* variable has only one outbound flow. A repeated attack can be represented by a periodically activated inbound flow that increases the attack intensity T, but this variation is not considered further in this chapter. Flows inside all other compartments are balanced.

The impact of the attack is captured by the parameter a. It measures the extent to which the water supply system is compromized. This parameter is large whenever many elements are damaged, when an element with high asset specificity is damaged, or when a large share of all drinking water was routed by a now damaged element. The effect rate σ measures how fast the attack damages the supply system. A thus affected system is restored at rate μ. Both rates depend on the number of elements that are affected and on the technical difficulty of restoring or replacing them.

The inverse of the decay rate ν describes the duration of the attack. It is typically short for demolition attacks and long in the case of sustained pollution. An attack is effective the effect rate σ exceeds the decay rate. Hence, the larger $(\frac{\sigma}{a\nu})$ is, the closer the effective damage is to the maximal damage a.

As the system is damaged, the population becomes affected at rate ϵ. These affected consumers recover at rate ρ. Further, the population becomes aware of the attack at rate χ, whereas this awareness vanishes at rate η.[3] The ratio $(1/\chi)$ measures the (typically short) time it takes to make consumers aware the water supply system is attacked. Whereas an attack that damages the system is self-revealing, implying immediate and full awareness among consumers, this awareness grows at a slower rate in the case of intentional pollution since consumers must first realize that their health issues are due to a contaminated water supply.

Finally, the damage caused by an attack is modeled in terms of the cost a consumer incurs as a result of both direct and ramification damage. Direct damage is captured by the cost parameter e which measures the direct cost per time unit and consumer. Ramification damage is captured by a conversion factor r that is specific to the attack vector. The model assumes that ramification damage only occurs if there was any preceding and nonzero direct damage.

[3]Since the physical and psychological stress for the population associated with an attack on their water supply is likely remembered for a long time, η is modeled as the smallest of all rates, and it is assumed to be significantly smaller than χ.

3 Model Dynamics and Damage Calculation

A set of differential equations is used to model the dynamics of the attack and effect propagation. First, the boundary conditions for all fractions must be met:

$$H + A = 1 \tag{1}$$

$$W + R = 1 \tag{2}$$

$$D + F = 1 \tag{3}$$

The dynamics of the attack (i.e., its decay over time) is given by

$$\frac{dT}{dt} = -\nu T \tag{4}$$

The dynamics of the system (i.e., the change over time of the fraction of the system that is working) is elaborated in detail in the technical appendix at the end of this chapter. It is given by

$$\frac{dW}{dt} = R\left(\mu D + \frac{\sigma}{a}T\right) - \sigma T \tag{5}$$

The dynamics of the population (i.e., consumers becoming affected and recovering over time) is given by

$$\frac{dH}{dt} = \rho A - \epsilon H R \tag{6}$$

Finally, the dynamics of the awareness (i.e., awareness about the attack growing and vanishing among consumers) is given by

$$\frac{dF}{dt} = \eta D - \chi F A \tag{7}$$

These equations are complemented with corresponding differential equations for those variables with two states, i.e. $\left(\frac{dR}{dt}\right)$, $\left(\frac{dA}{dt}\right)$, and $\left(\frac{dD}{dt}\right)$ are also specified. Since from $X + Y = cst.$ it follows that $\frac{dY}{dt} = -\frac{dX}{dt}$, the specification is obvious and therefore not expressly given here. Finally, the model sets the initial condition for the attack variable as $T(t = 0) = 1$.

Total direct damage at time t is obtained by scaling individual cost to the fraction of the affected population A and to the actual size of the entire population P, and by integrating this global damage over time, formally:

$$d_E(t) = ePA(t) \tag{8}$$

$$D_E(t) = \int_{t=0}^{t} d_E(t')dt' \tag{9}$$

The total direct damage of the attack is then given by the limit:

$$D_E^{tot} = \lim_{t \to \infty} D_E(t) \tag{10}$$

Using the assumption that ramification damage only occurs as a consequence of prior direct damage, any ramification damage at time t is linearly related to total direct damage at time t:

$$d_R(t) = r \int_{t'=0}^{t} D_E(t')dt' \tag{11}$$

Analogous to the specification of direct damage, total ramification damage is obtained by integrating over time and calculating the limit of this integration, formally:

$$D_R = \int_{t=0}^{t} d_R(t')dt' \tag{12}$$

$$D_R^{tot} = \lim_{t \to \infty} D_R(t) \tag{13}$$

4 Illustration

The analytical potential of the proposed model is illustrated by two basic scenarios. The first case, *demolition*, describes a terrorist attack by which a central element in a water supply system (e.g., a main pipe in the coarse distribution network) is physically destroyed. As a result, 80% of the system is affected ($a = 0.8$). The attack is assumed to be highly effective, such that the effect rate is high ($\sigma = 10$) and considerably exceeds the quotient $a\nu = 0.8$. A large share of the population is affected by the attack, and recovery is slow ($\epsilon/\rho = 3$). Since media broadcasts suggest the supply failure is the result of a terrorist attack, awareness quickly grows ($\chi = 1$) and it vanishes only at a negligible rate ($\eta = 0.001$).

The model is slightly extended to account for system operators' attempts to repair the damage. Since operators need time to assess the extent of the damage, organize equipment and schedule repairs, any repairs will be delayed. Therefore, operators will attempt to temporarily substitute water supply, such that effective recovery is much slower during this improvised substitution. Two recovery rates are introduced: μ_{sub} during the substitution phase (set at 0.01), and μ_{rep} once repairs begin (set at 0.5). Cost per time unit and consumer is set to 10 monetary units ($e = 10$), and for the sake of simplification, no ramification damage is assumed to materialize.

Figure 3 presents the simulation results for this scenario. The upper panel shows the attack potential and the fraction of the water supply system that is unaffected by the attack. The initial drop in the attack potential curve indicates an effective attack. It is followed by a phase in which temporary supply substitution can barely

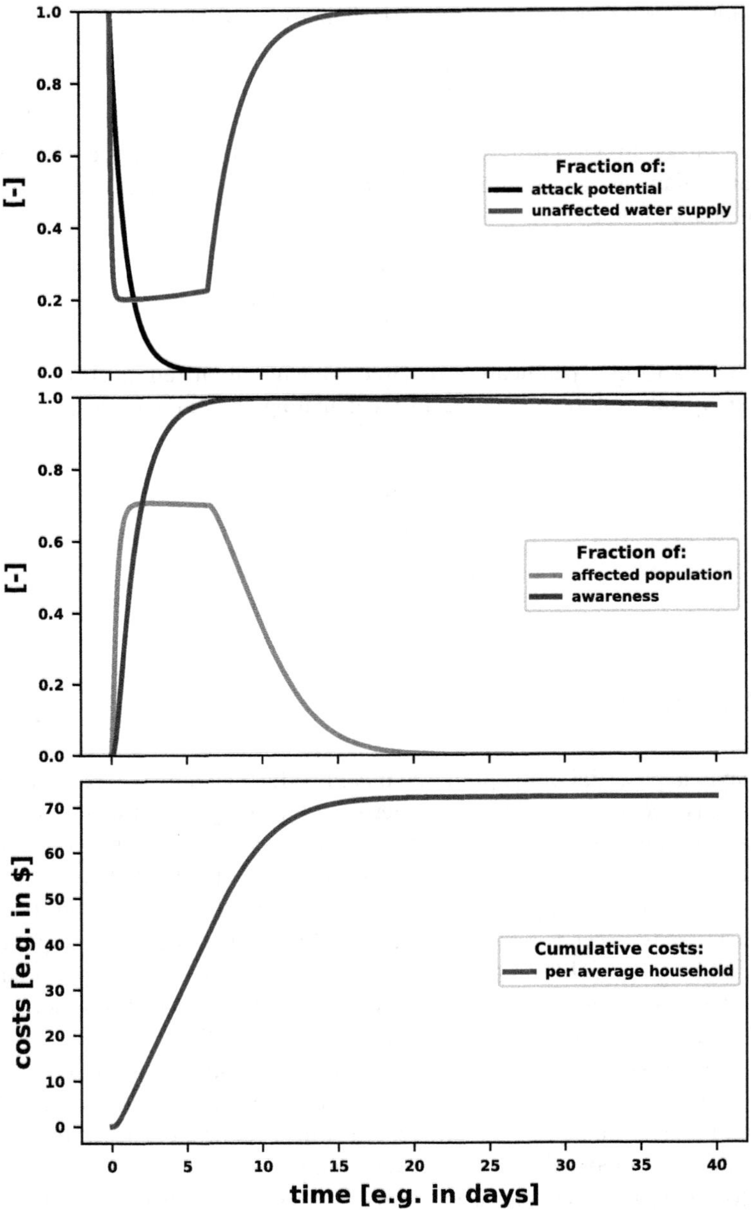

Fig. 3 Results for scenario *demolition*

contribute to system recovery. At about $t = 7$, the supply system is restored in full over the following days. The middle panel illustrates the large fraction of the population that is immediately affected by the attack. This fraction remains large until repairs start, indicating that temporary supply substitution has little effect on system recovery. Further, the sudden supply disruption lets the awareness level spike. The lower panel shows the cumulative direct cost of the attack per average household; it reaches a limit of about 70 monetary units by the time the system has fully recovered from the attack. The cumulative direct cost of the attack can be obtained by multiplying this value with the population size.

The second case, *pollution*, considers a scenario where an attacker silently injects harmful bacteria into a water tower that supplies a particular district of an urban area. The attack attempts to avoid the purification stage and prevent significant dilution; instead, the district-level distribution stage is targeted directly. As a result, the attack only affects 5% of the total water supply system ($a=0.05$). Since the bacteria are diluted at the distribution stage, the effect rate is significantly lower than in the *demolition* case ($\sigma = 1$). Since the injection happens quickly and takes effect immediately, the duration is set to ($1/\nu = 1$). However, while the bacteria cause serious illness, they can be neutralized by boiling or nanofiltrating the water, such that the system can recover quickly ($\mu = 0.5$).

When compared to the demolition case, the district population is affected at a much lower rate ($\epsilon = 0.15$), but those who do become ill take longer to recover ($\rho = 0.05$). Since the attack is initially undetected, the district population takes significant time to notice that the health problems they experience are due to contaminated water supplies. Hence, awareness increases much slower than in the demolition case ($\chi = 0.05$), but it decreases only marginally once the attack has been discovered ($\eta = 0.001$). As in the above case, cost per time unit and consumer is set to 10 monetary units ($e=10$), and for the sake of simplification no ramification damage is assumed to materialize.

Figure 4 presents the simulation results for this scenario. The upper panel shows that the attack potential is quickly reduced to zero, and the system as a whole is only marginally affected by the attack (this is because $a=0.05$). Since awareness grows only slowly, the affected part remains damaged for a prolonged period of time. In the middle panel, the fraction of the affected population is low since the attack is limited to the district-level water supply. Note that the awareness level increases only slowly; it reaches its maximum only when almost all affected individuals have recovered. This result is consistent with the expectation that consumers may not immediately relate illness symptoms to contaminated water supplies. The lower panel shows a similar development of cumulative cost as in the *demolition* scenario, but the growth of the damage-related costs is spread out over a significantly longer time period.

While the demolition scenario considers a highly effective attack on a large fraction of the supply system and the pollution scenario describes a mildly effective attack on a small fraction of the system, both lead to comparable total costs. In the *demolition*, case the quick raise of awareness leads to substantial efforts to repair the supply system and thus to a quick recovery. In the *pollution* case, on the other hand, the small fraction of the system remains affected over a prolonged period of time since awareness grows only slowly. Thus, the comparable total costs are generated

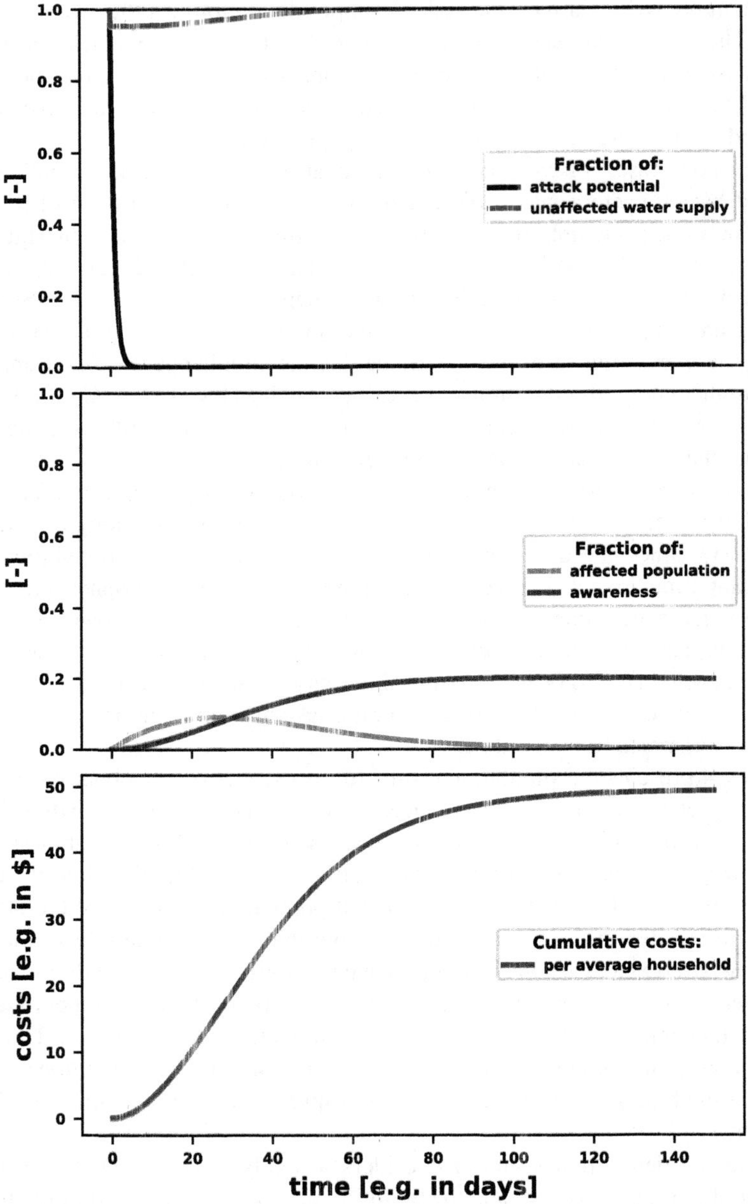

Fig. 4 Results for scenario *pollution*

in one case with high daily costs but over a relatively short amount of time ($\approx$15 days) and in the other with smaller daily costs but over a prolonged period ($\approx$150 days).

5 Discussion and Outlook

The model proposed here was applied to the specific context of an attack on an urban water supply system. Nevertheless, due to its high level of abstraction the model has benign information requirements. It can therefore be generalized to any scenario where a significant fraction of the population consumes some infrastructure good or service whose supply is disrupted.

At the same time, the model has some limitations that future research could address. While the high degree of abstraction makes the model generalizable, it also limits the applicability of the model to the analysis of idiosyncratic system designs. Specific adaptations of the model are required for more contextual analyses. For example, the compartment *system* could be replaced by an explicit model of a specific water supply system. Future work may also abandon the assumption that water is distributed homogeneously across the population, and adopt the Anytown model instead. In this case, the damage assessment would also have to be adapted, for example by differentiating between damages inflicted to consumers and those inflicted to industry, or by considering the specific geospatial context.

Further, since the model relies on linear differential equations, it assumes a linear relation between the change of a variable and the current value of that variable. In the case of a water supply system, this assumption implies that as soon as some fraction of the water distribution system is affected by an attack, it is repaired at a rate proportional to the awareness of the attack. Future research may contrast such linear relationships with nonlinear settings. For example, one might think of scenarios where an element is so vital to operations that the system cannot recover—even if awareness is at its maximum—until the vital element is repaired or replaced.

The model dynamics are flexible enough to accommodate such adaptations since the model is solved numerically. For the above example of a vital element, a custom recovery function could be designed that renders very small or even zero values until a replacement or repair can be made, and then renders values proportional to the fraction of the system affected by the attack. The illustration for the *demolition* scenario provided a minor adaptation in this respect, and future research may build on this conceptual idea.

While the model provides parameters and formulae for the calculation of ramification damage, this damage was omitted in both illustrations for the sake of simplicity. The cost estimates provided here are therefore limited to direct costs and likely present a conservative lower boundary of the actual total cost of an attack. Future research should develop methods to estimate and aggregate ramification damages into the proposed conversion factor. The adequate modeling of these damages may imply introducing more parameters that can capture the social and economic repercussions of an attack.

6 Technical Appendix

6.1 Derivation of System Dynamics

Even if the attack is successful from the attacker's point of view, it need not affect the complete water supply system. Hence, whenever $a < 1$, some fraction a of this system is affected by the attack whereas the remainder $(1 - a)$ is not. It follows that, whenever the rate of change of the working fraction of the supply system approaches $(1 - a)$, it must be rescaled to be equal to or larger than zero. The respective differential equation can be written as

$$\frac{dW}{dt} = \mu RD - \sigma f(W)T. \tag{14}$$

With $f(W) = \frac{1}{a}(W + a - 1)$, f is the required rescaled linear function since $f(W = 1) = 1$ and $f(W = 1 - a) = 0$. For a more concise formulation, one can exploit the fact that $W + R = 1$ and express the change in W as a function of the fraction of the system in need of repair, formally:

$$\frac{dW}{dt} = R\left(\mu D + \frac{\sigma}{a}T\right) - \sigma T \tag{15}$$

6.2 Effective Impact of an Attack

In order to determine the effective impact of an attack, the differential equations for the fraction of the system in need of repair can be used, assuming no recovery $(\mu = 0)$. In this case,

$$\frac{dT}{dt} = -\nu T \tag{16}$$

$$\frac{dR}{dt} = \sigma T\left(1 - \frac{R}{a}\right) \tag{17}$$

Combining (16) and (17) yields

$$\frac{dR}{dT} = -\frac{\sigma}{\nu}\left(1 - \frac{R}{a}\right) \tag{18}$$

Which, after separation of variables and subsequent integration, yields

$$a \ln(1 - \frac{R}{a}) = \frac{\sigma}{\nu} T + cst. \tag{19}$$

Using the initial conditions $T(t = 0) = 1$ and $R(t = 0) = 0$, the constant can be determined, and $R(T)$ can be written as:

$$R(T) = a \left(1 - e^{-\frac{\sigma}{a\nu}(1-T)}\right) \tag{20}$$

For $t \to \infty$, the attack strength T is reduced to zero, and hence $T \to 0$ yields

$$R_{effect} = a \left(1 - e^{-\frac{\sigma}{a\nu}}\right) \tag{21}$$

Note that whenever $\sigma >> a\nu$, the effective impact of the attack is roughly equivalent to its maximum effect size, i.e. $R \approx a$.

References

1. Esrey, S.A., Habicht, J.P.: Epidemiologic evidence for health benefits from improved water and sanitation in developing countries. Epidemiol. Rev. **8**(1), 117–128 (1986)
2. Jenerette, G.D., Larsen, L.: A global perspective on changing sustainable urban water supplies. Glob. Planet. Change **50**(3), 202–211 (2006)
3. Matlock, M., Thoma, G., Cummings, E., Cothren, J., Leh, M., Wilson, J.: Geospatial analysis of potential water use, water stress, and eutrophication impacts from US dairy production. Int. Dairy J. **31**, 78–90 (2013)
4. McDonald, R.I., Weber, K., Padowski, J., Floerke, M., Schneider, C., Green, P.A., Gleeson, T., Eckman, S., Lehner, B., Balk, D., Boucher, T., Grill, G., Montgomery, M.: Water on an urban planet: urbanization and the reach of urban water infrastructure. Glob. Environ. Change **27**, 96–105 (2014)
5. Muttiah, R.S., Wurbs, R.A.: Modeling the impacts of climate change on water supply reliabilities. Water Int. **27**(3), 407–419 (2002)
6. Sawka, M.N., Cheuvront, S.N., Carter Robert, I.: Human water needs. Nutr. Rev. **63**, 30–39 (2005)

Mass Casualty Treatment After Attacks on Critical Infrastructure: An Economic Perspective

Jean-Claude Metzger and Marcus Matthias Keupp

1 Introduction

Intentional attacks on critical infrastructure can cause mass casualties among civilians. Such attacks inflict economic loss in two different ways. First, such mass casualty incidents (MCIs) put significant strain on medical emergency services (MES) supply since such supply is not typically organized to consider extreme scenarios, implying resources for treatment are limited. Therefore, medical personnel must use triage to ration available supply and schedule treatment [1].

Second, as a consequence of the attack, a number of victims will not recover or remain permanently injured. In both cases, these victims represent an economic loss to the nation's labor force. As a result, the productivity of the economy suffers. Since the productivity of labor force participants differs according to whether they represent specialist, skilled, or unskilled labor, this loss is contingent on the number

Electronic Supplementary Material The online version of this article (https://doi.org/10.1007/978-3-030-41826-7_5) contains supplementary material, which is available to authorized users.

J.-C. Metzger
hemotune AG, Zurich, Switzerland
e-mail: jean-claude.metzger@hemotune.ch

M. M. Keupp (✉)
Department of Defense Economics, Military Academy at the Swiss Federal Institute of Technology Zurich, Birmensdorf, Switzerland
e-mail: mkeupp@ethz.ch

M. M. Keupp (ed.), *The Security of Critical Infrastructures*, International Series in Operations Research & Management Science 288,
https://doi.org/10.1007/978-3-030-41826-7_5

of victims in each group. Hence, intentional attacks on critical infrastructures may intend to disrupt economic productivity by targeting the labor force, such that persistent damage is inflicted. Since replacement time increases with labor force specialization, an MCI likely reduces labor productivity for a significant period of time [6].

Our analysis first draws up the event space of an MCI and then uses friction time analysis to model productivity loss. We then explore the effects of three different triage methods on economic loss reduction. In particular, we compare preferential to random treatment methods, investigating the extent to which these may reduce economic loss, if at the price of ethical dilemma.

2 The Consequences of Mass Casualty Incidents

Figure 1 draws up the event space after an MCI has occurred. A total number V of injured victims demands medical treatment. The limited medical emergency supply (MES) capacity M is deployed in order to treat as many victims as possible. If these victims are not treated within a particular timeframe, they cannot recover and hence these fulltime equivalents (FTEs) are lost ($V - M$). If they receive treatment, a share ($\beta \cdot M$) of victims under treatment does still not recover, and these FTEs are also lost. Another share ($\alpha \cdot M$) recovers but suffers from permanently reduced health over their remaining lifespan (partial recovery). Some of these victims will never be able to return to the workforce, hence an additional number ($\alpha \cdot \gamma \cdot M$) of FTEs is lost. The remaining victims, i.e. a share of ($(1 - \alpha - \beta) \cdot M$), fully recover. On the basis of this event space, our model explores the two major consequences of an MCI: First, the monetary loss to the economy as labor force participants must be replaced, and second, the strain such an event puts on medical supply capacity.

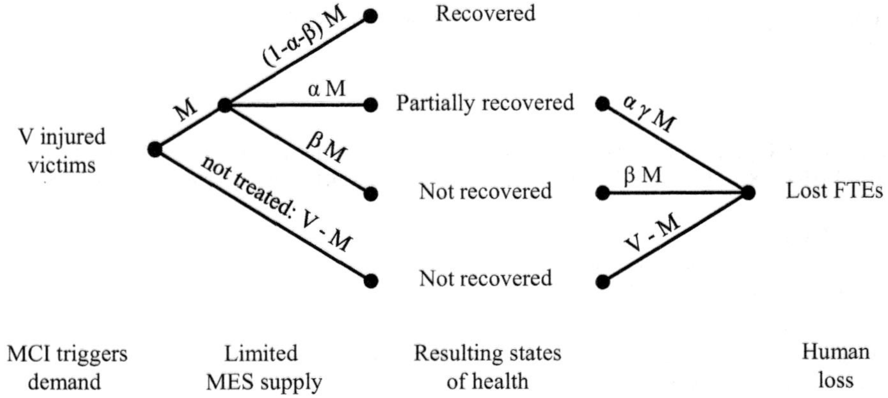

Fig. 1 Event space of victim treatment outcomes

Table 1 List of model parameters

Item	Parameter	Defined for
Population size	N	$\mathbb{N}^+$
Number of victims	V	$\mathbb{N}^+$
Number of groups with different average labor productivity	n	$\mathbb{N}^+ \in [0, V]$
Group number	i	$\mathbb{N}^+ \in [1, n]$
Group size (number of people in group i)	N_i	$\mathbb{N}^+$
Number of victims within group i	V_i	$\mathbb{N}^+ \in [0, V]$
Number of treated victims	M	$\mathbb{N}^+ \in [0, V]$
Lost full time equivalents	L	$\mathbb{R}^+ \in [0, V]$
Lost full time equivalents within group i	L_i	$\mathbb{R}^+ \in [0, N]$
Maximum duration of treatment	D	$\mathbb{N}^+$
Treatment duration	d	$\mathbb{N}^+, d < D$
Share of victims partially recovered after treatment	α	$\mathbb{R} \in [0, 1]$
Share of victims not recovered despite treatment	β	$\mathbb{R} \in [0, 1]$
Share of lost FTEs after partial recovery	γ	$\mathbb{R} \in [0, 1]$
Simplification parameter	η	$\mathbb{R} \in [0, 1]$
Average labor productivity of group i	h_i	$\mathbb{R}^+$
Lost labor productivity of all groups	H	$\mathbb{R}^+$
Lost labor productivity of group i	H_i	$\mathbb{R}^+ \in [0, H]$
Friction period to replace FTE in group i	T_i	$\mathbb{R}^+$
Friction period function type parameter	a	$\mathbb{R}^+, a > 0$
Friction period function parameter for scaling	c	$\mathbb{R}^+, c > 0$
Scaling factor of the sigmoid function	δ	$\mathbb{R}^+$
Total monetary loss	Π	$\mathbb{R}^+$
Monetary loss in group i	Π_i	$\mathbb{R}^+ \in [0, \Pi]$
Solow factor	ϵ	$\mathbb{R}^+, \epsilon > 1$
Lost labor productivity in all groups after Solow correction	H_ϵ	$\mathbb{R}^+, H_\epsilon \geq H$
Total monetary loss after Solow correction	Π_ϵ	$\mathbb{R}^+, \Pi_\epsilon \geq \Pi$

Table 1 provides an overview of all parameters used in our subsequent analysis of these two consequences.

2.1 *Monetary Loss to the Economy*

We assume that all victims, whether (if partially) recovered or not, were labor force participants. The total number of victims V can be subdivided into n groups that differ by their productivity levels h_i (for $i = 1 : n$ and with $h_1 > h_2 > \ldots > h_n$). The immediate loss of labor productivity over all n groups can be calculated as

$$H(t = 0) = \sum_{i=1}^{n} L_i \cdot h_i \tag{1}$$

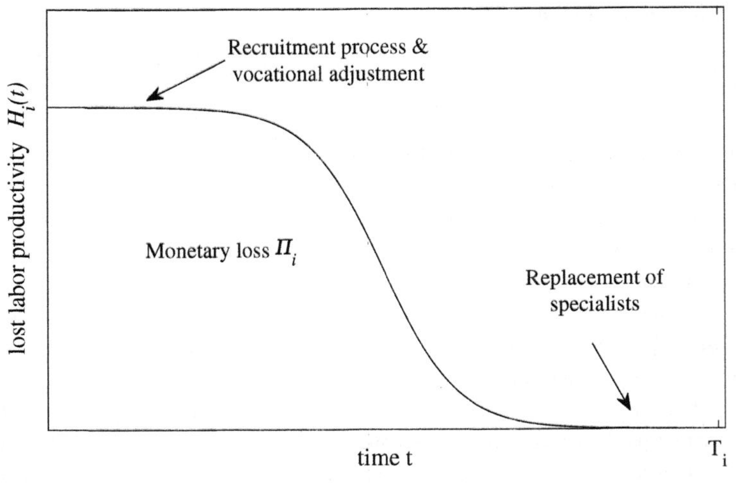

Fig. 2 Lost labor productivity $H_i(t)$ over time

where L_i reflects the lost full time equivalents in group i.

In principle, the impact of a loss of productive FTE for an economy could be modeled by considering the value of a statistical human life (e.g., [5, 9]). However, the reduction-in-loss estimates obtained by this method may be too high [6], and the replacement of large numbers of labor force participants requires significant time, both for the recruitment process and for vocational adjustment (friction time). In particular, specialists may be very hard to replace (if at all). We therefore prefer to use friction time analysis, proposing a scaled and shifted sigmoid function by which we can model the time-lagged replacement process [6, 10]. Figure 2 illustrates our approach.

As lost labor force participants are replaced, the loss of labor productivity in group i can be modeled as

$$H_i(t) = L_i \cdot h_i \cdot \left(1 - \underbrace{\frac{1}{1 + exp(\delta \cdot (1 - \frac{2t}{T_i}))}}_{\text{Scaled and shifted sigmoid function}}\right) \qquad t \in [0, T_i] \tag{2}$$

where T_i is the friction period and δ is a scaling factor that shapes the gradient of the curve. We shift and scale this function with $t' = \delta \cdot (2t/T_i - 1)$ such that $sigmoid(t') = 1/(1+exp(-t'))$ gives $f(t) = 1/(1+exp(\delta \cdot (1-2t/T_i)))$. Table 2 illustrates how this parameter shapes the share of FTEs replaced after a particular

Table 2 Share of FTEs replaced as a function of the sigmoid scaling factor δ

δ	3	4	4	6	7	8	9
$f(t = T_i)$ [%]	95.25	98.20	99.33	99.75	99.91	99.97	99.99

friction time has elapsed. As lost labor force participants are replaced, productivity loss decreases to zero as replacement time t converges to the friction period T_i.

T_i might differ among groups. Since replacing specialists probably takes much longer than replacing unskilled labor, friction time likely depends on both the number and the productivity of lost labor force participants that must be replaced. Hence, friction time can be specified as can be formulated as

$$T_i = c \cdot (L_i \cdot h_i)^a \tag{3}$$

where $a > 0$ and $c > 0$ are ancillary parameters that describe the capacity of the labor market to replace lost FTEs. The parameter c models the flexibility of the labor market. Larger values of c prolong friction time, for example in scenarios where the domestic labor market is unable to provide enough supply at short notice, or where bureaucratic or migration controls impede fast replacement of FTEs. The parameter a models the dependency type between the friction period and the lost labor productivity, such that $a = 1$ captures proportional and $a > 1$ disproportionate dependencies (e.g., when a severe epidemic wipes out many productive participants of the labor force). As these members are lost, the economy suffers a primary monetary loss due to lower labor productivity. The primary loss of group i can be calculated by integrating the lost labor productivity both over time, i.e. from the time the participants were lost ($t = 0$) until they were fully replaced ($t = T_i$), and over all groups

$$\Pi_i(T_i) = \int_0^{T_i} L_i \cdot h_i \cdot \left(1 - \frac{1}{1 + exp(\delta \cdot (1 - \frac{2t}{T_i}))}\right) dt = L_i \cdot h_i \cdot \frac{T_i}{2} \tag{4}$$

Integrating (3) into (4), the monetary loss in group i can be written as

$$\Pi_i = \frac{c}{2} \cdot (L_i \cdot h_i)^{a+1} \tag{5}$$

This loss is graphically represented in Fig. 2 by the area underneath the lost labor productivity curve $H_i(t)$.

Considering all groups, the overall labor productivity loss is

$$H(t) = \sum_{i=1}^{n} H_i(t) \qquad t \in [0, max(T_i)] \tag{6}$$

And thus the total primary monetary loss amounts to

$$\Pi = \sum_{i=1}^{n} \frac{c}{2} \cdot (L_i \cdot h_i)^{a+1} \tag{7}$$

However, in addition to this primary loss, there is also a secondary loss. Capital productivity also suffers as labor force participants are lost since machinery ceases to operate for a time or continues to be operated by less qualified staff (and hence at lower efficiency). Moreover, total factor productivity is reduced since lost labor force participants can no longer innovate. We consider this secondary loss by scaling primary loss with a group-specific ancillary parameter $\epsilon_i >= 1$, terming it Solow factor in honor of [8]. Total productivity and monetary losses are hence obtained after correcting (6) and (7) for such secondary loss:

$$H_\epsilon(t) = \sum_{i=1}^{n} H_i(t) \cdot \epsilon_i \qquad t \in [0, max(T_i)] \tag{8}$$

$$\Pi_\epsilon = \sum_{i=1}^{n} \frac{c}{2} \cdot \epsilon_i \cdot (L_i \cdot h_i)^{a+1} \tag{9}$$

2.2 *Strained Medical Emergency Services Capacity*

Supply for medical emergency services (MES) is limited, and hence only a limited number of victims can be treated within any given timeframe. This number M can be specified as a function

$$M = M(\frac{D}{d}, R) \tag{10}$$

where d is the treatment duration and D the time by which victims must have been treated to avoid certain death. Further, R comprises the available MES resources, i.e. personnel (doctors, nurses, etc.), infrastructure (hospitals, ambulances, etc.), and physical supplies (beds, equipment, drugs).

The event space we drew in Fig. 1 suggests that the total number L of lost labor force participants can be calculated as

$$\begin{aligned} L &= (V - M) + \beta \cdot M + \alpha \cdot \gamma \cdot M \\ &= V - M \cdot (1 - \beta - \alpha \cdot \gamma) \\ &= V - M \cdot \eta \end{aligned} \tag{11}$$

Note that the composite term $(1 - \beta - \alpha \cdot \gamma)$ is renamed to η to simplify the notation of the following equations. Stratifying L by groups yields

$$L_i = V_i - M_i \cdot \eta \tag{12}$$

where V_i is the number of victims in group i that require medical emergency service and M_i denotes the number of treated victims within group i. We now propose three methods to triage victims, and we explore the implications of each method for monetary loss. Thus, we analytically link human and economic loss, keeping medical supply constraints in mind. For all three methods, the number of victims treated in each group M_i is formally derived, then, using (12), the number of lost labor force participants can be calculated.

First In, First Out (FIFO) Triage methods such as START or SALT are typically recommended to optimize MES utilization [1, 2, 7]. Such concepts triage victims according to their level of injury and chances of survival. From an economic perspective, these treatments represent a random selection for which individual productivity is irrelevant; treatment is scheduled on a 'first come, first serve' basis.

Therefore, the number of victims randomly selected for treatment has a multivariate hypergeometric distribution [3], such that the number M_i of treated victims in each group i is

$$M_i = min(V_i, E[M_i]) = min(V_i, M \cdot \frac{V_i}{V}) \tag{13}$$

Preferential Treatment According to Productivity (PTAP) Treatment could also be rationed according to productivity levels. Under this scheme, victims belonging to the group with the highest labor productivity are treated first, those with the next highest are treated only if resources are still available, and so on until all resources are exhausted. The number of treated victims then is

$$M_i = min(V_i, max(0, M - \sum_{j=1}^{i-1} V_j)) \tag{14}$$

Minimization of Total Monetary Loss (MTML) A third triage option is to minimize total monetary loss to the economy, i.e. friction time is taken into account when scheduling treatment. Thus, the number of victims treated is obtained by using (12) in (9), which gives the optimization problem:

$$\min_{M_i} \sum_{i=1}^{n} \frac{c}{2} \cdot \epsilon_i \cdot ((V_i - M_i \cdot \eta) \cdot h_i)^{a+1} \tag{15}$$

Subject to:

$$\begin{aligned} &\sum_{i=1}^{n} M_i = M, \\ &M_i \in [0, V_i] \end{aligned} \tag{16}$$

The solution to this problem provides an optimal number of treatments M_i in each group i while minimizing total monetary loss Π_ϵ. This function is convex except for the cases of $a = 0$ and $a = 1$ which can be solved by Linear and Quadratic

Programming, respectively. Convex Programming is required to solve the problem for any a [4].

3 Illustration for Three Model Economies

We illustrate our concept by introducing the three model economies of Switzovenia, Tyrrhenia, and Aequatoria. These all differ in terms of population, labor productivity, and MES supply. While both Switzovenia and Tyrrhenia have small but highly productive populations, Aequatoria is a densely populated developing economy whose large unskilled labor force has low productivity. While MES supply is limited in both Aequatoria and Switzovenia, it is substantially larger in Tyrrhenia.

For each economy we simulate the impact of three distinct MCIs caused by deliberate attacks on critical infrastructures: A mass shooting in an underground network that causes 1000 victims, a series of bomb attacks on railway infrastructure that affects 10,000 victims, and an epidemic spread through intentionally contaminated drinking water that causes 100,000 victims.

3.1 *Parametrization*

The three model economies are specified by the parameters documented in Table 3. The population in each economy can be partitioned into (n = 3) groups (specialists, skilled labor, and unskilled labor) with different average productivity levels (h_1, h_2, h_3) with $h_1 > h_2 > h_3$.

Table 3 Specific parameters of model economies

Parameter	Switzovenia	Tyrrhenia	Aequatoria
Group size in millions $\{N_1, N_2, N_3\}$	{2, 2.5, 0.5}	{5, 12, 3}	{3, 10, 87}
Avg. labor prod. $\{h_1, h_2, h_3\}$ [$/h]	{100, 80, 55}	{100, 50, 30}	{85, 30, 8}
Solow factor $\{\epsilon_1, \epsilon_2, \epsilon_3\}$	{1.06, 1.05, 1.0}	{1.08, 1.04, 1.0}	{1.0, 1.0, 1.0}
Maximum number of treatments	5000	25000	500
Friction period parameter a	1	1	1
Friction period parameter c	0.007	0.0105	0.056
Scaling factor of the sigmoid function δ	5	5	5
Share of victims			
Partially recovered α	0.2	0.2	0.2
Not recovered β	0.1	0.1	0.1
Partially recovered but lost as FTEs γ	0.5	0.5	0.5

To simplify the computation, we set the ancillary parameter a to 1. Thus, the optimization problem can be solved by Quadratic Programming and noted in vector notation with $\mathbf{x} = [M_1, M_2, M_3]^\top$ and $\mathbf{v} = [V_1, V_2, V_3]^\top$ as

$$\min_{\mathbf{x}} = \frac{1}{2} \cdot \mathbf{x}^\top \cdot \mathbf{H} \cdot \mathbf{x} + \mathbf{f}^\top \cdot \mathbf{x} \tag{17}$$

Subject to:

$$\begin{aligned} \mathbf{A} \cdot \mathbf{x} &\leq b \\ \mathbf{0} \leq \mathbf{x} &\leq \mathbf{v} \end{aligned} \tag{18}$$

where

$$\mathbf{H} = c \cdot \eta^2 \cdot \begin{bmatrix} \epsilon_1 h_1^2 & 0 & 0 \\ 0 & \epsilon_2 h_2^2 & 0 \\ 0 & 0 & \epsilon_3 h_3^2 \end{bmatrix} \tag{19}$$

$$\mathbf{f} = -c \cdot \eta \cdot \begin{bmatrix} \epsilon_1 h_1^2 V_1 \\ \epsilon_2 h_2^2 V_2 \\ \epsilon_3 h_3^2 V_3 \end{bmatrix} \tag{20}$$

$$\mathbf{A} = \begin{bmatrix} 1 \cdots 1 \end{bmatrix} \tag{21}$$

$$b = M \tag{22}$$

For the case of Switzovenia, we set the ancillary parameter c such that such that the replacement of 1000 FTEs with an average labor productivity of $h_{avg} = h_2 = 80\$/\mathrm{h}$ takes 3 months (=548 working hours):

$$c = \frac{T_{avg}}{L \cdot h_{avg}} = \frac{548\,\mathrm{h}}{1000 \cdot 80\$/\mathrm{h}} = 0.007 \tag{23}$$

We assume this baseline value is exceeded by 150% in Tyrrhenia and by 800% in Aequatoria due to greater transaction cost and labor market inflexibility. Thus, we obtain ($c = 150\% \cdot 0.007 = 0.0105$) and ($c = 8 \cdot 0.007 = 0.056$), respectively.

3.2 Simulation Results

Tables 4, 5 and 6 detail the simulation results for all model economies. Victims, treated victims and lost FTEs are in thousands, and total monetary loss Π_ϵ is in millions.

Table 4 Simulation results for Switzovenia

Switzovenia		FIFO	PTAP	MTML
Shooting				
Victims	$\{V_1, V_2, V_3\}$	0.4, 0.5, 0.1	0.4, 0.5, 0.1	0.4, 0.5, 0.1
Treated victims	$\{M_1, M_2, M_3\}$	0.4, 0.5, 0.1	0.4, 0.5, 0.1	0.4, 0.5, 0.1
Lost FTEs	$\{L_1, L_2, L_3\}$	0.08, 0.1, 0.02	0.08, 0.1, 0.02	0.08, 0.1, 0.02
Total monetary loss	Π_ϵ	0.477	0.477	0.477
Bombs				
Victims	$\{V_1, V_2, V_3\}$	4, 5, 1	4, 5, 1	4, 5, 1
Treated victims	$\{M_1, M_2, M_3\}$	2, 2.5, 0.5	4, 1, 0	2.6, 2.4, 0
Lost FTEs	$\{L_1, L_2, L_3\}$	2.4, 3, 0.6	0.8, 4.2, 1	1.9, 3.1, 1
Total monetary loss	Π_ϵ	429	449	370
Epidemic				
Victims	$\{V_1, V_2, V_3\}$	40, 50, 10	40, 50, 10	40, 50, 10
Treated victims	$\{M_1, M_2, M_3\}$	2, 2.5, 0.5	5, 0, 0	5, 0, 0
Lost FTEs	$\{L_1, L_2, L_3\}$	38.4, 48, 9.6	36, 50, 10	36, 50, 10
Total monetary loss	Π_ϵ	109,872	107,940	107,940

Table 5 Simulation results for Tyrrhenia

Tyrrhenia		FIFO	PTAP	MTML
Shooting				
Victims	$\{V_1, V_2, V_3\}$	0.25, 0.6, 0.15	0.25, 0.6, 0.15	0.25, 0.6, 0.15
Treated victims	$\{M_1, M_2, M_3\}$	0.25, 0.6, 0.15	0.25, 0.6, 0.15	0.25, 0.6, 0.15
Lost FTEs	$\{L_1, L_2, L_3\}$	0.05, 0.12, 0.03	0.05, 0.12, 0.03	0.05, 0.12, 0.03
Total monetary loss	Π_ϵ	0.3	0.3	0.3
Bombs				
Victims	$\{V_1, V_2, V_3\}$	2.5, 6, 1.5	2.5, 6, 1.5	2.5, 6, 1.5
Treated victims	$\{M_1, M_2, M_3\}$	2.5, 6, 1.5	2.5, 6, 1.5	2.5, 6, 1.5
Lost FTEs	$\{L_1, L_2, L_3\}$	0.5, 1.2, 0.3	0.5, 1.2, 0.3	0.5, 1.2, 0.3
Total monetary loss	Π_ϵ	34	34	34
Epidemic				
Victims	$\{V_1, V_2, V_3\}$	25, 60, 15	25, 60, 15	25, 60, 15
Treated victims	$\{M_1, M_2, M_3\}$	6.2, 15, 3.8	25, 0, 0	15.5, 9.5, 0
Lost FTEs	$\{L_1, L_2, L_3\}$	20, 48, 12	5, 60, 15	12.6, 52.4, 15
Total monetary loss	Π_ϵ	54,810	51,621	47,544

These results suggest that the consequences of intentional attack depend on both the number of victims and the configuration of the model economy. If not more than 1000 victims suffer from the attack, in terms of lost FTEs there is no difference between the three triage concepts in both Switzovenia and Tyrrhenia, and differences are small for the case of Aequatoria. Total monetary loss is largest in Aequatoria and is also influenced by the triage method applied there, whereas there is no such influence in Switzovenia or Tyrrhenia. However, this picture changes

Table 6 Simulation results for Aequatoria

Aequatoria		FIFO	PTAP	MTML
Shooting				
Victims	$\{V_1, V_2, V_3\}$	0.03, 0.1, 0.87	0.03, 0.1, 0.87	0.03, 0.1, 0.87
Treated victims	$\{M_1, M_2, M_3\}$	0.01, 0.05, 0.44	0.03, 0.1, 0.37	0.03, 0.08, 0.39
Lost FTEs	$\{L_1, L_2, L_3\}$	0.02, 0.06, 0.52	0.01, 0.02, 0.57	0.01, 0.04, 0.55
Total monetary loss	Π_{ϵ}	0.644	0.608	0.598
Bombs				
Victims	$\{V_1, V_2, V_3\}$	0.3, 1, 8.7	0.3, 1, 8.7	0.3, 1, 8.7
Treated victims	$\{M_1, M_2, M_3\}$	0.01, 0.05, 0.44	0.3, 0.2, 0	0.25, 0.25, 0
Lost FTEs	$\{L_1, L_2, L_3\}$	0.29, 0.96, 8.35	0.06, 0.84, 8.7	0.1, 0.8, 8.7
Total monetary loss	Π_{ϵ}	165	154.1	153.8
Epidemic				
Victims	$\{V_1, V_2, V_3\}$	3, 10, 87	3, 10, 87	3, 10, 87
Treated victims	$\{M_1, M_2, M_3\}$	0.01, 0.05, 0.44	0.5, 0, 0	0.5, 0, 0
Lost FTEs	$\{L_1, L_2, L_3\}$	3.0, 10, 86.7	2.6, 10, 87	2.6, 10, 87
Total monetary loss	Π_{ϵ}	17,761	17,451	17,451

once the number of victims grows. For a scenario of 10,000 victims, there is a significant influence of the triage method in all three economies. Compared to FIFO, the MTML method reduces total monetary loss by 13.8% in Switzovenia and 6.7% in Aequatoria, while there is no influence in Tyrrhenia. This is due to the much larger capacity for treatment in this economy; the system has enough slack to satisfy all demand for treatment. In the extreme case of an epidemic with 100,000 victims, monetary loss is largest in Switzovenia since many highly productive labor force participants cannot recover. Given the larger capacity for MES supply in Tyrrhenia, monetary loss is 50.1% lower for random and 56% for MTML triage, but the loss is still significant. The relative differences between the three triage concepts are also largest in Tyrrhenia, whereas there is only a minor influence of triage on total monetary loss in Switzovenia and Aequatoria.

3.3 *Minimization of Monetary Loss*

Figures 3, 4, and 5 show simulation results for all three economies when victims are triaged such as to minimize total monetary loss to the economy. In each figure, the thin vertical line to the left-hand side of the diagram represents the capacity limit M up to which all victims can be treated (Switzovenia: 5000; Tyrrhenia: 25,000; Aequatoria: 500). In all analyses, these capacities are held constant whereas the number of victims varies. The upper plot shows how many victims from each of the three population subgroups (specialists, skilled and unskilled labor) are treated if MTML triage as defined in formulae 15 and 16 is applied. The lower plot shows

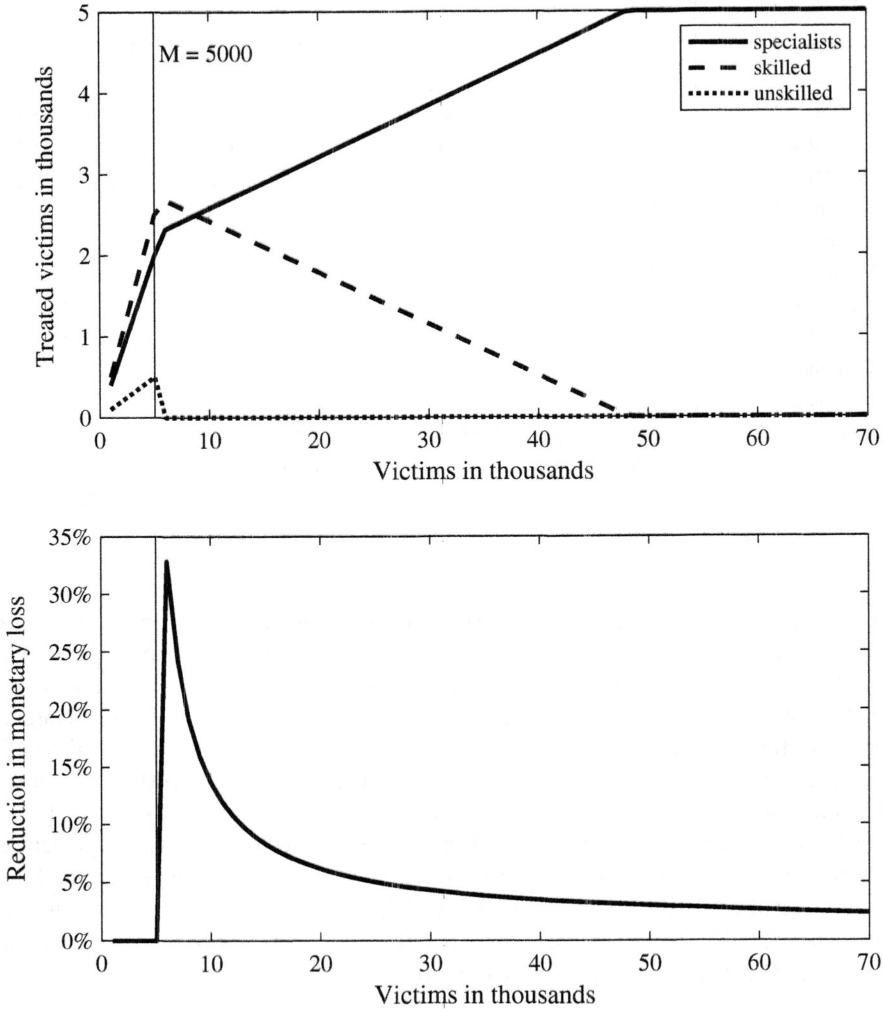

Fig. 3 Reduction of monetary loss in Switzovenia

the relative reduction of monetary loss which is calculated as the difference in loss between FIFO and MTML triage, i.e. $(\Pi_{\epsilon,FIFO} - \Pi_{\epsilon,MTML})/\Pi_{\epsilon,FIFO}$.

This relative difference is nil as long as the number of victims does not exceed MES supply; but if it does, then MTML triage reduces monetary loss by up to 32.8% in Switzovenia (48.4% in Tyrrhenia, 7.3% in Aequatoria). As the number of victims who seek treatment grows, the relative reduction of monetary loss converges to zero.

The analysis suggests that treatment scheduling is contingent on group membership once the number of victims exceeds MES supply in the respective economy. Whenever the number of victims V exceeds the capacity limit M, then MTML

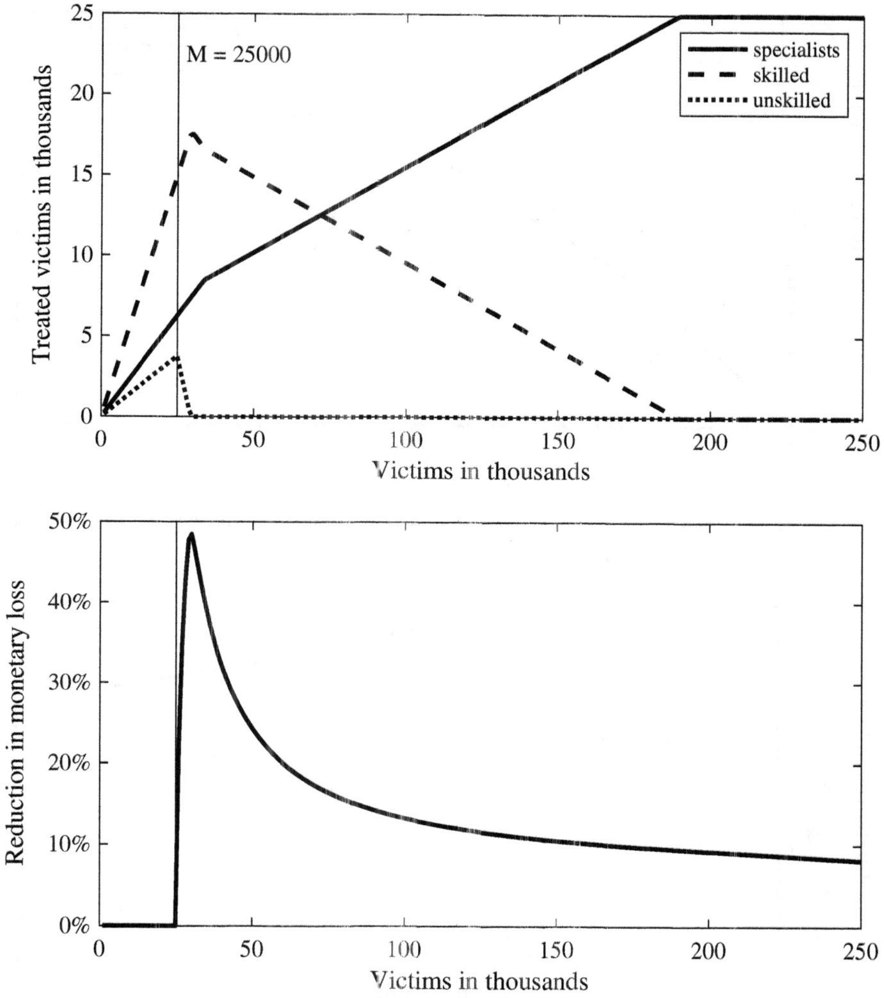

Fig. 4 Reduction of monetary loss in Tyrrhenia

triage suggests to first reduce treatment for unskilled labor (dotted lines in all figures), and then to reduce treatment for skilled labor (dashed lines). In other words, specialists receive preferential treatment, and treatment of the remaining labor force is rescheduled subject to remaining capacity. Should the number of victims in Switzovenia exceed 49,000 (in Tyrrhenia: 190,000; in Aequatoria: 22,800), MTML triage suggests to exclusively treat specialists.

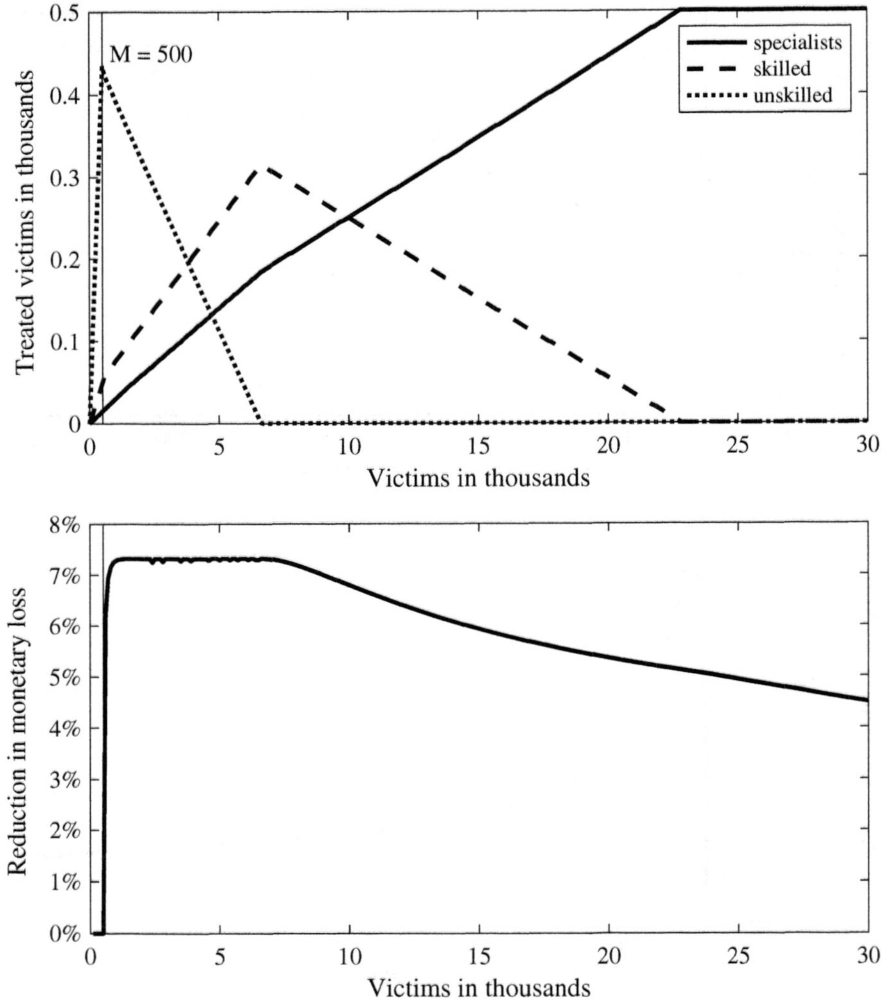

Fig. 5 Reduction of monetary loss in Aequatoria

4 Discussion

Our analysis suggests that whenever the number of victims inflicted by an MCI exceeds MES supply, a conflict between saving the economy from significant productivity loss and saving human lives exists. Using triage concepts such as our proposed MTML significantly reduces up to 48.4% of the monetary loss to the economy that is inflicted by an MCI. However, this triage also induces an ethical dilemma, since any preferential treatment on grounds of individual productivity is incompatible with the Hippocratic oath.

This dilemma can be somewhat mitigated if MES supply is increased by an additional emergency supply that can be made operational and scaled at short notice. However, such spare capacity would be expensive to build and maintain since it would barely be utilized in the absence of extreme events. Still, if the number of victims is very high, it will probably exceed any spare capacity. In this case, our MTML triage concept suggests that preferential treatment should be applied by treating the most productive members of the labor force first and then ration the remaining capacity among the less productive groups in order to maintain the productivity of the economy.

Without this minimization of friction time for specialists, the significant loss of labor force participants likely induces a productivity loss the neutralization of which will take a very long time. This perspective makes intentional attacks on critical infrastructure particularly dangerous, since the economic consequences of such an attack may change political majorities and society itself. It goes without saying that such extreme scenarios can only be imagined in the case of an uncontrolled epidemic, war, or massive terrorist attacks. Still, they illustrate the ethical dilemma any society would face under such circumstances. Hence, infrastructure defense is key to minimize the chance that such devastating attacks could ever occur.

The parametrization we provided is specific to the three model economies we conceptualized, but the simulation model is not. As the reduction of monetary loss is contingent on the number of victims, MES supply, group productivity levels, and friction time, we invite future research to feed data from real economies into our model, complementing our approach with additional illustrations. Further, our model could be refined by taking additional socioeconomic effects into account.

References

1. Bazyar, J., Farrokhi, M., Khankeh, H.: Triage systems in mass casualty incidents and disasters: a review study with a worldwide approach. Open Access Macedonian J. Med. Sci. **7**(3), 482 (2019)
2. Benson, M., Koenig, K.L., Schultz, C.H.: Disaster triage: Start, then save – a new method of dynamic triage for victims of a catastrophic earthquake. Prehosp. Disaster Med. **11**(2), 117–124 (1996)
3. Bishop, Y.M., Fienberg, S.E., Holland, P.W.: Discrete Multivariate Analysis: Theory and Practice. Springer Science & Business Media, New York (2007)
4. Boyd, S., Vandenberghe, L.: Convex Optimization. Cambridge University Press, Cambridge (2004)
5. Doucouliagos, C., Stanley, T., Giles, M.: Are estimates of the value of a statistical life exaggerated? J. Health Econ. **31**, 197–206 (2012)
6. Koopmanschap, M.A., Rutten, F.F., van Ineveld, B.M., Van Roijen, L.: The friction cost method for measuring indirect costs of disease. J. Health Econ. **14**(2), 171–189 (1995)
7. Lerner, E.B., Schwartz, R.B., Coule, P.L., Weinstein, E.S., Cone, D.C., Hunt, R.C., Sasser, S.M., Liu, J.M., Nudell, N.G., Wedmore, I.S., et al.: Mass casualty triage: an evaluation of the data and development of a proposed national guideline. Disaster Med. Public Health Prep. **2**(1), 25–34 (2008)
8. Solow, R.M.: A contribution to the theory of economic growth. Q. J. Econ. **70**(1), 65–94 (1956)

9. Viscusi, K., Aldy, J.: The value of a statistical life: a critical review of market estimates throughout the world. J. Risk Uncertain. **27**, 5–76 (2003)
10. Weisstein, E.W.: Sigmoid function. Technical report, MathWorld. http://mathworld.wolfram.com/SigmoidFunction.html. Accessed October 2019

Vulnerability and Resilience of National Power Grids: A Graph-Theoretical Optimization Approach and Empirical Simulation

Jean-Claude Metzger, Saša Parađ, Stefan Ravizza, and Marcus M. Keupp

1 Introduction

Modern societies must rely on a working electrical power distribution system, i.e. a power grid that supplies instantaneously all the required demand. System failure can lead to uncovered power demand, such that infrastructures and public services which rely on electrical power are significantly impaired or even terminated (e.g., public transport, drinking water supply, telecommunications, etc.).

Further, initial failure in a particular area of the power grid can result in a sequence of cascading failures that spreads through both the domestic and the international grid, implying black-outs in whole regions or even countries [12]. This effect is illustrated by actual black-out events from the recent past, e.g. in Italy [15], the north-east USA and Canada [13] and India [18]. These and other power grids have been investigated over the last two decades [7, 11]. The analysis

J.-C. Metzger
hemotune AG, Zurich, Switzerland
e-mail: jean-claude.metzger@hemotune.ch

S. Parađ
Valucor Group AG, Zurich, Switzerland

Valucor (FL) AG, Vaduz, Liechtenstein
e-mail: sascha.parad@valucor.ch

S. Ravizza
IBM Switzerland Ltd., Zurich, Switzerland
e-mail: stefan.ravizza@ch.ibm.com

M. M. Keupp (✉)
Department of Defense Economics, Military Academy at the Swiss Federal Institute of Technology Zurich, Birmensdorf, Switzerland
e-mail: mkeupp@ethz.ch

M. M. Keupp (ed.), *The Security of Critical Infrastructures*, International Series in Operations Research & Management Science 288,
https://doi.org/10.1007/978-3-030-41826-7_6

of power grids as graphs using graph theory is useful and productive (see [10] for a review). Prior research has analyzed topological patterns of nodes, edges and their links [1, 6]. Other studies provide dynamic analyses of potential black-out situations [7, 11]. Further, technical work has focused on the electro-physical properties of a power grid by enriching graphs with impedances [4] and complete AC models [3]. However, the majority of extant work focuses on a worst-case scenario by which the removal of a critical node or edge from the grid results in cascading failure that eventually causes a black-out. By contrast, in this chapter we propose that less-than-worst-case scenarios deserve equal attention. In particular, we focus on scenarios in which the grid can satisfy partially, but not completely, any given demand for power.

Power grids are subject to the fundamental electro-physical restriction that all power demand must be in equilibrium with all power supply at all times. If this condition is not met, the grid frequency will deviate from the ideal target value of $f = 50\,\text{Hz}$. A deviation as small as 2.5 Hz can already result in resonance oscillations and subsequent turbine damage [16].

Hence, a sudden drop of supply will result in a power shortage situation that requires shedding some of the electrical load (demand). By the same token, if a sudden drop in demand occurs, supply must also be reduced immediately. In both cases, uncovered demand (UD) results. The focus of our analysis is to provide a dynamic model of how UD develops as a result of node or edge removal.

We first discuss how a power grid network can be modeled as a graph and how linear programming can be used to simulate UD. Furthermore, quantitative measures are introduced which capture the reduction of grid performance as a function of node or edge removal. Section 3 presents how the vulnerability of a power grid can be analyzed by the systematic modeling of different attack strategies. Section 4 illustrates this analysis with topological and capacity data from the Swiss maximum voltage power grid. Section 5 develops some recommendations for building robust and resilient power networks.

2 Analyzing Power Grids Using Graph Theory

A power grid can be described as a set of elements that supply power (power plants), demand power (industry, individuals) or transform power between voltage levels. Those elements are connected to each other by power transmission lines that transfer power throughout the network. The totality of all elements and transmission lines can be modeled as a directed graph $G = (V, E)$, where V is a set of nodes and E the set of links between those nodes. Each transmission line is modeled by two directed edges that point to either the supplying or the receiving node.

Nodes can either supply to or demand power from the network or do both. Hence, for each node i the *net demand* is calculated as

$$y_i = supply_i - demand_i, \forall i \in N \tag{1}$$

where N is the total number of nodes.

While demand is modeled as a fixed value, the supply values of particular providers, such as pumped storage power stations, can vary between a minimum supply value $supply_i^{min}$ and a maximum supply value $supply_i^{max}$. Hence, the resulting net demand values y_i are bounded for each node i by

$$y_i^{min} \leq y_i \leq y_i^{max} \tag{2}$$

where $y_i^{min} = supply_i^{min} - demand_i$ and $y_i^{max} = supply_i^{max} - demand_i$.

Electricity imports from or to neighboring countries are modeled by the demand and supply of those (foreign) nodes that are adjacent to the focal country's border and connected to its internal power grid. Imported power is treated as supply and has therefore a lower and an upper supply boundary, while exported power is treated as demand and kept at a constant level $demand_i$.

The power flow of each edge is noted by x_{ij} for the edge transferring power from node i to node j and x_{ji} for the edge transferring power in the opposite direction, i.e. from node j to node i. The flows on those edges are also bounded by the physical capacity limit of the transmitting power line:

$$0 \leq x_{ij} \leq x_{ij}^{max} \tag{3}$$

One of the two flows between two nodes will always be zero while the other one defines the direction of the flow. If there is no power flow between two nodes then both edges will have the value zero.

Eventually, for each node i the difference of the outgoing and the incoming flows must equal the *net demand* of this node:

$$\underbrace{\sum_{(j,i)\in E} x_{ji}}_{outgoing\ flow} - \underbrace{\sum_{(i,k)\in E} x_{ik}}_{incoming\ flow} = y_i \quad \forall i \in N \tag{4}$$

Figure 1 shows a small example of a graph with seven nodes and fourteen edges. Node 7 is an auxiliary node that connects nodes 2, 4 and 5 to each other.[1]

2.1 Power Flow Calculation Using Linear Programming

In order to verify if the overall supply of a network can cover all demand by means of the existing transmission lines, the optimization problem specified by Eqs. (5)–(8) has to be solved. It is stated as a linear programming formulation where the overall

[1]While this auxiliary node neither demands nor supplies any power, it is required to reflect the tripartite connection between nodes 2, 4, and 5.

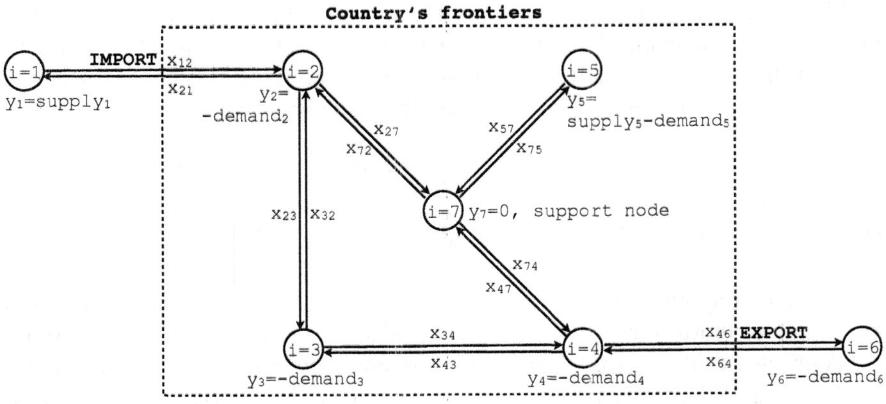

Fig. 1 This small sample network imports power from abroad via node 1 ($x_{12} = supply_1$ and $x_{21} = 0$) and exports power to node 6 ($x_{46} = -demand_6$ and $x_{64} = 0$). Nodes 2, 3 and 4 only demand power while node 5 supplies and demands power

power flow over all transmission lines is minimized (5). Hence, the overall loss from power transmission is minimized.[2] Inequalities (6) and (7) are calculated by placing Eq. (4) into the inequalities of Eq. (2). Equation (8) defines lower and upper bounds on the power flow variable x. It reflects the physical power flow limitations of the network's transmission lines.

Optimization problem (linear programming)

$$min \sum_{(i,j)\in E} x_{ij} \tag{5}$$

$$\underbrace{\sum_{(j,i)\in E} x_{ji}}_{outgoingflow} - \underbrace{\sum_{(i,k)\in E} x_{ik}}_{incomingflow} \leq y_i^{max} \quad \forall i \in N \tag{6}$$

$$- \underbrace{\sum_{(j,i)\in E} x_{ji}}_{outgoingflow} + \underbrace{\sum_{(i,k)\in E} x_{ik}}_{incomingflow} \leq -y_i^{min} \quad \forall i \in N \tag{7}$$

$$x_{ij}^{min} \leq x_{ij} \leq x_{ij}^{max} \quad \forall (i,j) \in E \tag{8}$$

An optimal solution for this LP not only proves that a network exists that can satisfy all demands. It also highlights which edges are transferring more power than others and hence illustrates that edges may differ in terms of their strategic

[2]By this approach, our model reflects engineers' attempts to minimize transmission loss as they operate real power networks.

importance for the network. The absolute power flow on a network's transmission line is calculated over the two edges connecting two nodes by $|x_{ij} - x_{ji}| \; \forall (i, j) \in E$.

2.2 (N-1) Analysis and Resulting Uncovered Demand

The failure of both nodes and edges can result in reduced network performance. An (N-1) analysis can identify the extent to which this is the case by analyzing the consequences of node removal for the remaining network's performance. Analogously, an (E-1) analysis can analyze those consequences when edges are removed. The node removal analysis comprises the following sequence of steps.

Step 1 Remove a node j and identify the edges connecting other nodes to node j. Delete also those connecting edges.
Step 2 Check if the remaining nodes and edges have been split into subgraphs.[3]
Step 3 Conduct for each subgraph the optimization problem as stated in Eqs. (5)–(8).
Step 4 If no solution to the optimization problem could be found, the demand of the subgraph is iteratively reduced by setting demands to zero (starting with the smallest demand within the subgraph) until a solution to the optimization problem is found or the demand of the subgraph cannot be reduced further.
Step 5 The covered demand and power flows of the subgraphs are stored.

Finally, we introduce the following quantitative measures for the analysis of the resulting graph or set of subgraphs.

Uncovered Demand (UD) Uncovered demand (UD) measures the reduced network performance, i.e. the percentage of any demand that cannot be covered after a node j has been removed:

$$UD = 100\% - \frac{100\%}{total\_demand_N} \cdot total\_demand_{(N-1)} \tag{9}$$

with

$$total\_demand_N = \sum_{i \in N} demand_i$$

$$total\_demand_{(N-1)} = \sum_{i \in N \setminus j} demand_i$$

[3]It is possible that the original graph is split into subgraphs upon node removal. For example, in Fig. 1 the removal of node 7 generates a subgraph that comprises only node 5, and another subgraph that comprises all other nodes.

This measure can be applied repeatedly, such that uncovered demand in the case of repeated node removal can also be calculated.

Residual Flow Capacity (RFC) Residual flow capacity (RFC) measures the extent to which any unused capacity is available on any transmission line $(i, j) \in E$:

$$RFC_{ij} = 100\% - \frac{100\%}{x_{ij}^{max}} \cdot (x_{ij}^{max} - x_{ij}) \tag{10}$$

This measure allows us to identify edges that are approaching their physical transmission capacity limit.

3 Vulnerability Analysis of Power Grids

Our analysis focuses on conscious and deliberate attacks against the power grid, whereas the analysis of random damage caused by natural disasters or hardware failure is beyond the scope of this chapter. Deliberate attack patterns target specific elements in the network that are easy to reach, have little resilience, or prove to be critical for network performance. In the following, we propose different operationalizations of such deliberate attack patterns, adopting the viewpoint of the attacker. A power grid can be deliberately attacked by removing single or multiple elements of the network, i.e. nodes, edges, or both.

3.1 Node Removal

Supply Removing those nodes which deliver maximum supply first can result in a nationwide low power situation. As a result, certain regions will be out of power, or government may ration the remaining capacity on the national level.

Demand Removing those nodes with the highest power demand first can result in local black-outs that affect areas with strong power demands, such as densely populated urban zones or industrial facilities.

Import Removing those nodes which provide import supplies first can also result in a nationwide low power situation. Whereas import nodes can be attacked both from within and beyond the national border, any national government can only protect nodes within the border. Hence, any country that must rely on foreign energy imports is particularly vulnerable if the attacker employs this strategy.

Export Removing those nodes which export power abroad first can result in power shortages or black-outs in neighboring countries. This effect also destabilizes the national grid, such that high demand for ancillary services that can compensate for the lack of demand is generated.

Topological An attacker striving to exploit the topological structure of the grid would minimize the number of attacked nodes while targeting those with the highest topological relevance for network performance. The relevance of each node can be measured by its *betweenness centrality* [7], which measures how often each node appears on a shortest path between any two nodes. Since there can be several shortest paths between two nodes s and t, the betweenness centrality of node v is:

$$C_B(v) = \sum_{s \neq t \neq v \in N} \frac{n_{st}(v)}{N_{st}} \tag{11}$$

where N_{st} is the total number of shortest paths from node s to node t and $n_{st}(v)$ is the number of those paths that pass through v. A high betweenness centrality value $C_B(v)$ implies that many shortest paths pass through the node v and therefore the node must have a topologically central position within the graph.

Whenever such central nodes are removed, the network loses multiple edges and the graph splits into subgraphs. As a result, regional power networks are disconnected from each other, implying the breakdown of the national transmission grid.

Terrorism An (N-1) analysis can be conducted for each node of a graph, i.e. a node is removed from the initial graph, the reduced graph is analyzed using the UD measure and afterwards the removed node is reintegrated before the next node is removed. As a result, discrete UDs are known, such that an attacker can target those with the highest UDs. This attack strategy can be deployed with little effort while it substantially reduces covered power demand. Contemporary computing equipment can calculate the respective UD values in a very short time. In our subsequent illustration, calculation for a power grid with 134 nodes and 394 edges was done in 38 s.[4]

Optimized Terrorism The above iterative approach can be extended in order to identify maximum UD when multiple nodes are removed. While computing time grows exponentially with network complexity (e.g. removing three nodes in a network with N nodes results in $N \cdot (N-1) \cdot (N-2)$ simulation runs), the power grid can be systematically analyzed in finite time to find those nodes whose joint removal implies maximum damage for the power grid.

3.2 *Edge Removal*

Transmission Lines with Maximum Power Flow Transmission lines can be easily attacked because they run outdoors and bridge long geographical distances. Whenever an edge is about to reach its maximum transmission capacity—as indi-

[4]Server infrastructure: 4x Intel Xeon Gold 6150 18C 165W 2.7 GHz CPU with 1.0 TB RAM.

cated by small RFC—and cannot be substituted by redundant edges, it constitutes a high-value target. The removal of such edges creates uncovered demand.

Transmission Lines with Maximum UD Similar to the node removal strategies *terrorism* and *optimized terrorism*, UDs can be calculated for both discrete and joint removal of edges. Hence, edges with the highest UDs are identified as attack targets. This identification also reveals edges critical for grid topology, e.g. those which import or export power, bridge subgraphs, or link significant supply and demand.

4 Simulation

The Swiss maximum voltage power grid transmits power by 380 kV and 220 kV transmission lines [16]. We modeled this grid as a directed graph with 159 nodes[5] and 394 bidirectional edges. Topological data for this network was obtained from a publicly available map created by the European Network of Transmission System Operators for Electricity [8]. Geocoordinates for each node were obtained from public Swisstopo data [5]. We imported these into Matlab R2017b and plotted them onto a map provided by d-maps.com [17]. Since we focus on the Swiss power grid, we modeled only nodes and edges within the national border, with the exception of 19 neighboring nodes in Germany, Austria, Italy and France that transmit imports and exports of power. Figure 2 superimposes our model onto a map of Switzerland.

4.1 Capacity Model

After this topological structure was defined, we attributed it with actual transmission flows and capacities. During this process, we made three assumptions to simplify the analysis.

First, we did not consider seasonal demand variation (e.g., higher power demand during the winter months due to heating). We can therefore work with annual demand and supply figures which are publicly available. Second, we did not consider dynamic electrophysical effects. Third, we assumed that any node connected to both a 380 kV and a 220 kV transmission line can transform any quantity of power between these voltage levels in either direction.

Energy Demand Energy demand was calculated for each node based on the overall energy consumption in Switzerland in 2013, i.e. a total consumption of 59,323 GWh [14]. We spread this national consumption over the cantons (federal states) of Switzerland by their respective population. We then further subdivided

[5]These 159 nodes comprise 134 physical supply and demand nodes as well as 25 auxiliary nodes we introduced to capture multiple connections.

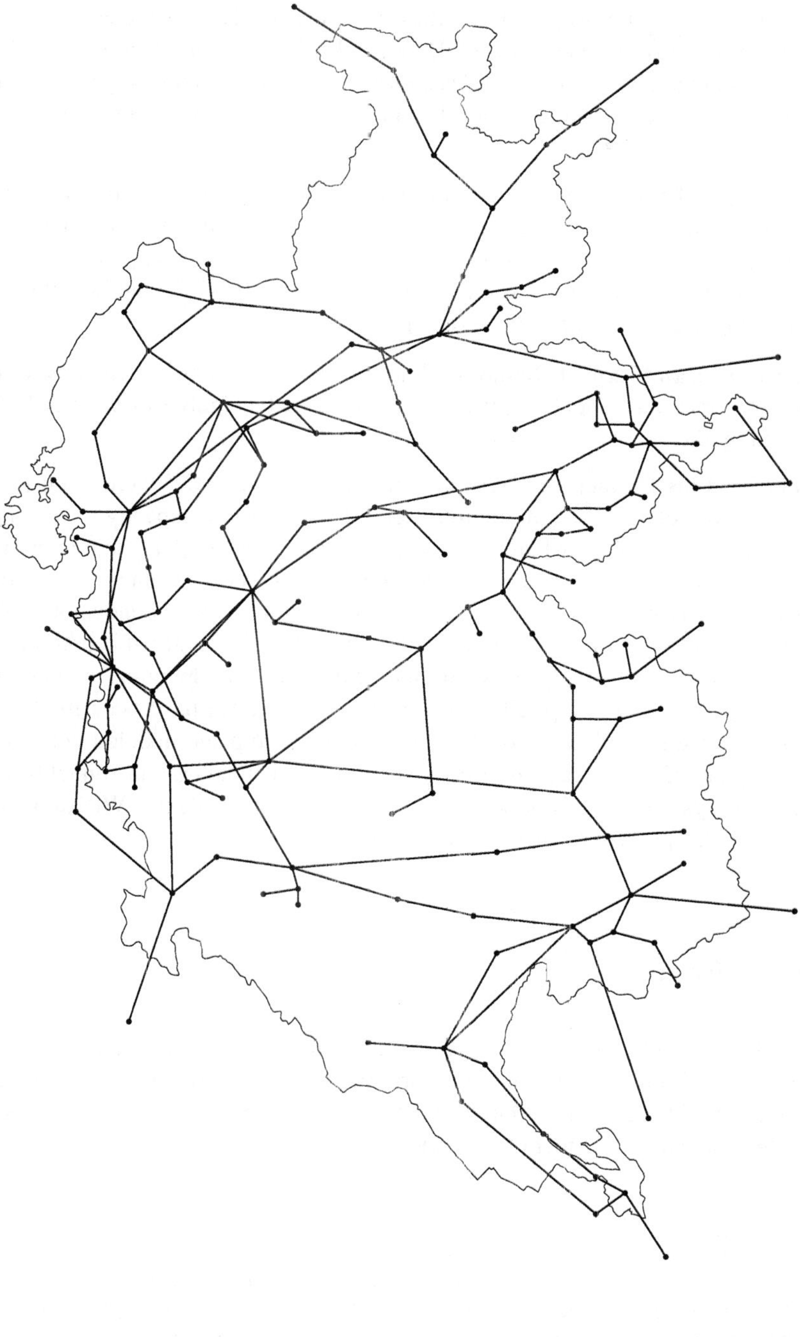

Fig. 2 The Swiss maximum voltage power grid as a graph with 159 nodes and 394 edges (simplified representation)

these cantonal consumptions according to the nodes present in each canton. The demands from cantons where no node is present were distributed to the demands of the surrounding cantons.

We excluded the ten most populous cities from this subdivision and added them separately to the closest node instead.[6] Hence, all nodes within a canton have the same energy demand but for those nodes closest to the most populous cities. These latter nodes are modeled with a higher demand to reflect the larger power demand of urban areas.

Energy Supply Energy supply by nuclear power stations and run-of-river and storage power plants is assumed to be constant and hence the minimal and maximal values are equal ($supply_i^{min} = supply_i^{max}$). For the supply of pump storage, the calculated values have been used as the maximal values $supply_i^{max}$ and the minimal values have been set to $supply_i^{min} = 0\,\text{GWh}$.

Import Supplies and Export Demands Import supplies and export demands were calculated based on the annual supply and demand of each neighboring country [17] and divided by the number of nodes in the respective country.

Transmission Line Capacities Transmission line capacities x_{ij}^{max} were calculated based on the formula for the maximum (thermal) transmission capacity [2, p. 27]: $Power = \sqrt{3} \cdot U \cdot 4 \cdot I_{max}$ where U is the voltage level and I_{max} is the maximum allowed current of a single conductor while the factor 4 in the formula relates to the number of conductors in the line, i.e. a conductor bundle of four conductors. We assumed the bundle was of type 243-AL1/39- ST1A since this material is used most frequently in maximum voltage transmission grids. The corresponding maximum current is $I_{max} = 645\,\text{A}$ [2, p. 20]. Each of the 380 kV lines have been modeled with four conductors while each of the 220 kV lines have been modeled with two conductors [9, p. 92]. The transmission capacity was calculated on an annual basis ($Power \cdot 365\,\text{days} \cdot 24\,\text{h/day} \cdot 3600\,\text{s/h}$) and transformed from Joule to GWh (division by 3.6E+12). This procedure gave the capacities shown in Table 1.

4.2 Calculation

We created two Excel worksheets, one with all topological node data, demands and supplies, and one with all transmission capacities of all edges. These two Excel worksheets were imported into Matlab R2017b using the Spreadsheet Import Tool to generate a database container (*.mat) file.

[6]For example, two nodes supply power to the canton of Geneva. This canton has 280,400 inhabitants, of which 189,033 dwell in the city of Geneva. One of the two nodes is closer to the city, hence, in our model this node supplies power to 329,233 inhabitants (280,400/2 + 189,033). The second node supplies power to the remaining 140,200 (280,400/2) inhabitants.

Table 1 Transmission line capacities

Line types	First line [kV]	Second line [kV]	Third line [kV]	Transmission capacity [GWh]
Line type 1a	220	None	None	4310
Line type 1b	380	None	None	14,900
Line type 2a	220	220	None	8620
Line type 2b	380	220	None	19,210
Line type 2c	380	380	None	29,800
Line type 3a	380	220	220	23,520
Line type 3b	380	380	220	34,110
Line type 3c	380	380	380	44,700

We then used the `graph` function to generate a Matlab graph structure. We used the `conncomp` function to analyze if a graph was split into subgraphs upon a particular removal strategy. For all graphs and subgraphs, we used the function `linprog` to solve the optimization problem as stated in (5) to (8).

Whenever a node or edge removal strategy involved multiple removals, this procedure was used iteratively. For the topological strategy, betweenness centrality was calculated by Matlab's `centrality` function. Finally, uncovered demand was calculated and plotted as a function of node or edge removal.

4.3 Results

4.3.1 Node Removal

We iteratively removed each node of the graph and analyzed whether the resulting graph had split into subgraphs. We then solved the linear program as stated in (5) to (8). If the resulting grid could not cover the full demand, this demand was reduced as described in step 4 of Sect. 2.2, i.e. by setting the demand of the node with the smallest demand to zero (load shedding). For security reasons, the following results are presented by node and edge coding id's only, and geocoordinates are omitted.

For each removed node, uncovered demand was calculated according to (9) as a percentage of total demand. Figure 3 presents the results of this (N-1) analysis. The grid exhibits significant scale free properties [9], i.e. very few nodes are of constitutive importance to the grid, and their removal may cause the network to collapse. In our calculation, the removal of 93 nodes (i.e., 69% of all nodes in the networks) caused UDs of less than 1%, whereas these increased to between 8.8% and 11.1% when one of the demand nodes D6, D9, D15, D17 or D18 was removed.

We then simulated each node removal strategy as outlined in Sect. 3.1. Each strategy was calculated in two variants in which three and five nodes were removed, respectively. After these multiple removals the graph was inspected for splitting into

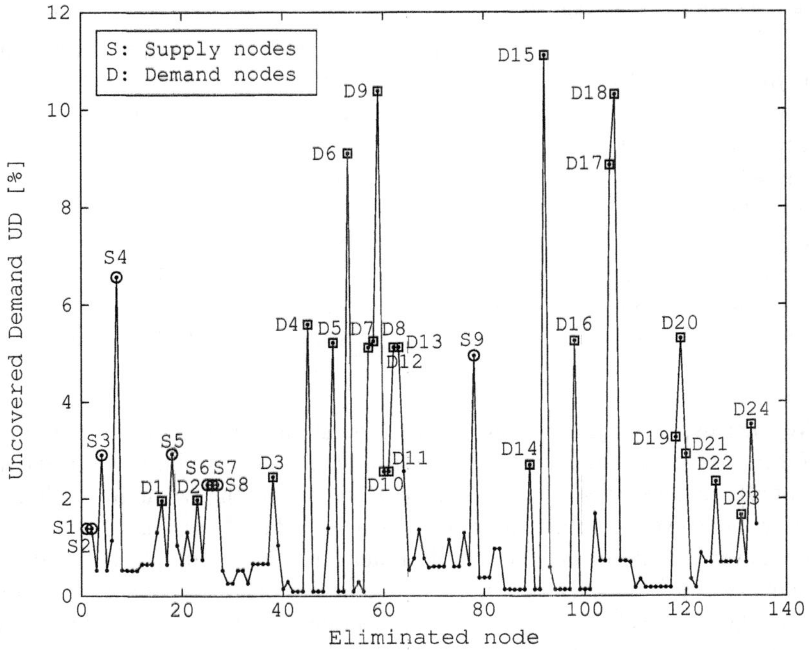

Fig. 3 Uncovered demand (UD) as a function of discrete node removal. We labeled nodes whose removal caused the largest uncovered demands by circles (supply nodes) and squares (demand nodes)

Table 2 Uncovered demands as a function of multiple node removal

Attack strategy	UD_{3nodes}	UD_{5nodes}
Supply	20.2%	25.1%
Demand	7.9%	13.3%
Import	15.5%	25.8%
Export	12.6%	20.7%
Topological	8.4%	20.3%
Terrorism	20.0%	26.1%

subgraphs; then, the optimization problem was solved. Table 2 presents the resulting uncovered demands by strategy and variation.

Removing nodes according to the *Supply*, *Import* and *Terrorism* attack strategies had the strongest negative effect on the Swiss power grid. By the removal of only five nodes (i.e., 3.7% of the grid), an uncovered demand of at least 25.1% results. By contrast, the removal of nodes with the highest demands according to the demand strategy resulted in the smallest UD values of all variants (7.9% and 13.3%, respectively).

Finally, the removal of those five nodes with maximum topological impact split the graph into six subgraphs and implied a loss of 62 edges, i.e. 15.7% of all edges.

When only three of these nodes were removed, the graph did not split, but still 32 edges were lost.

4.3.2 Edge Removal

Consistent with our explanations in Sect. 3.2, we ran two simulations for edge removal analysis. First, we simulated the discrete removal of edges with maximum transmission capacity and calculated the resulting UDs. Second, we performed an (E-1) analysis on the grid by discretely removing edges one by one, identifying those whose removal caused the highest UDs. Once these edges were known, they were eliminated from the graph to simulate the consequences for the grid.

The 394 bidirectional edges in our model correspond to 197 physical transmission lines in the grid. Figure 4 shows the absolute energy flows transmitted by these lines. It also gives the residual flow capacity (RFC) for each edge. With an average RFC of 86.6%, the grid seems to have much spare capacity by which power could be rerouted, and hence it appears relatively robust against random malfunction or loss of transmission lines. However, this picture changes when more deliberate attack patterns are considered.

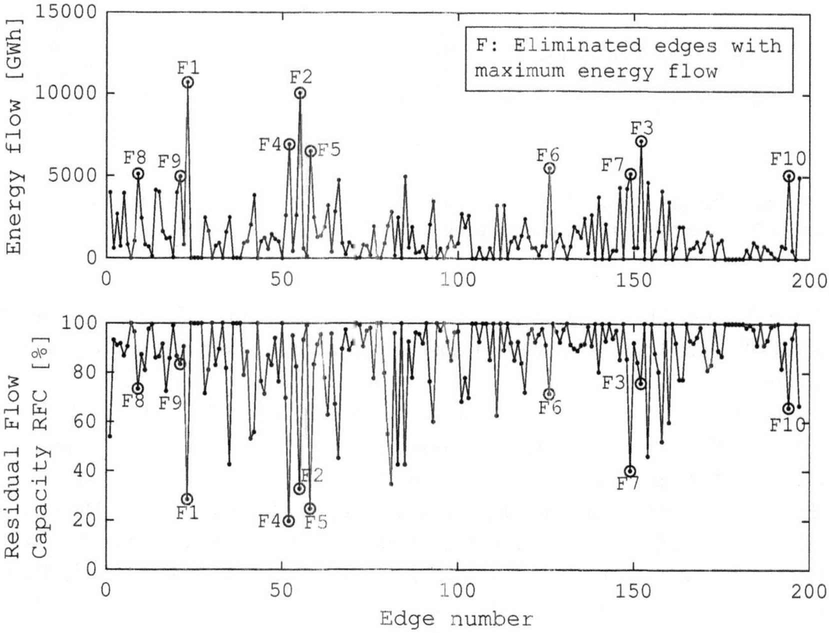

Fig. 4 The upper plot shows the energy flows of all the 197 transmission lines. The lower plot shows for each edge the Residual Flow Capacity as defined in Eq. (10) that relates the maximum flow values of the upper plot to the maximum flow capacities of each edge. The ten edges with the highest energy flow have been marked with a circle and labeled by *F* in both plots

Table 3 Uncovered demands (UD) after removing three, five or ten edges

Attack strategy	UD_{3nodes}	UD_{5nodes}	$UD_{10nodes}$
Maximum power flow	10.4%	15.6%	20.8%
Maximum UD	15.6%	20.6%	34.1%

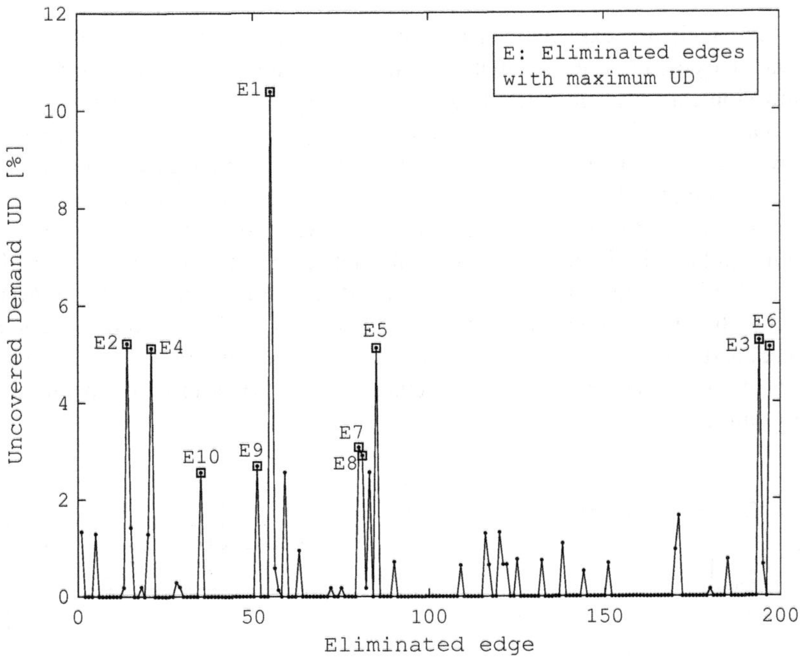

Fig. 5 Uncovered demand (UD) as a function of edge removal. Edges whose removal causes the highest UDs are marked with a square and labeled by E

Table 3 gives UDs when three or more edges are removed. For example, the removal of edges F1 to F10 which transmit the largest power flows in the network results in a UD of 20.8%.

Figure 5 presents the results of an (E-1) analysis for all 197 edges. The results corroborate the finding of the node removal analysis, i.e. the Swiss maximum voltage grid has significant scale free properties.

By contrast, some edges are of constitutive importance for the grid. The removal of any of the edges E2, E3, E4, E5 or E6 generates UDs of more than 5.1%, and the removal of E1 alone generates a UD of 10.4%. When those ten edges whose discrete elimination causes the highest respective UD values are removed in conjunction, a UD of 34.1% results (Table 3). This implies the grid is highly vulnerable, since the grid's transmission capacity can be reduced by a third by targeting only 5% of all edges.

5 Discussion

This simulation has modeled the Swiss maximum voltage transmission network as a graph and used linear programming techniques to analyze the resilience of this network. At a first glance, this grid appears relatively robust to cases of random and isolated component failure, since such events only result in minor performance loss. We find that the discrete removal of 69% of all nodes and 93% of all edges has a performance impact of close to nil, implying that power production can be managed and rerouted flexibly in the case of a probabilistic event.

However, this picture changes when deliberate attacks are considered. While the Swiss maximum voltage power grid is relatively robust against random failure of single components, deliberate attacks that follow a particular strategy can inflict significant damage to the grid. Both the node and the edge removal analyses demonstrate that significant uncovered demand is caused as a result of the removal of few yet topologically important elements. In particular, the node removal analysis suggests that removing supply (power-producing) elements from the network causes significantly more damage than removing demand (power-consuming) elements, such as urban areas. This implies the network we studied could adapt relatively well to demand failure by reducing supply, but would struggle to maintain performance upon supply failure.

Our modeling approach has made a number of simplifying assumptions that future research could relax. For example, we assumed that any node connected to both 220 kV and 380 kV lines has unlimited transformation capacity between these voltage levels. The resulting estimates for uncovered demand can thus be interpreted as best case scenarios, since the introduction of a restriction factor that limits transmission capacity puts further stress on the grid in the case of attacks. Future research may therefore expand our approach by putting more emphasis on the electro-physical and electro-dynamic restrictions of a power grid.

Prior literature has focused on the topological analysis of power grids, with the goal of identifying bottlenecks among both power supply and transmission elements [9, 12]. However, our results caution the reader to rely on topological analysis alone since this focus is unlikely to provide a full picture of the damage that deliberate attacks could cause. Our node removal analysis showed that, while the topological attack strategy causes an uncovered demand of 20.3% by removing five nodes with high betweenness centrality, the supply, import, and terrorism strategies inflict even greater damage. Hence, even a topological redesign of the network that emphasizes greater redundancy would not prevent such attacks. In this respect, the edge removal analysis shows that more edges than nodes must be removed to inflict similar damage, but since edges can be attacked more easily than nodes, targeted terrorism against transmission lines remains a feasible attack strategy.

The feasibility of deliberate attacks therefore confronts power grid operators with significant architectural challenges, and building resilient networks that can withstand deliberate attack patterns is at the core of this challenge. In all the analyzed attack patterns, the attacker has an advantage since the attacker chooses the strategy, the time and the intensity of the attack. The operators can neither foresee nor prevent such attacks with certainty. At the same time, an all-hazard approach that intends to protect the complete grid against any potential attack implies prohibitively high cost and hence is economically not viable for a grid operator even if such protective structures can be built. Hence, a more cost-effective approach is to increase the resilience of the network by reducing the damage any attack can infer onto the grid. As such resilience renders attacks futile, the attacker is also "educated" that any attack will be of little consequence. In this respect, three measures should be considered which, by themselves or in conjunction, should increase the resilience of any power grid.

First, operators can control temporary disequilibria between power supply and demand by applying ancillary services [2]. However, today's services were not designed to withstand deliberate attacks, and hence large-scale safety capacity should be created that can bridge supply gaps at any time and for longer periods of time. Our simulation suggests that deliberate attacks can cause uncovered demand that exceeds 20% of supply. In today's grids, such significant loss would immediately result in cascading load shedding, such that certain regions will be without power or power has to be rationed. Future safety capacity must be built to a scale that can cover such losses until the grid can be stabilized. Second, as existing power grid nodes and edges are replaced at the end of their technological lifecycle, future grid construction should strive to both reduce the betweenness centrality of nodes wherever possible and to add redundant edges with large residual flow capacity that can reroute power. This redundancy can be further strengthened by robust construction methods, e.g. by tunneling transmission lines through subsurface infrastructure instead of letting them run in open air. Of course, this robust construction comes at a price since air can no longer be used as an isolator, implying higher construction cost due to the adverse thermodynamic properties of subsurface transmission lines. Third, by definition the strategic importance of any transmission grid declines as the supply of power can be decentralized. Private and industrial consumers of energy should therefore emphasize the construction of autonomous and regional elements that can reliably supply power on a regional or local level even if the national grid should be compromised.

References

1. Albert, R., Albert, I., Nakarado, G.L.: Structural vulnerability of the north american power grid. Phys. Rev. E **69**(2), 025,103 (2004)
2. Ausbau elektrischer Netze mit Kabel oder Freileitung unter besonderer Berücksichtigung der Einspeisung Erneuerbarer Energien. http://www.izes.de/
3. Bernstein, A., Bienstock, D., Hay, D., Uzunoglu, M., Zussman, G.: Power grid vulnerability to geographically correlated failures – analysis and control implications. In: INFOCOM, 2014 Proceedings IEEE, pp. 2634–2642. IEEE, Piscataway (2014)
4. Bompard, E., Napoli, R., Xue, F.: Analysis of structural vulnerabilities in power transmission grids. Int. J. Crit. Infrastruct. Prot. **2**(1), 5–12 (2009)

5. Bundesamt für Landestopografie swisstopo. http://www.swisstopo.admin.ch
6. Crucitti, P., Latora, V., Marchiori, M.: Model for cascading failures in complex networks. Phys. Rev. E **69**(4), 045,104 (2004)
7. Cuadra, L., Salcedo-Sanz, S., Del Ser, J., Jiménez-Fernández, S., Geem, Z.W.: A critical review of robustness in power grids using complex networks concepts. Energies **8**(9), 9211–9265 (2015)
8. European Network of Transmission System Operators, ENTSO-E. https://www.entsoe.eu
9. Fischer, R., Kießling, F.: Freileitungen: Planung, Berechnung, Ausführung. Springer, Berlin (2013)
10. Mei, S., Zhang, X., Cao, M.: Power grid complexity. Springer Science & Business Media, New York (2011)
11. Pagani, G.A., Aiello, M.: The power grid as a complex network: a survey. Physica A Stat. Mech. Appl. **392**(11), 2688–2700 (2013)
12. Pahwa, S., Scoglio, C., Scala, A.: Abruptness of cascade failures in power grids. Sci. Rep. **4**, 3694 (2014)
13. Sachtjen, M., Carreras, B., Lynch, V.: Disturbances in a power transmission system. Phys. Rev. E **61**(5), 4877 (2000)
14. Schweizerische Gesamtenergiestatistik 2013, Swiss Federal Office of Energy. http://www.bfe.admin.ch/
15. Solé, R.V., Rosas-Casals, M., Corominas-Murtra, B., Valverde, S.: Robustness of the European power grids under intentional attack. Phys. Rev. E **77**(2), 026,102 (2008)
16. Stromübertragungsnetz zuständige Landesgesellschaft, Swissgrid AG. https://www.swissgrid.ch
17. Swiss national map from d-maps.com. http://www.d-maps.com/carte.php?num_car=24779&lang=de
18. Zhang, G., Li, Z., Zhang, B., Halang, W.A.: Understanding the cascading failures in Indian power grids with complex networks theory. Physica A Stat. Mech. Appl. **392**(15), 3273–3280 (2013)

A Robust Supply Chain Model for a National Economy with Many Goods, Multiple Import Routes, and Compulsory Stockpiling

Eva Morstein

1 Introduction

Robust supply chains can mitigate supply disruption risks, be these due to operational issues, natural disasters, or deliberately inflicted damage. The extant literature has mostly reviewed the construction of such robust supply chains from a private sector perspective. It therefore focuses on minimizing business losses and on the trade-off between supply chain resilience and related investment cost (e.g., [4–6, 10, 13]). In particular, this literature advises producers to make their supply chains more robust by targeted investments in their suppliers, by integrating redundant capacity, by diversifying suppliers, and by simulating threat scenarios and implied disruption probabilities [3, 7–9, 11, 12, 14, 15]. Quite often, these authors make strong assumptions that do not necessarily hold for complex supply chains. For example, both [8] and [7] assume suppliers have unlimited capacities, while [9] assume an evenly distributed demand.

This chapter proposes both an alternative view and a different level of analysis. A complete national economy is modeled as a supply chain, and supply chain disruption risk is conceived of as a threat to the effective delivery of goods and

Electronic Supplementary Material The online version of this article (https://doi.org/10.1007/978-3-030-41826-7_7) contains supplementary material, which is available to authorized users.

E. Morstein (✉)
Schweizerische Mobiliar Versicherungsgesellschaft AG, Bern, Switzerland

M. M. Keupp (ed.), *The Security of Critical Infrastructures*, International Series in Operations Research & Management Science 288,
https://doi.org/10.1007/978-3-030-41826-7_7

services to the population. This viewpoint makes the modeling of disruption risks and scenarios more demanding since a national economy typically imports many different goods (e.g., food, medical supplies, or fossil fuels). In such a setting, supply chain risk is not only related to the domestic distribution of goods, but also to the risk of import disruption, i.e. the risk that goods produced abroad cannot be delivered as a consequence of transportation shortage or blockage of import routes.

Moreover, many nations have implemented a system of compulsory stockpiling, whereby the state stores some quantity of essential goods in order to guarantee emergency supplies whenever significant disruptions occur. Any optimization procedure would have to take into account the existence of such additional stocks. To account for all of these issues, an extension of the model by Garcia-Herreros et al. [2] is proposed and specified by a mixed integer linear program (MILP).

2 Model Specification

The model proposed by Garcia-Herreros et al. [2] is a useful starting point for two reasons. First, it includes distribution centers (which are referred to as transshipment platforms in the remainder of this chapter) as a design decision. Second, it employs a Benders decomposition algorithm that reduces the computational complexity of finding optimal solutions for large-scale supply chains (see [1] for an extensive discussion). All in all, the model significantly improves supply chain resilience at a reasonable cost.

In this contribution, the original model is extended by relaxing some of its assumptions and by introducing novel elements. Moreover, the wording is slightly adapted to a setting where demand originates from different regions in the national economy. In the original model, supply is delivered to these regions by transshipment platforms which, in turn, receive their goods from different import routes which may be disrupted. Whenever an import route or transshipment platform cannot satisfy any particular demand, alternative routes and platforms are used. If, after this re-routing, there is any remaining (uncovered) demand, this demand is satisfied by a fictitious import route and a fictitious transshipment platform at a penalty cost.

The authors [2] assume that there exists only one producer of the goods that are to be distributed. Since firms in a national economy source goods and services from many different suppliers, the extension proposed in this chapter considers multiple producers. Further, they also assume a world of only two goods whose cost functions are interrelated. This assumption is relaxed by considering multiple and mutually independent goods produced by multiple suppliers. Finally, they assume production to be safe, whereas all supply chain risk is modeled at the distribution center stage. This restriction is relaxed here by modeling the possibility that not only transshipment centers, but also import routes themselves can be disrupted, e.g. as a consequence of war, natural disasters, technical failure, pandemics, or sanctions. The probability that any such disruption may occur is captured by different scenarios, each of which is given a particular probability.

Very few national economies operate in autarchy. This means that import is an important element of national supply, and therefore even a temporary disruption of import routes constitutes a significant supply risk. Further, both the structure and the number of different means of transport differ by country in terms of capacity, speed and cost. For example, water-bound flows of goods should take into account the fleet of ships available. The extension proposed here therefore considers the maximum capacity of each import route by factoring the speed and costs of different means of transport into total transport cost. Moreover, the flows from import routes to transshipment platforms are modeled, and new boundary conditions are proposed since goods can be imported by more than one import route.

Finally, the model by Garcia-Herreros et al. [2] does not consider external storage of goods (e.g., in warehouses). While this assumption may be acceptable for the case of private firms which try to minimize storage cost at all times, it may not apply to a national economy where stockpiling is a significant element of the security of supply. The purpose of a compulsory stockpile is to secure nationwide supplies by bridging bottlenecks in the case of longer interruptions. Hence, stockpiling typically concentrates on durable goods that can be stocked in large quantities and for longer periods of time, such as staple foods and fuels.

The extended model is specified by the following mixed integer linear program.

Sets

S scenarios
E import routes
U transshipment platforms
K regions
G goods

Parameters

N number of time periods
D_{kg} demand of region k for good g per time period
H_{ug} storage cost of good g in transshipment platform u per time period
F_e^1 fixed cost of import route e
F_u^2 fixed cost of transshipment platform u
V_{eg}^1 variable (capacity) cost per import route e and good g
V_{ug}^2 variable (capacity) cost per transshipment platform u and good g
T_{eug}^1 transport costs of import route e to transshipment platform u per good g
T_{ukg}^2 transport costs of transshipment platform u to region k per good g
C_{eg}^{max1} maximum capacity of import route e per good g
C_{ug}^{max2} maximum capacity of transshipment platform u per good g
C_g^{max3} maximum capacity of stockpile for good g
C_g^{min} minimum capacity of stockpile for good g
PL_g^1 stockpiling cost per thousand units of good g
PL_g^2 cost for requiring stockpiled goods per thousand units of good g
Π_s probability of scenario s

M_{seu} availability vector of import route e and transshipment platform u under scenario s
q number of import routes e
r number of transshipment platforms u

Decision Variables

$* w_e = \begin{cases} 1, \text{ if import route } e \text{ was selected} \\ 0, \text{ else} \end{cases}$
$* x_u = \begin{cases} 1, \text{ if transshipment platform } u \text{ was selected} \\ 0, \text{ else} \end{cases}$
$* d_{eg}$ storage capacity of good g in import route e
$* c_{ug}$ storage capacity of good g in transshipment platform u
$* z_{seug}$ quantity of good g transported from import route e to transshipment platform u under scenario s
$* y_{sukg}$ quantity of good g transported from transshipment platform u to region k under scenario s
$* l_g$ compulsory stock of good g
$* t_{skg}$ quantity of good g transported from stockpile to region k under scenario s

The model is formulated as follows

$$\begin{aligned}
\text{Min.} \; & \sum_{e=1}^{E-1} F_e^1 \cdot w_e + \sum_{u=1}^{U-1} F_u^2 \cdot x_u + \sum_{e=1}^{E-1} \sum_{g=1}^{G} V_{eg}^1 \cdot d_{eg} + \sum_{u=1}^{U-1} \sum_{g=1}^{G} V_{ug}^2 \cdot c_{ug} \\
& + N \cdot \sum_{s=1}^{S} \Pi_s \cdot \sum_{e=1}^{E} \sum_{u=1}^{U} \sum_{g=1}^{G} z_{seug} \cdot T_{eug}^1 \\
& + N \cdot \sum_{s=1}^{S} \Pi_s \cdot \sum_{u=1}^{U} \sum_{k=1}^{K} \sum_{g=1}^{G} y_{sukg} \cdot T_{ukg}^2 \\
& + N \cdot \sum_{s=1}^{S} \Pi_s \cdot \sum_{u=1}^{U} \sum_{g=1}^{G} H_{ug} \cdot \left(c_{ug} - \sum_{k=1}^{K} y_{sukg} \right) \\
& + \sum_{g=1}^{G} \left(l_g \cdot PL_g^1 + \sum_{s=1}^{S} \Pi_s \cdot \sum_{k=1}^{K} t_{skg} \cdot PL_g^2 \right) \\
& - \sum_{s=1}^{S} \Pi_s \cdot \sum_{g=1}^{G} \cdot \left(\sum_{k=1}^{K} t_{skg} \cdot \sum_{e=E}^{E} \sum_{u=U}^{U} T_{eug}^1 \right)
\end{aligned} \tag{1}$$

$$\text{s.t.} \; \sum_{u=1}^{U} y_{sukg} + t_{skg} = D_{kg} \tag{2}$$

$$\{s = 1, \ldots, S, k = 1, \ldots, K, g = 1, \ldots G\}$$

$$\sum_{k=1}^{K} y_{sukg} = \sum_{e=1}^{E} z_{seug} \tag{3}$$

$$\{s = 1, \ldots, S, u = 1, \ldots, U, g = 1, \ldots, G\}$$

$$\sum_{e=1}^{E} z_{seug} \leq C_{ug}^{max2} \tag{4}$$

$$\{s = 1, \ldots, S, u = 1, \ldots, U, g = 1, \ldots, G\}$$

$$d_{eg} \leq C_{eg}^{max1} \cdot w_e \tag{5}$$

$$\{e = 1, \ldots, E, g = 1, \ldots, G\}$$

$$c_{ug} \leq C_{ug}^{max2} \cdot x_u \tag{6}$$

$$\{u = 1, \ldots, U, g = 1, \ldots, G\}$$

$$z_{seug} \leq M_{seu} \cdot d_{eg} \tag{7}$$

$$\{s = 1, \ldots, S, e = 1 \ldots, E, u = 1, \ldots, U, g = 1, \ldots, G\}$$

$$\sum_{u=1}^{U} z_{seug} \leq d_{eg} \tag{8}$$

$$\{s = 1, \ldots, S, e = 1, \ldots E, g = 1, \ldots, G\}$$

$$\sum_{k=1}^{K} y_{sukg} \leq c_{ug} \tag{9}$$

$$\{s = 1, \ldots, S, u = 1, \ldots, U, g = 1, \ldots, G\}$$

$$\sum_{u=1}^{U} c_{ug} \leq \sum_{e=1}^{E} d_{eg} \tag{10}$$

$$\{g = 1, \ldots, G\}$$

$$w_e \leq \sum_{g=1}^{G} d_{eg} \tag{11}$$

$$\{e = 1, \ldots, E\}$$

$$\sum_{k=1}^{K} t_{skg} \leq l_g \tag{12}$$

$$\{s = 1, \ldots, S, g = 1, \ldots, G\}$$

$$t_{skg} \leq y_{sukg} \tag{13}$$

$$\{s = 1, \ldots, S, u = 1, \ldots, U, k = 1, \ldots, K, g = 1, \ldots, G\}$$

$$l_g \leq C_g^{max3} \tag{14}$$

$$\{s = 1, \ldots, S, g = 1, \ldots, G\}$$

$$l_g \geq C_g^{min} \tag{15}$$

$$\{s = 1, \ldots, S, g = 1, \ldots, G\}$$

$$w_e, x_u \in \{0, 1\} \tag{16}$$

$$\{e = 1, \ldots, E, u = 1, \ldots, U\}$$

$$c_{ug}, d_{eg}, z_{seug}, y_{sukg}, t_{skg} \in \mathbb{Z} \geq 0 \tag{17}$$

$$\{s = 1, \ldots, S, e = 1, \ldots, E, u = 1, \ldots, U, k = 1, \ldots, K, g = 1, \ldots, G\}$$

The structure of the program follows the approach of [2] by partitioning the objective function (1) into different cost blocks. For the sake of readability, they are organized by lines. The first line aggregates fixed and variable investment costs. The second line sums up all transport costs for deliveries from import routes to transshipment platforms, and the third line sums up those from transshipment platforms to regions. The fourth line sums up all storage costs in the transshipment centers. These are caused whenever the inflow of goods in particular scenarios is well below the maximum capacity of any particular transshipment platform. This lack of capacity utilization implies costs, e.g. for maintenance and electricity. The fifth line totals the cost of stocking goods in the stockpile and the cost of any deliveries from the stockpile to the regions. The sixth line corrects total cost for opportunity benefits since any delivery of goods from the stockpile substitutes for another delivery by an alternative import route or transshipment platform. Since the third line considers flows from transshipment platforms to regions but not those from import routes to transshipment platforms, this correction avoids an erroneous double consideration of the implied costs.

An optimal solution to this problem must take the following boundary conditions into account. First, constraint (2) ensures that the demand of all regions can be delivered by either traditional import routes or the stockpile. Constraint (3) specifies that the number of goods delivered to a transshipment platform must correspond to the number of goods shipped by this platform. Constraint (4) specifies that any quantity of goods delivered to a transshipment platform must not exceed its maximum capacity.

Constraints (5) and (6) guarantee that the capacities allocated to import routes and transshipment platforms do not exceed this maximum capacity, subject to the consideration of whether or not the model selected these import routes and transshipment platforms at all.

Constraints (7)–(9) guarantee that the quantities transported from one import route to all transshipment platforms and from one transshipment platform to all regions do not exceed their respective capacities. They also ensure that goods are only transported if the import route and transshipment platform in question are not disrupted. Constraint (10) specifies that any quantity of goods distributed to the regions must not exceed the quantity of goods imported by the import routes, and constraint (11) guarantees that the selection of import routes takes the storage capacity limits of these routes into account.

Constraints (12)–(15) refer to the compulsory stockpile. They stipulate that the total quantity transported from the compulsory stockpile to the regions must never exceed its total stock, and that any quantity transported from the compulsory stockpile to any region must never exceed the quantity delivered from the transshipment platform to the same region. In addition, the stockpile of each good must be above any minimum and below any maximum level of stock. Further, the costs of requiring goods from the compulsory stockpile must exceed the costs of requiring these from any transshipment platform since the stockpile must not be used to realize cost savings, but only as a lender of last resort. Also, the costs of delivering any goods from the compulsory stockpile should not exceed the penalty cost of any disrupted import route or transshipment platform. Finally, constraints (16) and (17) define all binary variables and the non-negativity and integer conditions of the decision variables. In addition, constraint (17) forbids reverse flows of any good from any region to any transshipment platform.

3 Application

A simple case provides a basic illustration of the model. It comprises two scenarios, one without and one with disruption, two import routes, one transshipment platform, three regions and one good (Sect. 3.1). The scalability of the model is demonstrated by considering a more complex case with 15 scenarios that might occur with different probabilities, nine import routes, ten transshipment platforms, four goods, six regions, and one compulsory stockpile per good (Sect. 3.2). Finally, a contingency analysis is provided within this complex case by considering different stockpile configurations (Sect. 3.3).

3.1 Simple Illustration

The model is illustrated using the national economy of Switzerland. This country is landlocked, but goods can be delivered from the seaport of Rotterdam to the river port of Basel by way of the river Rhine (water-bound import route). Once they arrive, the goods are either transferred to trucks and freight trains for subsequent inland transport, or added to a compulsory stockpile. In addition, an alternative import route by road exists. Demand for a single good g originates from region 1 (3 million units), region 2 (7 million units) and region 3 (4 million units). Import capacities for good g are 4 million units (water-bound route) and 6 million units (alternative route).

Normal operations are now affected by a distortion. Due to severe dryness over several weeks, the water level of the Rhine has dropped so much that all shipping traffic is stopped. In addition, an important sluice is out of operation due to maintenance work. Since the water-bound import route is now completely blocked, its import capacity is reduced to zero, whereas the alternative import route is not affected. Hence, any demand originating from the regions must now be satisfied by the alternative import route and by the compulsory stockpile. If their combined capacity cannot fully satisfy all demand, the remaining uncovered demand is delivered by a fictitious import route E and a fictitious transshipment platform U at a penalty cost. This scenario is parameterized with the following data (Tables 1, 2, 3, 4 and 5).

Figure 1 below provides a diagram of the optimal solution. The import capacity of the blocked water-bound route can be partially substituted by the alternative import route and the stockpile, but some uncovered demand remains that is delivered via fictional import route E and fictional transshipment platform U at a penalty cost.

More specifically, the demand originating from region 1 can be fully satisfied by the alternative import route. The stockpile can cover 50% of the demand originating from region 2, but the remaining uncovered demand of 3.5 m units is delivered at a penalty cost. The demand originating from region 3 can be partially satisfied by the alternative import route. After delivering 3 m units, this alternative route is at its maximum capacity of 6 m units since another 3 m units are shipped to region 1 via this route. The stockpile can cover an additional 0.5 m units, but since it delivers 3.5 m units to region 2 already, its capacity is now exhausted. As a result, the remaining uncovered demand of 0.5 m units is delivered at a penalty cost. The total cost for this optimal solution is approx. 491.8 m Swiss francs.

Table 1 Parameters and sets for the basic example

Parameter	Value	Unit
N	365	Days
D_1	3000	Units (thousands) per period
D_2	7000	Units (thousands) per period
D_3	4000	Units (thousands) per period
H_1	0.1	Swiss francs (thousands)
H_2	0	Swiss francs (thousands)
F_1^1	1000	Swiss francs
F_2^1	500	Swiss francs
F_1^2	500	Swiss francs
V_1^1	2	Swiss francs (thousands)
V_2^1	3	Swiss francs (thousands)
V_1^2	5	Swiss francs (thousands)
C_1^{max1}	6000	Units (thousands) per period
C_2^{max1}	8000	Units (thousands) per period
C_3^{max1}	1,000,000,000	Units (thousands) per period
C_1^{max2}	20,000	Units (thousands) per period
C_1^{max2}	1,000,000	Units (thousands) per period
C_g^{max3}	1,000,000	Units (thousands) per period
C_g^{min}	0	Units (thousands) per period
PL_g^1	50	Swiss francs (thousands)
PL_g^2	100	Swiss francs (thousands)
Π_1	0.7	
Π_2	0.3	
q	3	Import routes
r	2	Transshipment platforms

Table 2 Transportation cost from import routes to transshipment platforms

T_{eug}^1	u	
e	1	2
1	10	500
2	5	500
3	500	500

Table 3 Transportation cost from transshipment platforms to regions

T_{ukg}^2	k		
u	1	2	3
1	5	5	5
2	500	500	500

Table 4 First scenario without disruption

M_{1eu}	u	
e	1	2
1	1	1
2	1	1
3	1	1

Table 5 Second scenario with disruption of the water-bound import route

M_{2eu}	u	
e	1	2
1	1	1
2	0	1
3	1	1

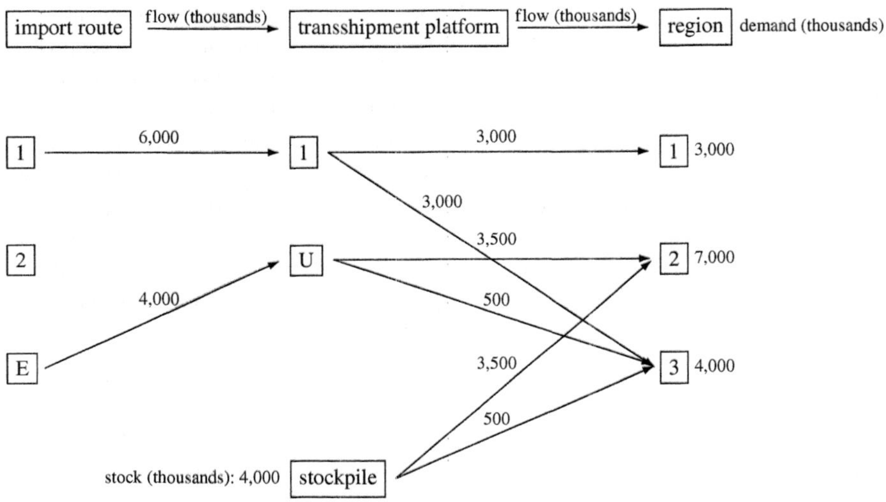

Fig. 1 Supply chain network with compulsory stockpiling and two import routes, one of which is disrupted

3.2 *Complex Disruption Case*

To illustrate the usability of the extended model and to demonstrate the importance of a resilient supply chain, fifteen different scenarios are specified, each of which has a particular probability. The scenarios cover situations from minor disturbances to complete network failure (viz. Table 6). Since complete breakdowns are less likely or occur less frequently, the probability with which a particular scenario occurs decreases as the number of interruptions increases. However, the probability also includes the geographical proximity of import routes. A major disruption in Basel may block multiple Basel-bound import routes, while import routes bound to other areas (e.g., Geneva) should not be affected. While the number of scenarios is limited to 15 in order to keep the model computable in this particular example, any

Table 6 Interruption scenarios and probabilities for the complex illustration

Scenario (S)	Probability (Π)	Disrupted U	Disrupted E	Example
1	50%	0	0	Normal operations
2	25%	1	0	Transshipment platform in Basel disrupted
3	15%	0	1	E_1 Waterbound import route to Basel disrupted
4	5%	0	1	E_2 Railway import route to Basel disrupted
5	2.5%	2	0	
6	1%	3	0	
7	0.6%	4	0	
8	0.4%	0	2	
9	0.2%	0	3	
10	0.165%	1	2	
11	0.1%	1	3	
12	0.01%	0	3	
13	0.01%	2	3	
14	0.01%	2	4	
15	0.005%	5	0	

supply chain can be modeled as long as the probabilities of interruptions are not underestimated.

These scenarios are applied to a fictitious national economy that has nine import routes and ten transshipment platforms. In this economy, demand for four discrete goods originates from six discrete regions, and one compulsory stockpile per good exists, the respective stock of which can range from zero to a specified maximum capacity.

First, a baseline case is calculated which assumes that no interruptions will ever occur. In the optimal solution for this baseline case, all compulsory stockpiles have an optimal stock of zero since all demand originating from the regions can be met by extant import routes and transshipment platforms. The values of the decision variables from this baseline case are then transferred into a scenario-based model which assumes that interruptions will occur according to the scenarios specified in Table 6. To simplify calculations, it is assumed that if an import route is interrupted, there is either no alternative import route (implying the goods cannot be delivered at all) or that delivery is only possible by a fictitious import route at a penalty cost. The same simplification applies to any interruption of any transshipment platform. This scenario-based model has an optimal solution. Calculation took less than 0.1 seconds on a 2016 Macbook Pro with a 3.1 GHz Intel Core i5 processor and 16 GB RAM. The model was implemented in AMPL (https://ampl.com) using a Gurobi solver. Table 7 below compares the optimal solution for the scenario-based model with the baseline case.

Table 7 Comparison of a scenario-based approach versus a baseline case without disruption

	Scenario-based	Baseline
# Binary variables	21	21
# Linear variables	11,008	816
# Conditions	10,234	770
Calculation time (seconds)	0.1	0.02
# Selected import routes[a]	8	6
# Selected transshipment platforms	9	7
Investment costs (Swiss francs)	1,620,140	809,038
Transport costs to transshipment platforms (Swiss francs)	251,993,000	283,714,000
Transport costs to regions (Swiss francs)	216,680,000	176,988,000
Storage costs (Swiss francs)	745,390	0
Stockpiling costs (Swiss francs)	395,536	0
Stockpiling savings (Swiss francs)	2,349,720	0
Penalty costs (Swiss francs)	71,481,600	319,585,000[b]
Total cost (Swiss francs)	540,565,946	781,096,038

[a]In the respective optimal solution, excluding the fictitious import route and transshipment platform.
[b]Upon implementation of the optimal solution for the baseline model into the scenario-based model.

The scenario-based model selects a larger number of import routes and transshipment platforms as it considers possible interruptions. In comparison to the baseline model, this consideration implies higher investment into compulsory stockpiling and transportation costs, but the supply chain is made significantly more robust. This result is reflected by the total penalty cost which is significantly lower than in the baseline case. In the baseline case, there is no storage and transportation cost for stockpiling. However, no penalty cost can be avoided by rerouting transport or using stockpiled goods once a disruption unexpectedly occurs. Hence, the modeling of interruption scenarios is productive since the investments in stockpiling are more than offset by saved penalty cost. All in all, my findings corroborate those of [2] by suggesting that while operators incur higher investment costs as they hedge supply chain risk, they can offset these investments by opportunity benefits which come as saved penalty costs.

3.3 *Contingency Analysis for Different Stockpile Configurations*

Table 7 illustrates the effect that a stockpile saves more costs than it causes. Hence, the impact of stockpiled goods on supply chain robustness is analyzed in greater detail. The optimal solution of the above scenario-based model is compared and contrasted with two alternative modifications of the compulsory stockpile. In the

Table 8 Contingency analysis for different stockpile inventory configurations

	Optimal	Maximum inventory	Minimum inventory
Calculation time (seconds)	0.1	0.4	0.3
# Import routes selected	8	8	8
# Transshipment platforms selected	9	9	9
Stockpile inventory for good 1 (thousands)	4024	1000	5000
Stockpile inventory for good 2 (thousands)	18,594	1000	19,000
Stockpile inventory for good 3 (thousands)	1644	999	2000
Stockpile inventory for good 4 (thousands)	14,880	1000	15,000
Stockpiling costs	395,536	40,399	413,916
Stockpiling savings	2,349,720	239,940	2,349,720
Total penalty costs	71,481,600	135,654,000	71,481,600

first modification, the stockpile inventory can range between a minimum of zero and a maximum of one million units per good. In the second modification, a minimum stockpile inventory must be maintained at all times. Models for this second modification were calculated with different minimum inventories. Table 8 compares the optimal solution from Sect. 3.2 with the optimal solutions for both modifications.

As the compulsory stockpile is not used for cost-saving purposes, a minimum or maximum level of stock has no influence on the choice of import routes and transshipment platforms and their capacities. Accordingly, the associated costs of these elements do not change. However, the effect of stockpile inventories on stockpile penalty costs is significant. Savings and penalty cost reductions are equally high for the optimal stockpile and any higher level of stock per good. It should be noted that for every good, the respective optimal inventories exceed the arbitrarily defined maximum of 1 million units per good that the first modification introduces.

Finally, the fact that penalty cost savings increase with increased stockpile inventories indicates that stockpiling creates redundancies which mitigate the effects of a disruption. However, the increase in stockpiling costs signals that this mitigation comes at the price of capital lockup. Hence, every increase in stockpile inventory should be justified by a corresponding interruption scenario.

4 Outlook

The proposed extension of the model by Garcia-Herreros et al. [2] is productive in several ways. It considers supply disruptions on two levels of the supply chain and introduces compulsory stockpiling. Further, the proposed extension is scalable to complex disruption cases, multiple goods and multiple import routes. Still, it is important to note that the results of the proposed extended model significantly depend on the specification of the disruption scenarios, as well as on the correct estimation of any probabilities associated with such scenarios. Future research also needs to find acceptable trade-offs between the number and the exhaustiveness of the disruption scenarios since a very large number of scenarios makes the assignment of specific probabilities difficult. Further, interdependencies between import routes and transshipment platforms must be modeled realistically in order to correctly estimate the extent to which (if any) imports can be rerouted.

Future research may further develop the extension proposed here by removing some of its limitations. In the model proposed computation time grows exponentially with the number of scenarios specified, the number of import routes, and the number of transshipment platforms. Hence, novel approximation algorithms and super-computing power may be required to adapt the extension proposed here to the analysis of highly complex supply chains. Finally, whenever a blocked import route implies an out-of-stock situation in any transshipment platform, the capacities of other import routes may be over-utilized as these platforms attempt to reroute imports. Hence, if blockages of import routes occur iteratively, a cascading effect may be caused that affects not only the focal, but also many other transshipment platforms. Future research should introduce additional elements into the extension proposed here to capture such dynamic effects.

References

1. Azad, N., Saharidis, G., Davoudpour, H., Malekly, H., Yektamaram, S.: Strategies for protecting supply chain networks against facility and transportation disruptions. An improved decomposition approach. Ann. Oper. Res. **210 Nr. 1**, 125–163 (2013)
2. Garcia-Herreros, P., Wassick, J.M., Grossmann, I.E.: Design of resilient supply chains with risk of facility disruptions. Ind. Eng. Chem. Res. **53**(44), 17240–17251 (2014)
3. Jabbarzadeh, A., Fahimnia, B., Sheu, J., Moghadam, H.S.: Designing a supply chain resilient to major disruptions and supply/demand interruptions. Transp. Res. B **94**, 121–149 (2016)
4. Kim, Y., Chen, Y.S., Linderman, K.: Supply network disruption and resilience: a network structural perspective. J. Oper. Manag. **33**, 43–59 (2015)
5. Kleindorfer, P., Saad, G.: Managing disruption risks in supply chains. Production Oper. Manag. Soc. **14**, 53–68 (2005)
6. Klibi, W., Martel, A., Guitouni, A.: The design of robust value-creating supply chain networks: a critical review. Eur. J. Oper. Res. **203**(2), 283–293 (2010)
7. Li, X., Ouyang, Y.: A continuum approximation approach to reliable facility location design under correlated probabilistic disruptions. Transp. Res. B **44**, 535–548 (2010)
8. Li, Q., Savachkin, A.: A heuristic approach to the design of fortified distribution networks. Transp. Res. Part E **50**, 138–148 (2013)
9. Meena, P., Sarmah, S., Sarkar, A.: Sourcing decisions under risks of catastrophic event disruptions. Transp. Res. Part E **47**, 1058–1074 (2011)
10. Park, Y., Hong, P., Roh, J.: Supply chain lessons from the catastrophic natural disaster in Japan. Bus. Horiz. **56**(1), 75–85 (2013)
11. Sadghiani, N.S., Torabi, S., Sahebjamnia, N.: Retail supply chain network design under operational and disruption risks. Transp. Res. Part E **75**, 95–114 (2015)

12. Schmitt, A., Singh, M.: A quantitative analysis of disruption risk in a multi-elechon supply chain. Int. J. Prod. Econ. **139**, 22–32 (2012)
13. Tang, C.: Perspectives in supply chain risk management. Int. J. Prod. Econ. **103**(2), 451–488 (2006)
14. Tomlin, B.: On the value of mitigation and contingency strategies for managing supply chain disruption risks. Manag. Sci. **52**(5), 639–657 (2006)
15. Torabi, S., Baghersad, M., Mansouri, S.: Resilient supplier selection and order allocation under operational and disruption risks. Transp. Res. Part E **79**, 22–48 (2015)

Assessing the Reliability of Street Networks: A Case Study Based on the Swiss Street Network

Philipp Baumann and Marcus M. Keupp

1 Introduction

Although street networks appear to be physically robust, intentional disruption can reduce their performance. To evaluate the reliability of a street network under extreme conditions, it is important to know the best possible performance of the network before and after a disruption. To determine this optimal performance of a street network, we solve the following planning problem. Given is a directed graph with arcs that represent street segments and nodes that represent intersections. Some nodes of the network act as origin or destination nodes. A predetermined amount of traffic must flow from each origin node to each destination node. Every arc of the graph is associated with a piecewise linear and convex function that determines the cost for a given amount of traffic. The goal is to determine the flow of traffic from origin to destination nodes such that total traffic cost is minimized. The resilience of a network can then be evaluated by comparing the total cost of traffic before and after the disruption.

Electronic Supplementary Material The online version of this article (https://doi.org/10.1007/978-3-030-41826-7_8) contains supplementary material, which is available to authorized users.

P. Baumann
Department of Business Administration, University of Bern, Bern, Switzerland
e-mail: philipp.baumann@pqm.unibe.ch

M. M. Keupp (✉)
Department of Defense Economics, Military Academy at the Swiss Federal Institute of Technology Zurich, Birmensdorf, Switzerland
e-mail: mkeupp@ethz.ch

M. M. Keupp (ed.), *The Security of Critical Infrastructures*, International Series in Operations Research & Management Science 288,
https://doi.org/10.1007/978-3-030-41826-7_8

The literature on street network reliability analysis can be roughly divided into two categories. The first category comprises approaches that identify vulnerabilities by analyzing the topology of the street network. Demšar et al. [6] use topological measures such as centrality and betweenness to identify critical nodes or arcs of a street network. They study the urban street network of the Helsinki Metropolitan Area in Finland. Duan and Lu [7] also analyze the robustness of street networks of six cities based on topological measures. They find that the level of granularity at which the network is represented has a strong impact on the identification of critical elements. A simplified representation of a street network could therefore lead to inaccurate conclusions. Jenelius and Mattsson [10] propose a grid-based method to identify areas in the network that are particularly vulnerable to large disruptions such as floods or heavy snowfall. They applied the method to a simplified representation of the Swedish street network. The second category comprises approaches that use optimization techniques to study the robustness of street networks. Brown et al. [5] propose bilevel and trilevel optimization models to identify vulnerabilities in critical infrastructure. Due to the computational complexity of these models, they are only applicable to small networks. Bell et al. [3] consider the problem of how to use a street network if information on several disruption scenarios is available. They present numerical results for an example that is based on the central London street network. Matisziw and Murray [13] propose an integer programming formulation for identifying important links in a truck transport network of Ohio, USA. Lou and Zhang [12] use mathematical programming to determine resilient transport networks under random and targeted attacks. Due to the computational complexity of the approaches in the second category, they are only applicable to relatively small street networks.

In this chapter, we propose an optimization-based decision support system that measures the resilience of a street network against user-defined disruptions. In contrast to existing optimization-based approaches, the proposed decision support system is applicable to nation-wide street networks. The system consists of a graph construction tool that transforms OpenStreetMap data into a directed graph, a simple traffic estimator that defines the traffic volume between origin-destination pairs, and a linear programming formulation that solves the above described planning problem and thus determines a minimum cost traffic flow from origin to destination nodes.

We used the proposed decision support system to analyze real-world street networks in Switzerland. For city-wide street networks, optimal traffic flows can be determined within seconds. The running time for large-scale networks increases considerably with the number of origin-destination pairs. Nevertheless, we were able to determine an optimal traffic flow for the entire Swiss street network with 380 origin-destination pairs.

The chapter is structured as follows. In Sect. 2, we describe the planning problem in detail. In Sect. 3, we describe how OpenStreetMap data is transformed into a directed graph. In Sect. 4, we show a simple method for estimating the traffic between origin-destination nodes. In Sect. 5, we introduce the linear programming formulation. In Sect. 6, we report the computational results. In Sect. 7, we conclude the chapter and provide some directions for future research.

2 Planning Problem

Given is a directed graph with arcs that represent street segments and nodes that represent intersections. Different types of traffic flow through this network. For example, one could differentiate between commercial traffic (trucks and coaches) and private traffic (cars). Some traffic types might not be allowed to traverse specific arcs of the street network (e.g., trucks are not allowed on residential streets). Some nodes of the graph represent origin nodes whereas others represent destination nodes. Traffic flows from origin nodes through the graph to destination nodes. Traffic matrices specify for each traffic type and each origin-destination pair the number of vehicles that flow from the respective origin node to the corresponding destination node. The numbers in the traffic matrices refer to a specific planning horizon which is typically a day. Every arc of the graph is associated with a piecewise linear and convex function that determines the cost for a given amount of traffic. For example, one could specify a piecewise linear function with two line segments for an arc such that the first 90,000 vehicles that traverse this arc within the planning horizon contribute 0.5 Swiss francs per vehicle and kilometer to total cost, whereas every additional vehicle contributes 50 Swiss francs per kilometer. The goal is to find the cheapest possible way to send each type of traffic from origin to destination nodes. This problem corresponds to a multi-commodity network flow problem with piecewise linear and convex costs.

3 Construction of Graph

An important component of the proposed decision support system is the graph that represents the street network. We suggest to use the Python package OSMnx [4] that retrieves spatial geometries from OpenStreetMap [14] and automatically converts them into a directed graph. The spatial geometries can be retrieved for a specific place, i.e., a city, a region or an entire country. Note that the retrieval of the OSM data for an entire country and the respective graph construction requires considerable running time and memory, especially when the option to include bikable and walkable paths is selected. We therefore suggest to include only drivable street types. Nodes and arcs in the directed graph are associated with several attributes. Tables 1 and 2 list some of these attributes for nodes and arcs, respectively.

The attribute *highway* is useful to control the complexity of the graph. For example, it is possible to represent only arcs whose *highway* attribute value is either motorway or motorway_link by removing all arcs with other *highway* attribute

Table 1 Node attributes

Attribute	Description
osmid	Unique OSM ID of node
x	Geographic longitude of node
y	Geographic latitude of node

Table 2 Arc attributes

Attribute	Description
osmid	Unique OSM ID of street
highway	Type of street (e.g., motorway)
maxspeed	Speed limit in km/h
lanes	Number of lanes (e.g., 2)
name	Name of street (e.g., Seedammstrasse)
oneway	Binary attribute that indicates if traffic flows only in one direction

values. The OSMnx package also provides a function to eliminate isolated nodes after the removal of a subset of arcs. Figure 1 shows the directed graph that represents the drivable street network of the city of Bern (Switzerland).

The motorway segments that lie within the shaded area of Fig. 1 are enlarged in Fig. 2. The magnification suggests that the graph not only contains nodes to represent intersections, but also a large number of nodes that approximate the curvature of the streets.

The OSMnx package provides a function to remove those nodes while keeping the information on the curvature of the streets. Figure 3 shows the simplified representation of the graph visualized in Fig. 2.

Finally, we add dummy nodes that represent origins (origin nodes) and destinations (destination nodes) of traffic flow. Origin nodes are connected to the rest of

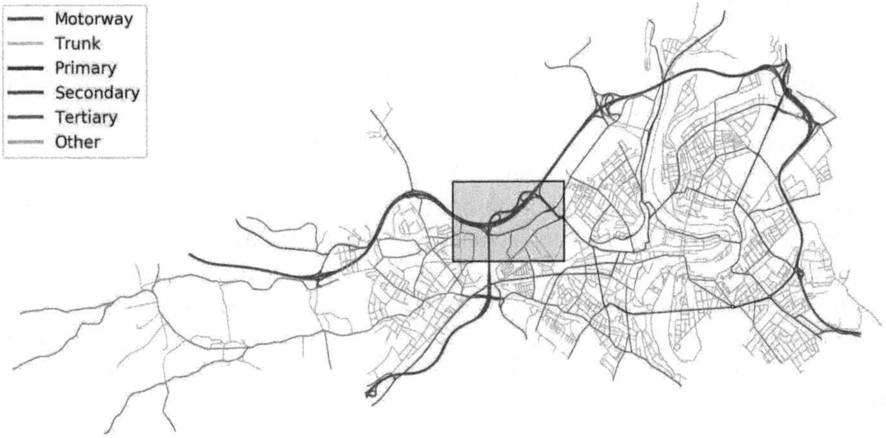

Fig. 1 Drivable street network of Bern (Switzerland) represented as a graph

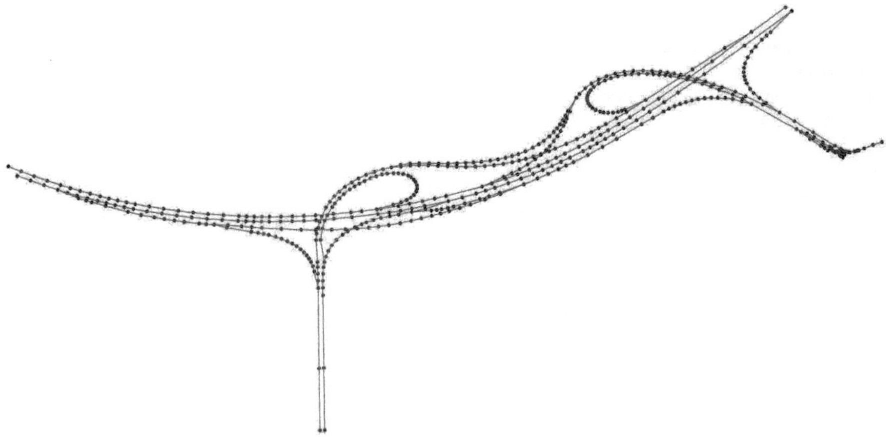

Fig. 2 Close-up of highlighted motorway segments

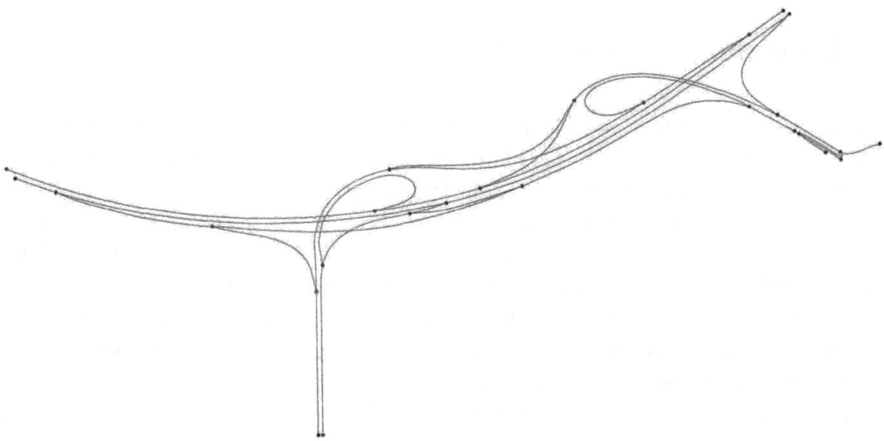

Fig. 3 Close-up of simplified graph representation

the graph by introducing arcs from the origin nodes to other nodes of the graph that are within close proximity of the origin nodes. Destination nodes are connected to the rest of the graph by introducing arcs from other nodes that are within close proximity of the destination nodes to the destination nodes. Note that traffic can only flow from origin nodes to the other nodes and from other nodes to destination nodes. Figure 4 visualizes a graph that contains such an origin node.

The daily throughput capacity of the arcs is not contained in the OSM data, such that it has to be determined by the analyst. In the computational analysis that we perform in Sect. 6 of this chapter, we estimate these daily throughput capacities for each arc based on the attributes *highway* and *lanes*.

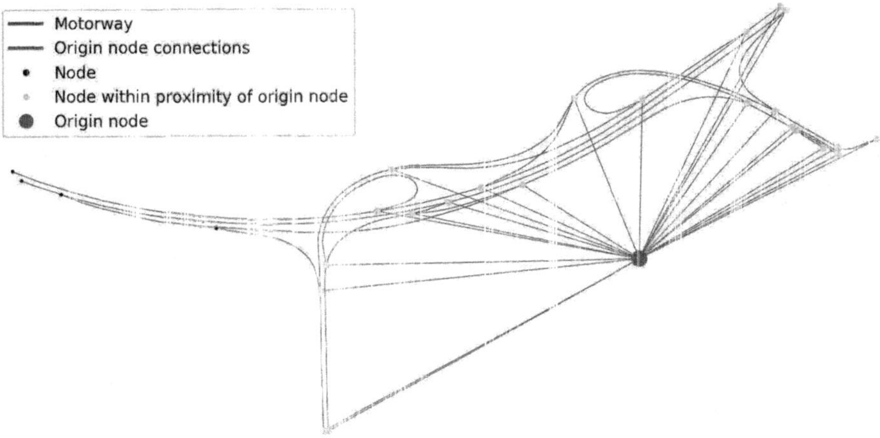

Fig. 4 Illustration of an origin node

4 Estimation of Traffic Matrices

The second component of our decision support system are so-called traffic matrices. There is one traffic matrix for each traffic type. This matrix specifies a daily traffic volume for each origin-destination pair. Hence, the size of the matrix depends on the number of origins and destinations the analyst considers. We denote the traffic matrix by T. Several approaches have been proposed to estimate the entries of the traffic matrix (see [16]). We use a simple gravity model to estimate the traffic matrix. Gravity models have been successfully used in social science research to model the movement of goods, information, or individuals between geographic regions (e.g., [18]) and, more recently, also for estimating traffic matrices (e.g., [9]).

The basic idea of a gravity model is that the amount of traffic from a given origin to a given destination is proportional to the total traffic to the destination. Analogously to [8], we model the traffic between two cities to be proportional to the product of the two populations divided by the distance between the two cities. Hence, the traffic volume from city i to city j is computed by (1):

$$T_{ij} = \sigma \frac{P_i P_j}{d_{ij}}, \tag{1}$$

where σ denotes a normalization factor, d_{ij} denotes the distance between city i and city j, and P_i and P_j denote the population of city i and city j, respectively. Ideally, the normalization factor σ is chosen such that when the resulting traffic volumes T_{ij} are routed along the shortest paths between the cities, the resulting total traffic volume for individual arcs corresponds roughly to the data from automatic traffic counting stations for these arcs.

5 Formulation of Traffic Flow Model

The third component of our decision support system is an optimization model that determines a flow of traffic from the origins to the destinations at minimal cost. We propose an extension of the well-known multi-commodity network flow model (see [1]). This extension entails using piecewise-linear functions to compute the total cost of the network flow. In Sect. 5.1, we introduce the notation of the model. In Sect. 5.2, we describe the constraints of the model. In Sect. 5.3, we discuss the objective function of the model.

5.1 Notation

Sets

V	Nodes
K	Types of traffic (e.g., commercial traffic or private traffic)
K_a	Types of traffic allowed on arc $a \in A$
V^O	Origin nodes
V^D	Destination nodes
V^R	Regular nodes (neither origin nor destination nodes)
A	Arcs
A_i^{in}	Incoming arcs of node $i \in V$
A_i^{out}	Outgoing arcs of node $i \in V$
O	Origin-destination pairs
O_i^{org}	Origin-destination pairs that have node $i \in V^O$ as origin
O_i^{des}	Origin-destination pairs that have node $i \in V^D$ as destination
S_a	Segments of arc $a \in A$

Parameters

T_{ko}	Traffic volume of type k for origin-destination pair $o \in O$
c_{as}	Cost per vehicle that moves along segment $s \in S_a$ on arc $a \in A$
b_{as}	Upper bound on traffic volume that moves along segment $s \in S_a$ on arc $a \in A$

Variables

x_{aks}	Total flow of type $k \in K_a$ on arc $a \in A$ through segment $s \in S_a$
x_{ako}	Total flow of type $k \in K_a$ on arc $a \in A$ associated with origin-destination pair $o \in O$
x_a	Total flow on arc $a \in A$

5.2 Constraints

Constraints (2) ensure that the total flow along an arc $a \in A$ is equal to the sum of the flows through the different segments of this arc.

$$x_a = \sum_{s \in S_a;\ k \in K_a} x_{aks} \qquad (a \in A) \tag{2}$$

Constraints (3) guarantee that the total flow along an arc $a \in A$ is equal to the sum of the flows of different types through this arc.

$$x_a = \sum_{o \in O;\ k \in K_a} x_{ako} \qquad (a \in A) \tag{3}$$

Constraints (4) enforce for each arc $a \in A$ that the sum of flow of type $k \in K_a$ across all segments $s \in S_a$ is equal to the sum of the flow of type $k \in K_a$ across all origin-destination pairs $o \in O$.

$$\sum_{s \in S_a} x_{aks} = \sum_{o \in O} x_{ako} \qquad (a \in A;\ k \in K) \tag{4}$$

Constraints (5) guarantee for each origin node $i \in V^O$ that the outgoing traffic volume of type $k \in K$ is equal to the sum of the traffic volume of this type for all destinations.

$$\sum_{a \in A_i^{\text{out}}} x_{ako} = T_{ko} \qquad (i \in V^O;\ k \in K;\ o \in O_i^{\text{org}}) \tag{5}$$

Constraints (6) prevent traffic flow from starting from the wrong origin node.

$$\sum_{a \in A_i^{\text{out}}} x_{ako} = 0 \qquad (i \in V^O;\ k \in K;\ o \in O \setminus O_i^{\text{org}}) \tag{6}$$

Constraints (7) guarantee for each destination node $i \in V^D$ that the incoming traffic volume of type $k \in K$ is equal to the sum of the traffic volume of this type from all origins.

$$\sum_{a \in A_i^{\text{in}}} x_{ako} = T_{ko} \qquad (i \in V^D;\ k \in K;\ o \in O_i^{\text{dest}}) \tag{7}$$

Constraints (8) guarantee for each regular node $i \in V^R$ that the incoming traffic volume of each type $k \in K$ is equal to the outgoing traffic volume of this type.

$$\sum_{a \in A_i^{\text{in}};\ s \in S_a} x_{aks} = \sum_{a \in A_i^{\text{out}};\ s \in S_a} x_{aks} \qquad (i \in V^R;\ k \in K) \tag{8}$$

Constraints (9) guarantee for each regular node $i \in V^R$ that the incoming traffic volume of a specific origin-destination pair $o \in O$ is equal to the outgoing traffic volume of this origin-destination pair.

$$\sum_{a \in A_i^{\text{in}};\ k \in K_a} x_{ako} = \sum_{a \in A_i^{\text{out}};\ k \in K_a} x_{aks} \qquad (i \in V^R;\ o \in O) \tag{9}$$

Constraints (10) impose upper bounds on the flow through each segment $s \in S_a$ of arc $a \in A$.

$$\sum_{k \in K_a} x_{aks} \leq b_{as} \qquad (a \in A;\ s \in S_a) \tag{10}$$

5.3 *Objective Function*

The objective function computes the total cost of the flow in the network:

$$\sum_{a \in A} \sum_{k \in K_a} \sum_{s \in S_a} c_{as} x_{aks} \tag{11}$$

The complete linear programm reads as follows:

$$\text{TF} \begin{cases} \text{Min.} & (11) \\ \text{s.t.} & (2)\text{–}(10) \\ & x_{aks} \geq 0 \quad (s \in S_a;\ a \in A;\ k \in K_a) \\ & x_{ako} \geq 0 \quad (a \in A;\ k \in K_a) \\ & x_a \geq 0 \quad (a \in A) \end{cases}$$

6 Computational Results

In this section, we test the proposed decision support system with artificial and real-world data. In Sect. 6.1, we illustrate the proposed traffic model with a simple example. In Sect. 6.2, we use the street network of the city of Bern to demonstrate how the resilience of a network can be evaluated. In Sect. 6.3, we demonstrate the scalability of the proposed decision support system by applying it to the nation-wide street network of Switzerland. Finally, in Sect. 6.4, we discuss how the proposed decision support system could potentially be applied to train networks. We implemented all parts of the decision support system in Python 3.6 and used the Gurobi (7.5.2) solver. All computations were performed on a workstation with Intel Xeon CPUs (model E5-2667 v2) with clock speed 3.30 GHz and 256 GB of RAM.

6.1 Illustrative Example

We consider a directed graph that has four regular nodes, three origin, and three destination nodes. The graph is shown in Fig. 5.

For each arc between regular nodes, a piecewise-linear convex cost function with two segments defines the total cost for a given flow of traffic. Figure 6 displays such a cost function for an arbitrary arc a.

Table 3 provides the parameters of the cost functions for different street types. Note that the flow on arcs that connect origin and destination nodes with the rest of the graph is not bounded and does not incur any cost.

Finally, Tables 4 and 5 specify the traffic matrices for private and commercial traffic, respectively. Private traffic can use any street type and commercial traffic is

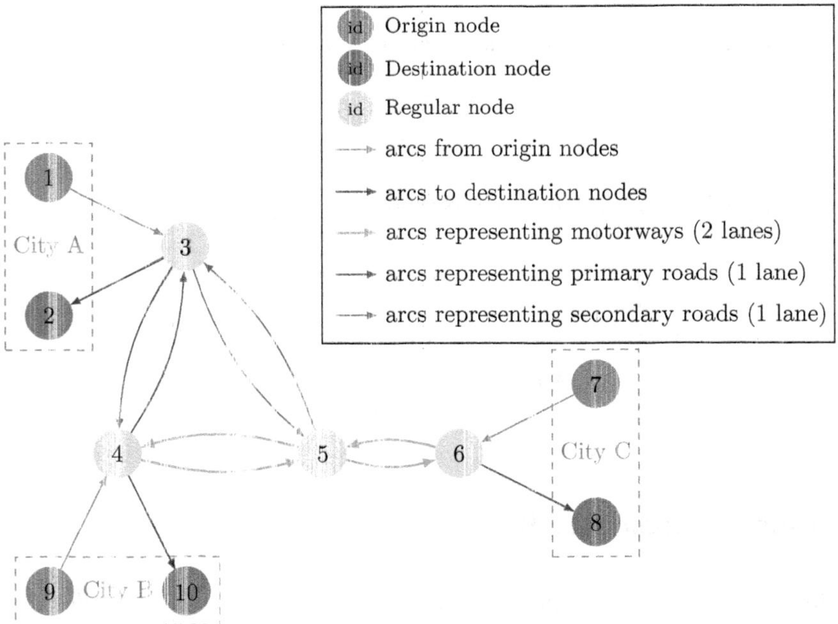

Fig. 5 Graph of illustrative example

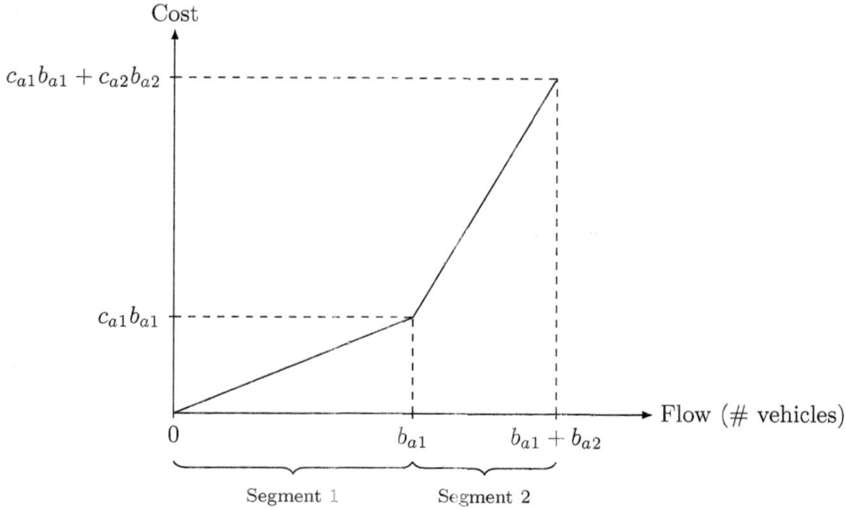

Fig. 6 Piecewise linear convex cost function of arc a with two segments

Table 3 Illustrative example: parameters of cost function for different street types

	Segment 1		Segment 2	
Street type	b_{a1}	c_{a1}	b_{a2}	c_{a2}
Motorway (2 lanes)	50,000	0.5	50,000	1.5
Primary (1 lane)	30,000	0.5	30,000	1.5
Secondary (1 lane)	15,000	0.5	15,000	1.5

Table 4 Illustrative example: traffic matrix for private traffic [1000 vehicles]

	A	B	C
A	0	15	20
B	15	0	25
C	20	25	0

Table 5 Illustrative example: traffic matrix for commercial traffic [1000 vehicles]

	A	B	C
A	0	3	4
B	3	0	5
C	4	5	0

restricted to motorways and primary streets. Figure 7 shows an optimal solution to the illustrative example that we obtained in less than a second.

6.2 Application to the Street Network of the City of Bern

In this section, we demonstrate how our decision support system can be used to assess the resilience of a street network against a disruption (e.g., a major accident).

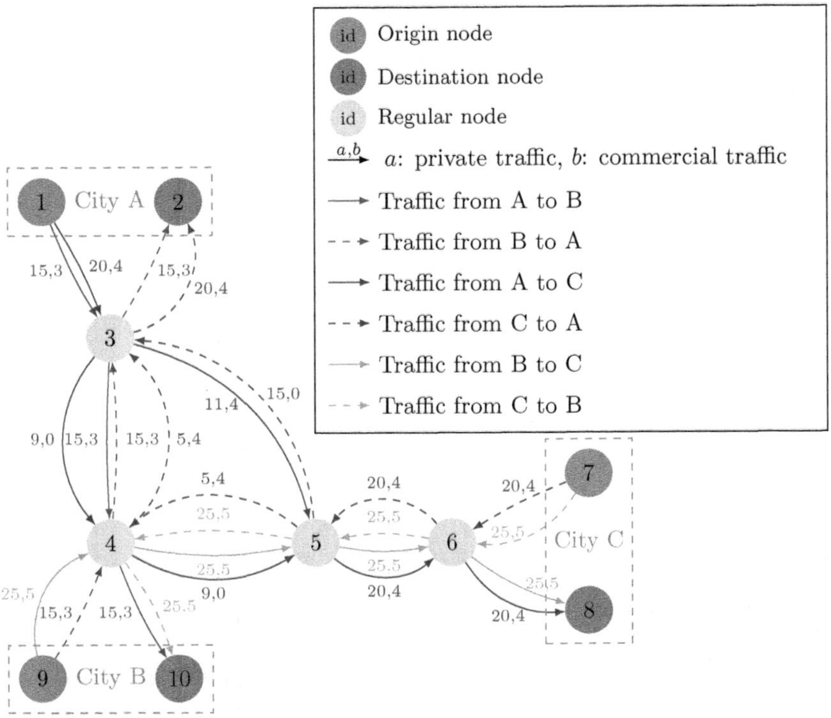

Fig. 7 Graph of illustrative example

For this analysis, we consider the street network of the city of Bern. The proposed model TF is used to determine an optimal traffic flow before and after the disruption. A small difference between the total cost of traffic in these discrete states indicates high resilience and vice versa. The graph is constructed such that it represents all motorways, trunks, primary, secondary, tertiary, and residential streets within the city boundaries. Unclassified streets were eliminated. After simplification and before adding origin and destination nodes, the graph comprises 2733 nodes and 6805 arcs with a total length of 759.6 km.

We also created four artificial cities to capture transit traffic flowing through the city of Bern. This transit traffic originates from adjacent areas to the northeast (from Zurich and Basel), southeast (from Thun), northwest (from Lausanne), and southwest (from Fribourg). For each artificial city, we add one origin and one destination node to the graph. These nodes are connected as described in Sect. 3 to all nodes that lie within a certain radius around the origin and destination nodes. Consistent with the illustrative example above, arcs that connect origin and destination nodes with regular nodes have infinite capacity and zero cost. Table 6 details for each city the longitude and latitude of the origin-destination nodes, the population, and the radius. We determined the populations such that the optimal flow of traffic before the disruption does not exceed any capacity limit. Based on

Table 6 Location, population, and radius of artificial cities

City	Name	Latitude	Longitude	Population	Radius [m]
1	Traffic from Fribourg	46.932808	7.405586	15,000	1000
2	Traffic from Zurich and Basel	46.976864	7.467384	45,000	1000
3	Traffic from Thun	46.935052	7.471473	15,000	1000
4	Traffic from Lausanne	46.959727	7.389250	20,000	1000

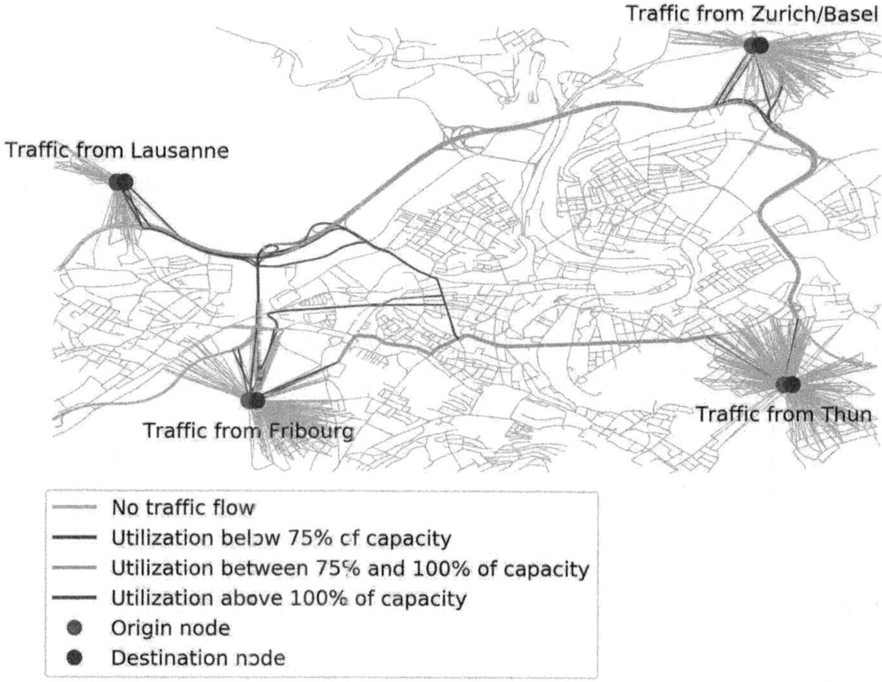

Fig. 8 Optimal traffic flow before disruption

the population and the location of the artificial cities, the traffic matrix is computed using formula (1) with $\sigma = 0.00035$. For the sake of simplicity, we did not distinguish here between different types of traffic. Note that in Figs. 8 and 9 the longitude of the destination nodes is increased by 0.001 in order to distinguish them from the origin nodes.

Consistent with our illustrative example, a piecewise-linear convex cost function with two segments defines for each arc between regular nodes the total cost for a given flow of traffic. The first segment represents fluid, the second segment congested traffic. Table 7 provides for each street type and segment the daily capacity and the costs per vehicle and kilometer.

We derived the maximum capacities for the first segments according to the Road Task Force report's technical note [15]. Note that these numbers are rough estimates; they could be refined by considering additional information such as the attribute

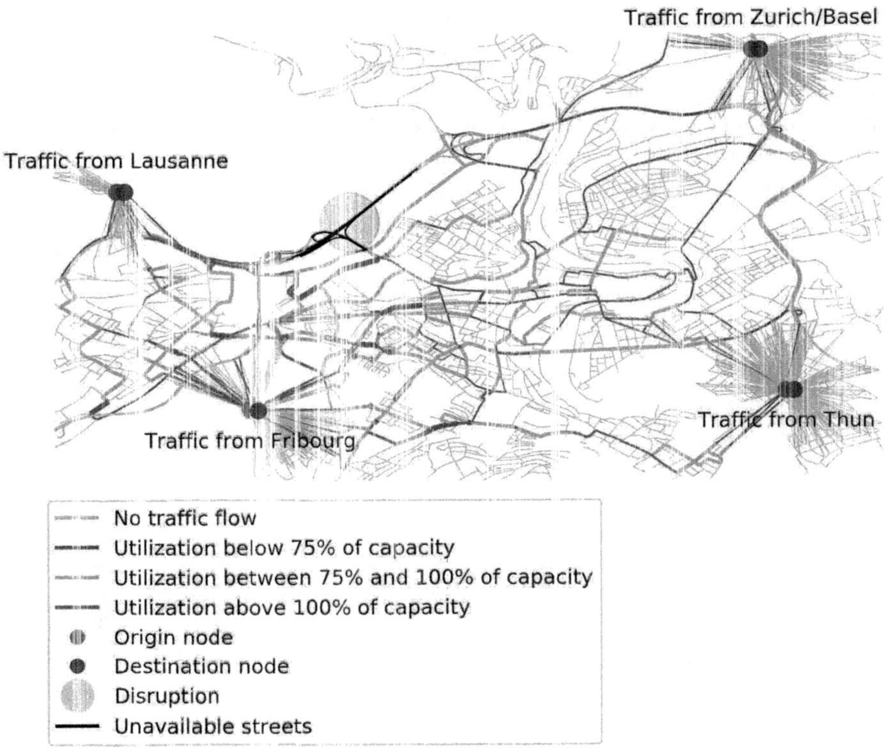

Fig. 9 Optimal traffic flow after disruption

Table 7 Capacity (# vehicles per day) and cost (per vehicle and km) for different street types

	Segment 1		Segment 2	
Street type	Capacity	Cost	Capacity	Cost
Motorway (more than two lanes)	90, 000	0.5	∞	50
Motorway (up to two lanes)	60, 000	0.5	∞	50
Motorway_link	50, 000	1.5	∞	150
Trunk/Trunk_link	50, 000	1.5	∞	150
Primary/Primary_link	30, 000	2.0	∞	200
Secondary/Secondary_link	15, 000	3.0	∞	300
Tertiary/Tertiary_link	10, 000	4.0	∞	400
Other	5000	5.0	∞	500

maxspeed and data from automatic traffic counters. The capacity of the second segment is infinite, such that a feasible solution always exists. The costs per vehicle and kilometer for the first segment are derived from average cost calculations in [19]. For the second segment, we multiplied this number with a factor of 100 to account for additional fuel consumption and reduced workforce productivity. By considering these cost types, we follow the approach of [2].

Table 8 Numerical results

Instance	#Vars	#Constrs	Time [sec]	Total cost	#Congested arcs
Before disruption	114,801	73,250	1.5	1,506,024.7	0
After disruption	85,905	56,982	1.7	7,520,532.9	68

A disruption is specified in terms of location, as indicated by its geographical coordinates, and in terms of magnitude, as measured by its radius. All arcs that have at least one endpoint within the radius of the disruption are assumed to be affected. We set the capacity of all affected arcs to zero. In our example, we assume that the disruption takes place at (46.955839, 7.417909) and has a radius of 400 m.

We applied model TF to determine an optimal traffic flow before and after the disruption. Table 8 presents the number of variables (#Vars), the number of constraints (#Constrs), the running time (Time) in seconds, the value of the objective function (Total cost) and the number of congested arcs (#Congested arcs) for the case without disruption and the case with disruption.[1]

The results suggest that the disruption significantly increases the total cost of traffic flow. Since it dissects the motorway which links the eastern and western city areas, all motorway traffic must be rerouted through primary and secondary streets. As a result, 68 arcs are congested, implying that the city's street network is not particularly resilient to disruptions of this magnitude. Figures 8 and 9 show the optimal flow of traffic before and after the disruption.

6.3 *Application to the Swiss Street Network*

To demonstrate the scalability of the decision support system, we applied it to four large-scale problem instances that are all based on the nation-wide street network of Switzerland. The graph depicting this network is constructed such that it represents all motorways, trunks, primary, secondary, and tertiary streets of Switzerland. Other street types such as unclassified or residential streets were eliminated. After simplification and before adding origin and destination nodes, the graph consists of 26,294 nodes and 61,980 arcs with a total length of 45,291.8 km. Figure 10 shows the graph of the Swiss street network.

The problem instances differ with respect to the number of cities that are considered. The largest instance considers the 20 most populated cities in Switzerland. Smaller instances consider only a subset of these cities. Table 9 reports for each instance the considered cities and the normalization parameter σ that was used

[1] We obtained the best performance in terms of running time by choosing the interior point method *Method=2* of the Gurobi solver with the following specification: *Presolve=1*, *Crossover=0*, *AggFill=5*, *PrePasses=1*. We refer the reader to the documentation of the Gurobi solver at http://www.gurobi.com/ for a detailed explanation of these options.

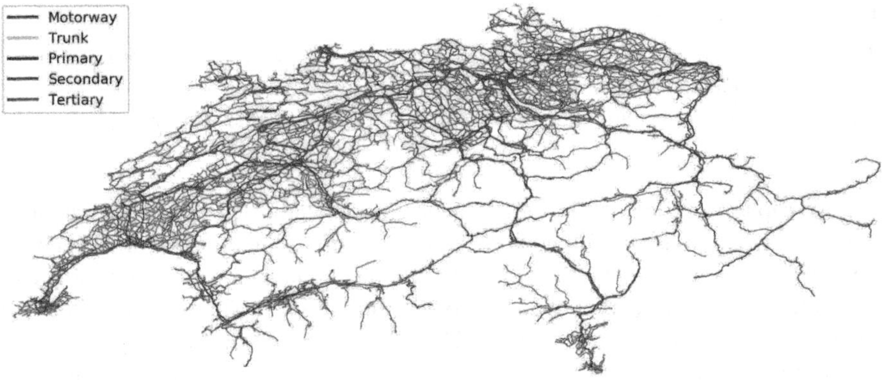

Fig. 10 Graph of the Swiss street network

Table 9 Large-scale problem instances

Instance	Cities	Normalization parameter σ
1	5 most populated cities	0.00005
2	10 most populated cities	0.00004
3	15 most populated cities	0.00003
4	20 most populated cities	0.00002

to compute the respective traffic matrix. For the sake of simplicity, we did not distinguish here between different types of traffic.

Origin and destination nodes are added for each city as described in Sect. 6.2. Table 10 contains for each city the longitude and latitude of the origin-destination nodes, the radius, and the population. We obtained population figures from the Swiss Federal Statistical Office [17] and the coordinates from the website https://www.latlong.net/. The traffic matrix is computed according to formula (1) with the normalization parameter specified in Table 9.

The cost of traffic is determined as in Sect. 6.2, using the data specified in Table 7.

We applied model TF to all four instances, using the same Gurobi solver settings as specified in footnote 1, and solved each instance to optimality. Table 11 presents for each instance the number of origin-destination pairs (#O/D pairs), the number of variables (#Vars), the number of constraints (#Constrs), the running time (Time) in minutes, and the value of the objective function (Total cost).

From these results, we can conclude that optimal solutions can be obtained in reasonable running time even for very large street networks. The running time, however, increases considerably with the number of origin-destination pairs. Figure 11 shows the optimal flow of traffic for the largest instance with 20 cities.

Table 10 Location, population, and radius of the 20 largest cities in Switzerland

City	Name	Latitude	Longitude	Population	Radius [m]
1	Zurich	47.376887	8.541694	402, 762	4028
2	Geneva	46.204391	6.143158	198, 979	1990
3	Basel	47.559599	7.588576	175, 940	1759
4	Lausanne	46.519653	6.632273	137, 810	1378
5	Bern	46.953547	7.440301	133, 115	1331
6	Winterthur	47.498820	8.723689	109, 775	1098
7	Lucerne	47.050168	8.309307	81, 592	816
8	St. Gallen	47.424482	9.376717	75, 481	755
9	Lugano	46.003678	8.951052	63, 932	639
10	Biel	47.136778	7.246791	54, 456	545
11	Thun	46.757987	7.627988	43, 568	436
12	Koeniz	46.925634	7.416721	40, 938	409
13	La Chaux-de-Fonds	47.103489	6.832784	38, 965	390
14	Fribourg	46.806477	7.161972	38, 829	388
15	Schaffhausen	47.695890	8.638049	36, 148	361
16	Vernier	46.212264	6.105269	34, 983	350
17	Chur	46.850783	9.531986	34, 880	349
18	Uster	47.348275	8.717874	34, 319	343
19	Sion	46.233122	7.360626	33, 999	340
20	Neuchâtel	46.989987	6.929273	33, 772	338

Table 11 Numerical results

Instance	#O/D pairs	#Vars	#Constrs	Time [min]	Total cost [million]
1	20	1, 486, 348	873, 250	0.72	33.7
2	90	6, 042, 808	2, 715, 760	9.74	70.2
3	210	13, 866, 784	5, 873, 842	111.00	76.9
4	380	24, 984, 042	10, 348, 938	965.77	56.4

6.4 *Application to Train Networks*

A major advantage of the proposed decision support system is that it is not restricted to street networks. Particularly, it can be used (with some modification) to study train networks as well. We predict that the OSMnx package can be extended such that it transforms spatial OpenStreetMap information on train routes and networks directly into graphs. Alternatively, OpenRailwayMap could be used as a source for raw data as it contains detailed information on the world's railway infrastructure. A third option would be to extract the graph from timetable data as described in [11]. Characteristics of a railway system could be incorporated in the traffic flow model by modifying some constraints or changing the objective function. For example, one could introduce capacities that are shared by several arcs to model the flexibility of railway operators to determine whether a track is used in both directions or

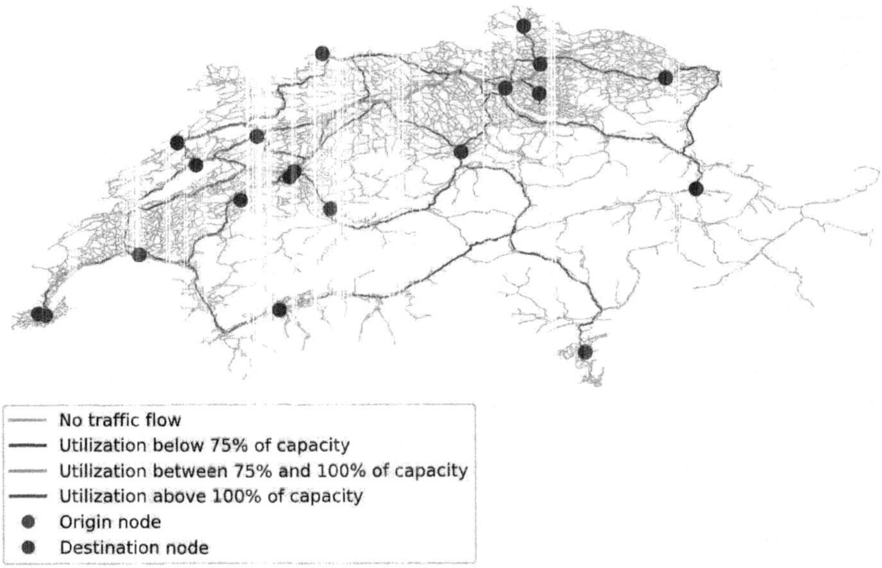

Fig. 11 Optimal traffic flow for instance 4. Note that the origin nodes are co-located with the destination nodes and hence not visible

only in one direction. Additional insights could be gained by considering a traffic system that comprises both street and railroad networks. This integration would allow researchers to investigate higher-order combination effects, e.g. the blockade or destruction of a road-rail bridge on which both vehicles and trains run.

7 Conclusion

We proposed a decision support system that can be used to evaluate the resilience of street networks based on publicly available data. The system consists of three main components: a directed graph that represents the street network, a traffic matrix that defines the traffic volume between origin-destination pairs, and an optimization model that determines an optimal flow of traffic from the origins to the respective destinations. We applied the system to real-world street networks to demonstrate how the model can be used to study the impact of a disruption and to illustrate the scalability of the optimization model. An optimal flow of traffic between 380 origin-destination pairs was determined in a few hours for a nationwide street network with 26,294 nodes and 61,980 arcs.

We suggest that future research could extend our approach by developing more sophisticated traffic matrix estimation techniques that also incorporate available traffic counts for specific street segments, by developing a dynamic traffic flow model that accounts for transfer times, and by applying our decision support system to train networks.

References

1. Ahuja, R.K., Magnanti, T.L., Orlin, J.B.: Network Flows: Theory, Algorithms, and Applications. Prentice Hall, Upper Saddle River (1993)
2. Ali, M.S., Adnan, M., Noman, S.M., Baqueri, S.F.A.: Estimation of traffic congestion cost-a case study of a major arterial in Karachi. Procedia Eng. **77**, 37–44 (2014)
3. Bell, M., Kanturska, U., Schmöcker, J.D., Fonzone, A.: Attacker–defender models and road network vulnerability. Philos. Trans. R. Soc. Lond. A Math. Phys. Eng. Sci. **366**(1872), 1893–1906 (2008)
4. Boeing, G.: Osmnx: New methods for acquiring, constructing, analyzing, and visualizing complex street networks. Comput. Environ. Urban. Syst. **65**, 126–139 (2017)
5. Brown, G., Carlyle, M., Salmerón, J., Wood, K.: Defending critical infrastructure. Interfaces **36**(6), 530–544 (2006)
6. Demšar, U., Špatenková, O., Virrantaus, K.: Identifying critical locations in a spatial network with graph theory. Trans. GIS **12**(1), 61–82 (2008)
7. Duan, Y., Lu, F.: Robustness of city road networks at different granularities. Physica A Stat. Mech. Appl. **411**, 21–34 (2014)
8. Dwivedi, A., Wagner, R.E.: Traffic model for USA long-distance optical network. In: Optical Fiber Communication Conference, pp. 156–158. Optical Society of America, Washington (2000)
9. Feldmann, A., Greenberg, A., Lund, C., Reingold, N., Rexford, J., True, F.: Deriving traffic demands for operational ip networks: methodology and experience. IEEE/ACM Trans. Networking (ToN) **9**(3), 265–280 (2001)
10. Jenelius, E., Mattsson, L.G.: Road network vulnerability analysis of area-covering disruptions: a grid-based approach with case study. Trans. Res. Part A Policy Ractice **46**(5), 746–760 (2012)
11. Kurant, M., Thiran, P.: Extraction and analysis of traffic and topologies of transportation networks. Phys. Rev. E **74**(3), 036,114 (2006)
12. Lou, Y., Zhang, L.: Defending transportation networks against random and targeted attacks. Transp. Res. Rec. J. Transp. Res. Board **2234**, 31–40 (2011)
13. Matisziw, T.C., Murray, A.T.: Modeling s–t path availability to support disaster vulnerability assessment of network infrastructure. Comput. Oper. Res. **36**(1), 16–26 (2009)
14. OpenStreetMap contributors: Data retrieved from https://planet.osm.org (2017). https://www.openstreetmap.org
15. Roads Task Force: Technical note 10-what is the capacity of the road network for private motorised traffic and how has this changed over time. Transport for London (2013)
16. Roughan, M., Thorup, M., Zhang, Y.: Traffic engineering with estimated traffic matrices. In: Proceedings of the 3rd ACM SIGCOMM Conference on Internet Measurement, pp. 248–258. ACM, New York (2003)
17. Swiss Federal Statistical Office STAT-TAB, o.d.: Ständige und nichtständige Wohnbevölkerung nach institutionellen Gliederungen, Geburtsort und Staatsangehörigkeit (in German). https://www.pxweb.bfs.admin.ch/pxweb/de/?rxid=954e2c03-0a80-4dba-ba74-b4dbbc2a0b6e. Accessed 30 Jan 2018
18. Tinbergen, J., Heckscher, A.: Shaping the World Economy: Suggestions for an International Economic Policy. Literary Licensing, LLC, Whitefish (2012)
19. Venetz, D.: Ein Durchschnittsfahrzeug kostet 70 Rappen pro Kilometer: schnelle und einfache Berechnung der Kilometerkosten. [An average vehicle costs 70 centimes per kilometer: quick and easy calculation]. Touring Club Suisse, Vernier (2017)

Securing the Air–Ground Link in Aviation

Martin Strohmeier, Ivan Martinovic, and Vincent Lenders

1 Introduction

As an increasingly interconnected and digitalized global system of systems, aviation faces new challenges. Passengers, airlines and air navigation service providers (ANSPs) all demand more connectivity; passengers for their entertainment needs, airlines for increased serviceability and more efficient operations, and ANSPs to help facilitate the safe control of the ever increasing flight traffic.

Recently, security researchers in both academia and industry have increasingly treated the aviation system as national and supra-national critical infrastructure similar to power grids, telecommunication and public health infrastructure. Responsible for this renewed focus on aviation security are new technological developments, which have shifted the threat model away from traditional electronic warfare and towards an easy accessibility of wireless systems by a wide variety of threat actors [109]. The ubiquitous availability of low-cost software-defined radio transceiver (SDR) technology enables both innocent amateurs and malicious actors to compromise civil aviation security.

Academic and industrial research on such matters has picked up significantly over the past decade, and those who argue that airports and aircraft are secure with current defenses slowly become the minority. However, there is still a large knowledge and awareness gap in the broader industry on this topic. Until recently, voices from outside and within the industry have been ignored too often and

M. Strohmeier (✉) · V. Lenders
armasuisse W + T, Thun, Switzerland
e-mail: martin.strohmeier@armasuisse.ch; vincent.lenders@armasuisse.ch

I. Martinovic
Department of Computer Science, University of Oxford, Oxford, UK
e-mail: ivan.martinovic@cs.ox.ac.uk

M. M. Keupp (ed.), *The Security of Critical Infrastructures*, International Series in Operations Research & Management Science 288,
https://doi.org/10.1007/978-3-030-41826-7_9

necessary actions such as information sharing have not been taken or delayed considerably.

It is commonly held that reminding passengers about any potential dangers of flying is likely to be detrimental to the aviation industry as a whole. Consequently, the main goal with regards to cybersecurity is to not scare the public at all costs. In a traditionally very secretive industry, this means that public information is scarce and often unreliable, and cybersecurity is no exception.

In this work, we compile and systematize the existing sources on the topic of wireless security in civil aviation. We first compile recent academic research on vulnerabilities but also real-world reports on possible incidents, such as news articles and analyses conducted by aviation authorities. Then, we discuss the existing strategies suggested by researchers to address the problems of integrity, authenticity and confidentiality. Our aim is to fill the knowledge and awareness gaps that exist around the security and privacy of commonly used communication technologies in aviation. Similarly, we hope to provide a reliable resource for aspiring researchers who look to get started in this field and who seek to understand its most important issues.

To make these contributions, we survey the literature on reported security incidents and privacy breaches and link this evidence to extant research on security and privacy in aviation. We use these insights to create a taxonomy of feasible countermeasures, and we develop recommendations for future aviation security research.

The remainder of this chapter is organized as follows: Sect. 2 discusses and classifies known vulnerabilities and incidents. Section 3 then outlines the existing research on security before it examines the work on privacy. Finally, based on the insights from this discussion, Sect. 4 defines a research agenda for both areas.

2 Classification of Air–Ground Link Incidents and Vulnerabilities

We first survey and systematize all incidents and vulnerabilities across the technologies that underpin modern air traffic management (ATM) that have been reported in the past. We first consider those that impact the security of the system, followed by privacy-related incidents. Table 1 provides a short glossary of the surveyed technologies.

2.1 Security Incidents

Table 2 lists reported incidents and vulnerabilities relating to air–ground links, with attack vectors including denial of service (DoS), jamming, injection and intrusion.

Table 1 Glossary of the analyzed technologies

Abb.	Technology
ACARS	Aircraft Communications Addressing and Reporting System
ADS-B	Automatic Dependent Surveillance-Broadcast
CPDLC	Controller-Pilot Data Link Communication
MLAT	Multilateration
PSR	Primary Surveillance Radar
SSR	Secondary Surveillance Radar
TCAS	Traffic Alert and Collision Avoidance System
VHF	Very High Frequency (voice transmission)

Table 2 Reported security incidents and vulnerabilities related to different air traffic control (ATC) technologies

Technology	Type	Vector	Description	Sources
ADS-B	Vulnerability	Injection	Analysis of different types of message injection in theory and in lab	[19, 88]
	Vulnerability	Jamming	Analysis of jamming with SDR in lab	[56]
	Exploit	Injection	Software enabling ADS-B spoofing with SDRs	[20]
SSR	Incident	DoS	Ground-based over-interrogation of aircraft transponders, causing real-world radar failures.	[85]
	Vulnerability	Jamming, Injection	Lab analysis by German Aerospace Center	[78]
PSR	Vulnerability	Jamming	Traditional electronic warfare	[1–3]
MLAT	Vulnerability	Injection	Proof of concept of an attack on MLAT system in lab	[70, 94]
VHF	Incident	Injection	Spoofing of ATC in Turkish airspace and at Melbourne airport	[100, 134]
	Incident	DoS	Regular communication interference from pirate radio stations and other unlicensed transmitters	[101]
ACARS	Vulnerability	Intrusion	Remote intrusion in lab into flight management system	[118]
	Vulnerability	Injection	Analysis of different types of message injection theoretically and in lab	[12, 86, 137]
CPDLC	Incident	Injection	Delayed CPDLC messages received undetected at aircraft hours later	[5, 93]
	Vulnerability	Jamming, Injection, DoS	Lab analyses conducted by several different aviation authorities	[23, 78]

Additionally, eavesdropping is possible for all considered technologies as none of them uses encryption. While we believe that eavesdropping is not a direct security issue, it does compromize the privacy of both passengers and airline staff. We discuss these implications in Sect. 2.2. It is noteworthy that there have been no academic studies or public incident reports with regards to TCAS, although its vulnerability is similar to the SSR and ADS-B technologies whose information TCAS uses.

2.1.1 ADS-B

The introduction of ADS-B has motivated much research on aviation security. Talks by hackers and academics pointed out the absence of any security in the protocol by the early 2010s (e.g. [19]). Later works analyzed the concrete physical circumstances (distance, sending power) required to manipulate the 1090 MHz ADS-B channel and showed concrete laboratory attacks [56, 88]. The use of ADS-B is only mandatory since 2020, and it is not yet used widely in airline operations. Therefore, no security incidents have been reported to date. However, exploit kits, i.e., tool boxes for SDRs, which enable the spoofing of ADS-B messages are available online (e.g., [20]), such that attacks are presumably only a matter of time.

2.1.2 SSR

While there are no dedicated attack tool boxes available for SSR/Mode S, it shares the same fundamental protocol characteristics with ADS-B. Thus, sending and exploiting Mode S is trivially possible by adapting existing scripts such as [20] or others. Consequently, an analysis by the German Aerospace Center [78] showed that radio frequency interference is possible, enabling ghost aircraft, jamming, or transponder lockouts. There has been one widely reported real-world incident related to SSR jamming and over-interrogation, causing several aircraft to vanish from controllers' radar screens in Central Europe on two separate occasions in June 2014 [85]. The subsequent investigation by the European Aviation Safety Agency could not identify the culprit for this SSR over-interrogation but found it was unlikely the attack was malicious. Still, cybersecurity experts stress that such malicious attacks would be generally feasible [85].

2.1.3 PSR

PSR takes a special role in our survey, since attacks are not feasible with standard software-defined radio transmitters. PSR detection is based on the reflection of its own signals, thus there is no message content that could be injected or modified. It is true that PSR can be jammed, but this requires sophisticated and powerful military equipment. See [1–3] for a detailed account of primary radar jamming and electronic warfare. Since we want to focus on civil aviation, and since there is little research about attacks on PSR, we do not consider this topic any further.

2.1.4 MLAT

Multilateration uses the signals of other wireless protocols, such as SSR or ADS-B. Thus, MLAT is often considered as a verification technology for unauthenticated wireless links [44]. Even if the contents of, e.g., an ADS-B message are wrong, the location of the sender can still be identified. Thus, MLAT offers security by physical layer properties (specifically, by the propagation speed of electromagnetic waves) which are difficult to manipulate. However, real-world MLAT systems must rely on combining location and message content data as they attempt to authenticate the identification and altitude of a target. This dependability makes these systems as vulnerable to exploits as Mode A/C/S or ADS-B. Additionally, a well-coordinated and synchronized attacker may manipulate the time of arrival of a message at the distributed receivers of an MLAT system and hence may falsify location data [70].

2.1.5 VHF

VHF has long been subject to radio interference due to its analogue nature and well-known technological underpinning. Indeed, in a recent survey, aviation experts regarded VHF as the most untrustworthy communication with the highest likelihood of both benign and malicious interference [113], such as spoofed voice communication. For example, the impersonation of air traffic controllers in Turkish airspace [100] and at Melbourne airport [134] caused significant stress among real controllers. Further, VHF communication is regularly interfered with by non-licensed emitters such as pirate radio stations, implying additional workload for controllers who must identify such frequency abuse [101].

2.1.6 ACARS

ACARS vulnerabilities have been described as early as 2001 when a U.S. military official pointed out that forged ATC clearances may be issued by unauthenticated data links [86]. In 2013, Hugo Teso used second-hand hardware to show the potential of using ACARS to remotely exploit a Flight Management System (FMS). Recently, [137] has analyzed the injection of outside ACARS messages into an FMS in both theory and practice.

2.1.7 CPDLC

CPDLC is a relatively new technology; hence, it has only recently been scrutinized by security experts, partly because fully implemented decoders for SDRs have not been openly available. Nonetheless, CPDLC generally offers no authentication or confidentiality and hence is subject to the same attack vectors that are used to compromise ACARS. The German Aerospace Center has recently addressed some vulnerabilities of CPDLC [78], highlighting the ease with which this technology can be spammed and spoofed. While there are no public reports of malicious interference, the robustness of CPDLC against outside interference is questionable. To date, several investigations have been launched into duplicate, delayed or lost CPDLC messages as well as into logins to unauthenticated ground stations [5, 93]. These problems, while yet benign, illustrate the vulnerabilities of the system.

2.2 Privacy Incidents

Table 3 lists the known privacy-related incidents and vulnerabilities with respect to air traffic control communication. We can broadly classify these privacy issues into tracking-related and data link-related leaks. The overwhelming majority of the surveyed privacy incidents relates to the possibility of aircraft tracking, while very few studies discuss aircraft user privacy breaches by compromised data links.

2.2.1 Tracking-Related Privacy Leaks

Privacy is at risk predominantly because almost all ATC technologies allow non-aviation actors to closely track flight movements. Many websites on the Internet (e.g., *Flightradar24*, *ADS-B Exchange*, or the *OpenSky Network*) exploit one or several of these technologies, and they provide easy access to immediate, highly detailed and continuous tracking data. When this information is combined with data from other comprehensive sources (including authoritative ones such as the FAA [29]), individual aircraft users can be tracked at little cost [109].

ACARS transmits flight data, e.g., flight plans, by unencrypted data links, such that aircraft identifications, movements and locations are revealed to the public. The system therefore became an attractive high-value target. Novel SDR technology allows any outside listener to receive ACARS data links. As shown in [95–97], location data sent via satellite can be received far beyond the line-of-sight required for other technologies.

ADS-B has been held responsible for significant tracking and privacy issues ever since it became operational. As authorities in the US, Europe and many other airspaces make the use of ADS-B mandatory in all flights under instrument flight rules, even so for military, government or corporate flights, the effort required to track sensitive aircraft data has decreased substantially. There are reports of sensitive

Table 3 Reported privacy leaks and confirmed vulnerabilities on ATC technologies

Technology	Type of leak	Description of privacy leak	Ref's
ACARS	Tracking	Tracking sensitive aircraft using ACARS	[95, 97]
	Data	Personal data leakage on non-commercial and commercial aircraft	[95, 97, 121]
	Tracking, Data	Weak proprietary cryptography broken	[96]
ADS-B	Tracking	Leak of military operations	[15, 16]
	Tracking	Tracking of personal/governmental assets	[25]
	Tracking	Circumvention of aircraft blocking	[52]
	Tracking	Tracking of business assets	[79]
	Tracking	De-anonymization of transponder IDs	[87]
	Tracking	Fingerprinting of aircraft transponders	[57, 105]
SSR & MLAT	Tracking	Tracking of surveillance drones	[109]
VHF	Tracking	Aircraft tracking using voice recognition	[42]
ATC (general)	Tracking	Correlating CEO vacations with press releases	[131]
	Tracking	Analysis of CEO private aircraft use	[61]
	Tracking	Corporate aircraft movement tracking for merger data	[62, 114]
	Tracking	Large-scale analysis of effects of government and military aircraft tracking	[114, 115]
	Tracking	Use of aircraft blocking to hide merger negotiations	[18]
	Tracking	Analysis of aircraft patterns to uncover surveillance operations	[7]

military missions that were exposed by expoiting ADS-B information (e.g., [16]). Journalists have set up ADS-B receivers and Twitter bots which publicly announce the presence of government aircraft at Geneva airport. These data leaks are not only a privacy concern for users, but they have also been used as evidence in court [25]. Moreover, the public reporting of CEOs' corporate aircraft use has caused reputation and business loss [79]. The National Business Aviation Association (NBAA) has repeatedly criticized that ADS-B data intercepts are compromising the privacy of their members. In particular, they note that attempts to block online services from using these data can be circumvented [52]. Studies on ADS-B have shown that procedures designed to protect privacy in the ADS-B Universal Access Transceiver (UAT) data link are flawed [87] since pseudonyms can be correlated with real transponder IDs. Aircraft transponders can be fingerprinted on the physical and data link layer, such that aircraft can be tracked even if real transponder IDs are unknown [57, 105].

SSR/MLAT: Even if aircraft are not equipped with ADS-B, their location can be obtained by Mode S. Hence, the movements and locations of non-updated military aircraft can be exposed once multiple stations are able to receive the same signal. For example, the combination of SSR and MLAT data on the *Flightradar24* website allowed the public to track movements of the border surveillance drones of the Swiss armed forces [109].

VHF: While VHF remains the most important ATC communication option to date, both its analogue nature and the fact that transmissions are not encrypted enable almost anyone to listen into local voice communication and identify aircraft registration codes. Websites such as *LiveATC*[1] publicly broadcast ATC communication transmitted by VHF. An experimental approach demonstrated that voice recognition algorithms can be used to automate and scale a tracking approach, even if blocking techniques designed to prevent public websites from accessing the data are used [42].

ATC (general): Many privacy issues are rather associated with ATC as a system than with any particular technology. Three studies have used a list of all civil flights in the United States between 2007 and 2011 that the Wall Street Journal obtained from the FAA following a Freedom of Information Act request. Journalists have used this dataset to track CEOs' private aircraft use. The publication of these data led to accusations of under-reported CEO income and increased scrutiny of corporate flight departments [61]. Other authors have used this dataset to establish a correlation between CEOs' holiday schedules and their companies' news announcements to predict stock price volatility [131]. Finally, the data have been used to correlate merger and acquisition activities with corporate flights [62], motivating later research that used ADS-B data to investigate the same issue [114].

Reports indicate that some companies are aware of this vulnerability and therefore attempt to prevent the exposure of their aircraft on public tracking websites [18]. Lastly, aircraft movement data obtained from the ATC system has been used to uncover government and military operations [114, 115] as well as surveillance operations by police entities [7].

2.2.2 Leaks of Personal Data

There have been only sporadic reports of privacy leaks on data links, despite the popularity of ACARS decoders such as acarsd.[2] A Swiss pilot magazine reports several incidents such as the transmission of credit card data, and it describes Internet forums where aviation enthusiasts share potentially sensitive ACARS messages [121]. Academic work has addressed the same issue in a more systematic way. The authors in [95, 97] examine the usage of ACARS in Central Europe. They analyze messages transmitted by VHF and satellite communication, showing that sensitive data such as credit card details, medical records, and passenger manifests were transmitted. In a related study [96], the authors show that there is a clear demand for privacy by ACARS users as some of them use mono-alphabetic

[1] https://www.liveatc.net.

[2] http://www.acarsd.org.

substitution ciphers in an attempt to protect their communication. Naturally, this approach is highly insecure and leaks both tracking information and personal data.

3 Defense

3.1 Security Countermeasures

We create a novel taxonomy that partitions the literature on countermeasures to security and privacy threats into four categories (viz. Table 4). We use this taxonomy to illustrate current research directions.

3.1.1 Cyber-Physical Security

While security has always been a major issue in computer networking, and academic research has developed countless strategies to secure and authenticate data and users, many of these are either bound to the traditional wired paradigm or difficult to deploy in a legacy-oriented aviation environment.

Cyber-physical systems (CPS) such as ATC combine computation and physical processes. Integrated feedback loops between these elements secure system monitoring and control. While classical attacker-defender models for wired networks have been developed, these can be too prohibitive since they do not consider the fact that in wireless networks there are always (if inadvertent) listeners. Hence, new solutions beyond cryptographic measures are required that can take into account the peculiarities of wireless communication. Such a cyber-physical approach to security

Table 4 Existing research on security for ATC technologies

Cyber-Physical Security	
Physical Layer	[9, 34, 50, 54–56, 58, 59, 70–72, 75 80, 90, 94, 106, 117, 124, 127, 133]
Localization	[26, 28, 67, 68, 89, 107, 112]
Watermark/Fingerprinting	[27, 39, 41, 83, 105, 133]
Machine Learning	
Classification	[30, 73, 100, 133]
Anomaly Detection	[30, 38, 54, 55, 59, 106, 108, 111]
Non-technical Measures	
Formal Methods	[12, 66, 69, 76, 116, 119]
Policies/Procedures	[17, 60, 74, 78, 98, 103, 123]
Cryptography	
Cryptographic Measures	[4, 8, 11, 13, 21, 22, 31–33, 35, 37, 43, 45–49, 53, 63, 64, 77, 82, 84, 86, 92, 102, 108, 120, 125, 128–130, 132, 135, 136]

should focus on attack detection in the first place and only deploy additional security measures if these are deemed necessary. Thus, the performance and the security requirements of the CPS may be balanced. To date, the extent research interest on CPS can be partitioned into three (if partially overlapping) areas: physical layer security, localization, and watermarking/fingerprinting.

Physical Layer Security

Physical layer security has recently emerged as a complementary technique to improve the communication security of wireless networks. A fundamentally different approach to cryptography, it establishes secrecy by exploiting the physical layer properties of the channel [138]. It is particularly attractive for the legacy systems found in aviation as it does not require changes to communication protocols or aircraft. The work in this area has identified several methods by which spoofing attacks can be identified, such as time differences of arrival [9, 70, 106], Doppler shifts [34, 90], direction of arrival [124], or angle of arrival [71]. Some authors [72, 117] further suggest the use of beamforming to detect spoofing attacks. Several works also exploit physical layer characteristics to improve defenses against jamming [56, 58, 127].

Localization

The opportunities the physical layer offers to increase security can also be exploited to verify aircraft location data. Hence, the veracity of ADS-B position messages can be checked. As localization is a relatively mature area of research, technical implementations based on multilateration have been realized. This approach seems promising since it is based on physical constants and constraints that are difficult to manipulate (e.g., the speed of light). For the case of ATC, most works have exploited time differences of arrival, often in the form of traditional multilateration [26, 67, 68] but also by alternative techniques [89, 107, 112]. Other approaches have used the angle of arrival to localize aircraft and to verify their position claims [28].

Watermarking/Fingerprinting

Watermarking and fingerprinting are two related approaches that both can identify or authenticate wireless devices and their users. Watermarking installs deliberate markers in the communication process that can be used by authentication algorithms. Fingerprinting exploits technological imperfections of the hardware and software that enable communication. Both techniques can verify the authenticity of the participants' transceivers on the ground and on the aircraft. Hence, they can be deployed to detect both malicious and inadvertent intrusion. Several studies have investigated the option to watermark VHF communication in an attempt to introduce speaker verification[27, 39, 41, 83]. Further, two studies considered the feasibility of fingerprinting the ADS-B protocol. One of them proposes to exploit differences in transponder implementations on the data link layer [105], another approach uses behavioral differences in the frequencies exhibited by different aircraft transponders [57]. Note that none of these approaches offer perfect security, since attackers with a large resource endowment may mimic both watermarks and fingerprints.

3.1.2 Machine Learning

The use of machine learning for security purposes has found widespread adoption over the past years, in particular with respect to intrusion detection in networked systems. Two approaches have been used to detect attacks on wireless aviation systems. The first is classification, whereby the characteristics of particular legitimate users are segmented and verified against these saved patterns. The other is anomaly detection, whereby the parameters of the normal state of the system are learned over time, and deviations from these patterns are marked as an anomaly and potential security concern.

Classification

Currently, classification approaches have mostly been applied to human users using the VHF channel. The authors in [30, 73, 100] use behavioral biometric voice data from pilots communicating via VHF radio to tell apart speakers on the VHF channel in an attempt to verify them and detect potential imposters. Very recent approaches have attempted to classify and segment standardized digital communication using deep learning on ADS-B signal characteristics [133].

Anomaly Detection

Some of the above-cited studies attempt to detect abnormal stress levels and distress in the pilot's voices over VHF radio [30, 100], thereby seeking to detect anomalies with regards to legitimate channel use. In contrast, the authors in [106, 111] suggest to use analogue physical layer features such as received signal strength and time differences of arrival collected from ADS-B/SSR data to learn about the space of states normally occupied by aircraft and detect subsequent diversions from this normal state. Finally, the authors in [38] apply long short-term memory networks to detect spoofed ADS-B location messages in the flight tracks of commercial aircraft.

There are many explanations for irregular aircraft movement, which is why anomaly detection is only one of several elements of an intrusion detection system. Careful calibration and engineering are required to prevent false positives.

3.1.3 Non-technical Measures

Much contemporary research focuses on non-technical measures by which the air-ground link can be secured. By the term 'non-technical', we refer to approaches that prefer formal and procedural reform of extant ATC technology landscapes over the development of new technical systems or technologies.

Formal Methods

Early academic work has described changes to user experience following the introduction of formal security requirements into an ATC system and explored whether ADS-B position reports should be used as a primary position source for aircraft [76]. More recently, the authors of [66] conducted a risk and requirements analysis of the ATM system, using VHF communication as a case study.

As the popularity of this research field grows, and as users become more experienced and deploy novel technological tools, research is now at a point where security standards can formally be verified. A complete formal verification of the ACARS Message Security standard ARINC 823 [12] identified several weaknesses that can be exploited. While the analysis confirms the security properties of the protocol, it also highlights that improvements must be made. Other work proposes the use of ontologies [69], modal logic [119], and dynamic queue networks [116] to validate different aspects of the information flow on the air–ground link.

Policies/Procedures

As new systems and technical changes to existing technologies are difficult to deploy in the real aviation environment, researchers have proposed policies and procedures which might improve the security of wireless communications. An overview of security-related initiatives of aviation authorities and the industry can be found in [60].

Both aviation professionals and passengers should be educated about ADS-B security problems [103], and flight simulators should simulate cyberattacks [74, 98]. Further, aviation authorities are advised to release test-run data and mitigation options, to increase the awareness of security vulnerabilities, and to continuously operate primary surveillance radars [103, 123]. While the last recommendation is costly and thus offsets the efficiency advantage of introducing improved protocols, it is mentioned by the FAA as a potential intermediate solution until the 2020 ADS-B adoption requirement [14]. Finally, it is suggested that the next generation of ATC technology should be designed with cyberattacks and radio frequency interference in mind [78, 104].

3.1.4 Cryptography

Cryptography is the most effective measure by which communication can be secured in any scenario. As a result, it is used widely in research that focuses on improving the security of wireless aviation protocols, nonwithstanding some significant obstacles that many analysts have cited (e.g., [108, 125]). Cryptography can effectively secure the content of any digital communication by integrity, authentication, and confidentiality. In particular, there is no alternative means by which confidentiality can be guaranteed. Unfortunately, to date only the ARINC 823 standards on ACARS message security [21, 22], have proposed to introduce cryptograhpic measures, and these standards have not yet been adopted in practice [97].

Earlier work has suggested experimental solutions that might address the security problems of unencrypted communication in both ACARS [86], ADS-B [45], and CPDLC [33, 64, 77] technology. Once the security problems of ADS-B came to the fore, many researchers focused on the development of extant and future protocols. They propose to introduce identity-based encryption [37, 40, 120, 128, 129], format preserving encryption [4, 31, 32, 43] and retro-active key publication [11, 92, 108]. There has also been research on public key infrastructures in the aviation context [53, 136] and the use of blockchain technology [8, 84]. While much work has addressed the downsides of cryptographic countermeasures and their incompatibility with current systems [92, 130, 132], to the best of our knowledge these studies have not yet been considered in detail by aviation authority committees.

3.2 *Privacy Countermeasures*

Studies that aim to protect the privacy of aircraft users and stakeholders can be categorized into two fundamental areas: First, those which analyze countermeasures to the tracking of private and government aircraft, and second, those which strive to provide greater confidentiality for sensitive data that are sent to or from aircraft.

3.2.1 Countermeasures Against Tracking

Recent works have analysed industry initiatives that propose mitigate the problem of tracking sensitive private and public aircraft. They found that these proposals are likely ineffective in realistic threat scenarios [114]. Alternative proposals in the academic literature can be partitioned into technical and non-technical countermeasures.

Technical Measures

Turn Position Broadcasting Off Since the use of ADS-B is not yet mandatory in all airspaces, around 30% of all aircraft do not broadcast their position [91]. However, since the use of ADS-B is now mandatory in Western airspaces, this share can be expected to decrease; moreoever, there are alternative means by which aircraft can be easily tracked.

Pseudonymous Identifiers Only the UAT data link offers pseudonymous identifiers by design. This link is used by some aircraft under visual flight rules in the US. It offers a built-in privacy mechanism that generates a non-conflicting, random, temporary identifier that inhibits third-party tracking [65]. Unfortunately, this approach is both limited to general aviation aircraft in the US and ineffective as the aircraft's real identifiers can be recovered [87]. Furthermore, the FAA warns that the use of this feature may have serious negative consequences [6]:

> We do not recommend integrating the anonymity features, as the operator will not be eligible to receive ATC services, may not be able to benefit from enhanced ADS-B search and rescue capabilities, and may impact ADS-B In situational awareness benefits.

On the level of the aircraft call sign, commercial firms offer solutions which assign the aircraft to an anonymous "DOTCOM" airline [122], and thus anonymize its call sign. While this approach has potential benefits compared to other blocking solutions, aircraft still broadcast their real transponder IDs, such that this method only neutralizes very weak attacks.

Encryption While few works have actively proposed and developed cryptographic solutions specifically tailored to prevent tracking, the full encryption of a message's identifying information may constitute an effective method. Consequently, cryptographic solutions as discussed in Sect. 3.1.4 may also be effective. However, practical compatibility and implementation problems will likely require separate solutions that can safeguard privacy in both SSR, ADS-B, ACARS, CPDLC and even VHF communication.

Non-technical Measures

Web Tracker Blocking Many stakeholders seek to prevent the live and public display of their aircraft on websites such as *Flightradar24* by using block lists. For a history and legal analysis of the FAA's blocking program in the USA, see [36]. However, the effectiveness of this approach is questionable [114], since such obscuration can be circumvented by alternative data sources (e.g., personal SDR receivers or non-compliant websites).

Ownership Obscuration Some stakeholders use third-party entities to register their aircraft and conceal the real owner from public records. Popular methods include the use of offshore shell companies, special aircraft registration services, wealth management companies and trusts. This approach can help obscure the movements of their owners, however, a single slip of operational security can permanently destroy this advantage.[3]

Commercial Air Transport The most straightforward and effective approach to neutralize the above privacy concerns is to forego the use of designated aircraft. Instead, more anonymous and non-exclusive means of transport could be used. As such radical measures may compromise the security or privacy of the user, they may not be feasible in many cases.

Recommendations

The literature has further discussed potential directions in aviation privacy: In the short term, regulation may mitigate the privacy impact of large-scale tracking. Governments may legally restrict and regulate entities (such as web trackers) which share data about aircraft movements.

In this respect, more dedicated efforts are required that may, for example, introduce mandatory requirements or enforce significant penalties[114]. Still, as legal norms differ internationally, and as aircraft data can be freely accessed on the Internet, the international enforcement of such regulation remains difficult. Thus, in the longer term, technical solutions should be developed to provide privacy guarantees; a robust pseudonym system could limit the tracking of aircraft over time. There is no critical technical or procedural need to have a consistent, publicly known identifier for any aircraft. On the contrary, there is evidence that authorities have assigned alternative identifiers to aircraft deployed in sensitive (e.g., military) flights [24]. Hence, a more flexible identification and assignment policy could disentangle aircraft identification from flights patterns. This measure alone would greatly reduce the security risk of ATC-based flight tracking.

Only the combination of technical and regulatory measures will create effective privacy solutions for ATC systems [114]. While regulatory measures may address data collection by state agencies, technical measures are still required to prevent data collection by unauthorized third parties.

3.2.2 Privacy for Data Links

In the long term, encryption is the sensible, mature and effective solution to achieve confidentiality in wireless networks. In the short term, as there may be no suitable implementations available, changes in procedures and awareness can at least mitigate the most significant concerns.

Such short-term measures should focus on educating avionics users to not use ACARS or CPDLC to send sensitive information. In fact, this requirement has been

[3]Examples of such slips include pictures and reports by traditional planespotters upon landing, investigative journalism, or posts on social media.

voiced as early as 1998 [81, 126]. For example, a Swiss pilot has documented a case study where sensitive credit card data transmitted by plain-text ACARS messages were intercepted [121]. The author subsequently suggests not to use ACARS free-text messages to send credit card information or names of passengers and crew. The article also suggests to prefer telephone lines on the ground and satellite links over VHF. However, a recent study has found that this suggestion is ineffective [97].

While cryptographic solutions are desirable in the long term, the deployment of related technology and protocols is in its infancy. Besides the ARINC 823 standards on ACARS Message Security [21, 22, 102], which have seen no adoption in practice, no currently used aviation standard proposes cryptographic measures. This leads to a proliferation of several proprietary encryption standards to protect ACARS and/or CPDLC, none of which has been independently verified. Instead, researchers have shown that these standards can be easily compromized [96]. While recent proposals for novel data link technology, such as L-DACS and AeroMACS, do consider encryption as a standard measure (e.g., [63]), the technology required to build such solutions is still in its early development phase.

4 Research Agenda

Our survey suggests that the reporting and data sharing on security vulnerabilities and incidents should be improved. A number of contemporary initiatives are already responding to this call. In Europe, the European Air Safety Agency (EASA) has created the European Centre for Cyber Security in Aviation (ECCSA); while the US-based Aviation Information Sharing & Analysis Center (A-ISAC) aims to distribute crucial cybersecurity information among members. However, a free global platform that integrates and shares such data among all stakeholders has not yet been realized.

Second, we suggest that the aviation industry should reconsider its approach to aviation security. Just as technology firms have evolved from producers of consumer goods to providers of global IT infrastructure, airlines and operators should embrace cooperation with academic research to transform the industry such that it can provide effective cybersecurity.

Third, many authors have pointed out that security is not safety, hence the production of effective security solutions requires a different mindset. Some intersections between these field have been identified early on [99]. While extensive development, testing and certification cycles boosted flight safety performance to record levels, measures traditionally deployed for physical flight safety (e.g., redundancy) are ineffective against malicious actors in the radio and cyber spheres. Indeed, the available (consumer) technology significantly outpaced aviation communication systems, leaving the latter dangerously vulnerable [51]. As a result, there are some fundamental gaps in the literature, which we propose should be addressed by the following agenda.

4.1 Security

There is very little research that focuses on the security of the collision avoidance system TCAS. While there are also no explicit (public) reports on security incidents related to TCAS, the system uses both SSR and ADS-B to communicate, hence, it is exposed to all physical and cyber-related vulnerabilities these technologies entail [10, 110]. In light of the safety criticality of the system, active steps to secure it should be strongly considered.

Further, the application of formal methods to verify security claims in aviation protocols should considered. Such verification procedures can help minimize the risk of technology development failure as novel technology such as L-DACS is deployed throughout the aviation industry. To date, we are not aware of any study that has proposed short-term, transparent, and readily applicable solutions for the ACARS and CPDLC protocols. While there are many proposed approaches based on cyber-physical security or machine learning for all ATC technologies, there have been no attempts to transfer such research in order to protect the integrity of data transmitted on the data link. While cryptographic solutions are desirable in the long term, short-term solutions should focus on alternative technological approaches since the ACARS message security standard has not been adopted to date, and since early attempts to encrypt ACARS messaging were found to be flawed [96].

4.2 Privacy

Privacy research has shown that both innocent and malicious actors can compromise aircraft and passenger privacy by correlating publicly available or leaked data and metadata. This problem is due to the simple fact that the data links used to transmit information cannot consider even basic privacy requirements. To date, little academic work has focused on mitigating these disadvantages. While many studies attempt to improve the integrity and authenticity of ATC systems, few have explicitly looked at the confidentiality of ATC data or the anonymity of its users. To date, the aviation industry still prefers open systems in an attempt to maximize safety by maximizing global compatibility [109]. As a result, this compatibility focus is at odds with demands for more privacy and security. Privacy leaks may be less obvious, but they still compromise the safety of aircraft users. As the number of reported cyber- and radio-related incidents of data interception and manipulation increases, a shift of the research focus towards privacy issues seems desirable.

References

1. Adamy, D.: EW 101: A First Course in Electronic Warfare. Artech, Norwood (2001)
2. Adamy, D.: EW 102: A Second Course in Electronic Warfare. Artech, Norwood (2004)

3. Adamy, D.: EW 103: Tactical Battlefield Communications Electronic Warfare. Artech, Norwood (2008)
4. Agbeyibor, R., Butts, J., Grimaila, M., Mills, R.: Evaluation of format-preserving encryption algorithms for critical infrastructure protection. In: International Conference on Critical Infrastructure Protection, pp. 245–261. Springer, Heidelberg (2014)
5. Airways New Zealand: FANS1/A Problem Reporting (2018). http://www.fans-cra.com/report/de-identified/list/
6. Airworthiness Approval of Automatic Dependent Surveillance - Broadcast (ADS-B) Out Systems. Tech. Rep. 20-165, Federal Aviation Administration (2010)
7. Aldhous, P.: BuzzFeed News trained a computer to search for hidden spy planes. This is what we found. Buzzfeed News (2017). https://www.buzzfeed.com/peteraldhous/hidden-spy-planes
8. Arora, A., Yadav, S.K.: Batman: Blockchain-based aircraft transmission mobile ad hoc network. In: Proceedings of 2nd International Conference on Communication, Computing and Networking, pp. 233–240. Springer, Singapore (2019)
9. Baker, R., Martinovic, I.: Secure location verification with a mobile receiver. In: Proceedings of the 2nd ACM Workshop on Cyber-Physical Systems Security and Privacy, pp. 35–46. ACM, New York (2016)
10. Berges, P.M.: Exploring the vulnerabilities of traffic collision avoidance systems (TCAS) through software defined radio (SDR) exploitation. Ph.D. thesis, Virginia Tech (2019)
11. Berthier, P., Fernandez, J.M., Robert, J.M.: Sat: Security in the air using tesla. In: 36th Digital Avionics Systems Conference. IEEE, Piscataway (2017)
12. Blanchet, B.: Symbolic and computational mechanized verification of the ARINC823 avionic protocols. In: 30th Computer Security Foundations Symposium. IEEE, Piscataway (2017)
13. Bresteau, C., Guigui, S., Berthier, P., Fernandez, J.M.: On the security of aeronautical datalink communications: problems and solutions. In: 2018 Integrated Communications, Navigation, Surveillance Conference (ICNS), pp. 1A4–1. IEEE, Piscataway (2018)
14. Carey, B.: FAA no longer expected to retire radars. Aviation Week (2018). https://aviationweek.com/awincommercial/faa-no-longer-expected-retire-radars
15. Cenciotti, D.: Forget any security concern and welcome Air Force One on Flightradar24! The Aviationist (2011). https://theaviationist.com/2011/11/24/af1-adsb
16. Cenciotti, D.: Online flight tracking provides interesting details about Russian air bridge to Syria. The Aviationist (2015). https://theaviationist.com/2015/09/11/ads-b-exposes-russian-air-bridge-to-syria/
17. Chivers, H.: Control consistency as a management tool: the identification of systematic security control weaknesses in air traffic management. Int. J. Crit. Comput. Based Syst. **6**(3), 229–245 (2016)
18. City, A.M.: Drugs giant AbbVie flicks privacy switch on corporate jet (2014). http://www.cityam.com/1405384925/drugs-giant-abbvie-flicks-privacy-switch-corporate-jet
19. Costin, A., Francillon, A.: Ghost is in the air(traffic): on insecurity of ADS-B protocol and practical attacks on ADS-B devices. In: Black Hat USA, pp. 1–12 (2012)
20. Crescentvenus: Wireless Attack Launch Box (WALB) (2018). https://github.com/crescentvenus/WALB
21. DataLink Security, Part 1 - ACARS Message Security. Tech. Rep. 823P1, ARINC (2007)
22. DataLink Security, Part 2 - Key Management. Tech. Rep. 823P2, ARINC (2008)
23. Di Marco, D., Manzo, A., Ivaldi, M., Hird, J.: Security testing with controller-pilot data link communications. In: 2016 11th International Conference on Availability, Reliability and Security (ARES), pp. 526–531. IEEE, Piscataway (2016)
24. Directorate of Air Traffic Management: Automatic Dependent Surveillance-Broadcast (ADS-B). Tech. rep., Airports Authority of India, New Delhi (2014)
25. Dupraz-Dobias, P.: Swiss officials just seized 11 of the world's most expensive cars from this African president's son. Quartz (2016). https://goo.gl/rR34aP

26. El Marady, A.A.W.: Enhancing accuracy and security of ADS-B via MLAT assisted-flight information system. In: 2017 12th International Conference on Computer Engineering and Systems (ICCES), pp. 182–187. IEEE, Piscataway (2017)
27. Fantacci, R., Menci, S., Micciullo, L., Pierucci, L.: A secure radio communication system based on an efficient speech watermarking approach. Secur. Commun. Netw. **2**(4), 305–314 (2009)
28. Faragher, R., et al.: Spoofing mitigation, robust collision avoidance, and opportunistic receiver localisation using a new signal processing scheme for ADS-B or AIS. In: 27th International Technical Meeting of The Satellite Division of the Institute of Navigation (2014)
29. Federal Aviation Administration: Aircraft Registry (2017). https://www.faa.gov/licenses_certificates/aircraft_certification/aircraft_registry/
30. Finke, M., Stelkens-Kobsch, T.H.: A practical example for validation of ATM security prototypes. CEAS Aeronaut. J. 1–14 (2018). https://doi.org/10.1007/s13272-017-0275-y
31. Finke, C., Butts, J., Mills, R.: ADS-B encryption: confidentiality in the friendly skies. 8th Annual Cyber Security and Information Intelligence Research Workshop (2013)
32. Finke, C., Butts, J., Mills, R., Grimaila, M.: Enhancing the security of aircraft surveillance in the next generation air traffic control system. Int. J. Crit. Infrastruct. Prot. **6**(1), 3–11 (2013)
33. Getachew, D., Griner, J.H. Jr.: An elliptic curve based authentication protocol for controller-pilot data link communications. In: Integrated CNS Conference & Workshop (2005)
34. Ghose, N., Lazos, L.: Verifying ADS-B navigation information through Doppler shift measurements. In: 34th IEEE/AIAA Digital Avionics Systems Conference (DASC) (2015)
35. Gurtov, A., Polishchuk, T., Wernberg, M.: Controller–pilot data link communication security. Sensors **18**(5), 1636 (2018)
36. Gurtovaya, O.: Maintaining privacy in a world of technological transparency: The barr program's ups and downs in changing times. J. Air L. Com. **77**, 569 (2012)
37. Hableel, E., Baek, J., Byon, Y.J., Wong, D.S.: How to protect ADS-B: confidentiality framework for future air traffic communication. In: Computer Communications Workshops (2015)
38. Habler, E., Shabtai, A.: Using LSTM encoder-decoder algorithm for detecting anomalous ADS-B messages. Preprint (2017). arXiv:1711.10192
39. Hagmuller, M., Hering, H., Kropfl, A., Kubin, G.: Speech watermarking for air traffic control. In: IEEE European Signal Processing Conference (2004)
40. He, D., Kumar, N., Choo, K.K.R., Wu, W.: Efficient hierarchical identity-based signature with batch verification for automatic dependent surveillance-broadcast system. IEEE Trans. Inf. Forensics Secur. **12**(2), 454–464 (2017)
41. Hering, H., Hagmüller, M., Kubin, G.: Safety and security increase for air traffic management through unnoticeable watermark aircraft identification tag transmitted with the VHF voice communication. In: 22nd IEEE/AIAA Digital Avionics Systems Conference (DASC) (2003)
42. Hoffman, D., Rezchikov, S.: Busting the BARR: Tracking "Untrackable" Private Aircraft for Fun & Profit. In: DEF CON 20, Las Vegas (2012)
43. Huang, R.S., Yang, H.M., Wu, H.G.: Enabling confidentiality for ADS-B broadcast messages based on format-preserving encryption. In: Applied Mechanics and Materials, vol. 543, pp. 2032–2035. Trans Tech Publ (2014)
44. International Civil Aviation Organization (ICAO): Guidance material: security issues associated with ADS-B. Tech. rep., Montreal (2014)
45. Jochum, J.R.: Encrypted Mode Select ADS-B tactical military situational awareness. Master's thesis, Massachusetts Institute of Technology, Cambridge (2001)
46. Kacem, T., Wijesekera, D., Costa, P.: Integrity and authenticity of ADS-B broadcasts. In: IEEE Aerospace Conference (2015)
47. Kacem, T., Wijesekera, D., Costa, P.: Key distribution scheme for aircraft equipped with secure ADS-B in. In: 2017 IEEE 20th International Conference on Intelligent Transportation Systems (ITSC), pp. 1–6. IEEE, Piscataway (2017)

48. Kacem, T., Wijesekera, D., Costa, P., Carvalho, J., Monteiro, M., Barreto, A.: Key distribution mechanism in secure ADS-B networks. In: IEEE Integrated Communications, Navigation and Surveillance Conference (ICNS) (2015)
49. Kenney, L., Dietrich, J., Woodall, J.: Secure ATC surveillance for military applications. In: IEEE Military Communications Conference (MILCOM), pp. 1–6. IEEE, Piscataway (2008)
50. Kim, Y., Jo, J.Y., Lee, S.: ADS-B vulnerabilities and a security solution with a timestamp. IEEE Aerosp. Electron. Syst. Mag. **32**(11), 52–61 (2017)
51. Kirschbaum, J.: Urgent need for DOD and FAA to address risks and improve planning for technology that tracks military aircraft. Tech. Rep. GAO-18-177, United States Government Accountability Office (2018)
52. Laboda, A.: Unencrypted ADS-B OUT confounds aircraft blocking. NBAA Convention News (2015)
53. Lee, S.H., Han, J.W., Lee, D.G.: The ADS-B protection method for next-generation air traffic management system. In: Ubiquitous Computing Application and Wireless Sensor. Springer, Dordrecht (2015)
54. Leonardi, M.: ADS-B anomalies and intrusions detection by sensor clocks tracking. IEEE Transactions on Aerospace and Electronic Systems (2018)
55. Leonardi, M., Di Fausto, D.: ADS-B signal signature extraction for intrusion detection in the air traffic surveillance system. In: 2018 26th European Signal Processing Conference (EUSIPCO), pp. 2564–2568. IEEE, Piscataway (2018)
56. Leonardi, M., Piracci, E., Galati, G.: ADS-B vulnerability to low cost jammers: risk assessment and possible solutions. In: IEEE Tyrrhenian International Workshop on Digital Communications-Enhanced Surveillance of Aircraft and Vehicles (TIWDC/ESAV), pp. 41–46. IEEE, Piscataway (2014)
57. Leonardi, M., Di Gregorio, L., Di Fausto, D.: Air traffic security: aircraft classification using ADS-B message's phase-pattern. Aerospace **4**(4), 51 (2017)
58. Leonardi, M., Piracci, E., Galati, G.: ADS-B jamming mitigation: a solution based on a multichannel receiver. IEEE Aerosp. Electron. Syst. Mag. **32**(11), 44–51 (2017)
59. Li, T., Wang, B.: Sequential collaborative detection strategy on ADS-B data attack. Int. J. Crit. Infrastruct. Prot. **24**, 78–99 (2019)
60. Mahmoud, M., Pirovano, A., Larrieu, N.: Aeronautical communication transition from analog to digital data: a network security survey. Elsevier Comput. Sci. Rev. **11**, 1–29 (2014)
61. Maremont, M., McGinty, T.: Corporate jet set: leisure vs. business. Wall Street J. (2011). https://www.wsj.com/articles/SB10001424052748703551304576260871791710428
62. Maremont, M., McGinty, T.: Ready for departure: M&A airlines. Wall Street J. (2011). https://www.wsj.com/articles/SB10001424052702303499204576389923856575528
63. Mäurer, N., Bilzhause, A.: A cybersecurity architecture for the L-band digital aeronautical communications system (LDACS). In: Digital Avionics Systems Conference. IEEE, Piscataway (2018)
64. McParland, T., Patel, V., Hughes, W.J.: Securing air-ground communications. In: 20th IEEE/AIAA Digital Avionics Systems Conference (DASC), vol. 2 (2001)
65. Minimum operational performance standards for Universal Access Transceiver (UAT) Automatic Dependent Surveillance – Broadcast. Tech. Rep. DO-282B, RTCA, Inc (2011)
66. Montefusco, P., Casar, R., Koelle, R., Stelkens-Kobsch, T.H.,: Addressing security in the ATM environment: from identification to validation of security countermeasures with introduction of new security capabilities in the ATM system context. In: 11th International Conference on Availability, Reliability and Security (ARES), pp. 532–541. IEEE (2016)
67. Monteiro, M., Barreto, A., Division, R., Kacem, T., Carvalho, J., Wijesekera, D., Costa, P.: Detecting malicious ADS-B broadcasts using wide area multilateration. In: 34th IEEE/AIAA Digital Avionics Systems Conference (DASC) (2015)
68. Monteiro, M., Barreto, A., Kacem, T., Wijesekera, D., Costa, P.: Detecting malicious ADS-B transmitters using a low-bandwidth sensor network. In: IEEE International Conference on Information Fusion (Fusion) (2015)

69. Morel, L.P.: Using ontologies to detect anomalies in the sky. Ph.D. thesis, École Polytechnique de Montréal (2017)
70. Moser, D., Leu, P., Lenders, V., Ranganathan, A., Ricciato, F., Capkun, S.: Investigation of multi-device location spoofing attacks on air traffic control and possible countermeasures. In: 22nd Annual International Conference on Mobile Computing and Networking (MobiCom) (2016)
71. Murphy, T., Harris, W.: Device, system and methods using angle of arrival measurements for ADS-B authentication and navigation (2014). https://www.google.com/patents/US20140327581. US Patent App. 13/875,749
72. Naganawa, J., Tajima, H., Miyazaki, H., Koga, T., Chomel, C.: ADS-B anti-spoofing performance of monopulse technique with sector antennas. In: 2017 IEEE Conference on Antenna Measurements & Applications (CAMA), pp. 87–90. IEEE, Piscataway (2017)
73. Neffe, M., Van Pham, T., Hering, H., Kubin, G.: Speaker segmentation for air traffic control. In: Speaker Classification II. Springer, Berlin (2007)
74. Nguyen, D., Shelton, J.W., Mitchell, T.M.: System and method for evaluating cyber-attacks on aircraft (2017). US Patent 9,836,990
75. Nguyen, A.Q., Amrhar, A., Zambrano, J., Brown, G., Landry, R. Jr., Yeste, O.: Application of phase modulation enabling secure automatic dependent surveillance-broadcast. J. Air Transp. Manag. **26**(4), 157–170 (2018)
76. Nuseibeh, B., Haley, C.B., Foster, C.: Securing the skies: in requirements we trust. IEEE Comput. **42**(9), 64–72 (2009)
77. Olive, M.L.: Efficient datalink security in a bandwidth-limited mobile environment-an overview of the Aeronautical Telecommunications Network (ATN) security concept. In: 20th IEEE/AIAA Digital Avionics Systems Conference (DASC), vol. 2, pp. 1–10 (2001)
78. Osechas, O., Mostafa, M., Graupl, T., Meurer, M.: Addressing vulnerabilities of the CNS infrastructure to targeted radio interference. IEEE Aerosp. Electron. Syst. Mag. **32**(11), 34–42 (2017)
79. Palan, D., Boldt, K.: Abflug in höhere Sphären. Manager Magazin (2012). http://www.manager-magazin.de/lifestyle/reise/a-827947-6.html
80. Park, P., Khadilkar, H., Balakrishnan, H., Tomlin, C.J.: High confidence networked control for next generation air transportation systems. IEEE Trans. Autom. Control **59**(12), 3357–3372 (2014)
81. Pascoe, K.: ACARS and error checking (2015). http://www.flight.org/acars-and-error-checking
82. Patel, V.: ICAO air-ground security standards strategy. In: IEEE Integrated Communications, Navigation and Surveillance Conference (ICNS) (2015)
83. Prinz, J., Sajatovic, M., Haindl, B.: S/sup 2/EV-safety and security enhanced ATC voice system. In: IEEE Aerospace Conference (2005)
84. Reisman, R.: Blockchain serverless public/private key infrastructure for ADS-B security, authentication, and privacy. In: AIAA Scitech 2019 Forum, p. 2203 (2019)
85. Results from EASA technical investigation on the radar detection losses in June 2014 in Central Europe. Tech. Rep. ED0.1-2014-ed04.00, European Aviation Safety Agency (2014)
86. Risley, C., McMath, J., Payne, C.B.: Experimental encryption of aircraft communications addressing and reporting system (ACARS) aeronautical operational control (AOC) messages. In: Digital Avionics Systems Conference (2001)
87. Sampigethaya, K., Taylor, S., Poovendran, R.: Flight privacy in the nextgen: challenges and opportunities. In: Integrated Communications, Navigation and Surveillance Conf. (2013)
88. Schäfer, M., Lenders, V., Martinovic, I.: Experimental analysis of attacks on next generation air traffic communication. In: International Conference on Applied Cryptography and Network Security (ACNS), pp. 253–271. Springer, Berlin (2013)
89. Schäfer, M., Lenders, V., Schmitt, J.: Secure track verification. In: IEEE Symposium on Security and Privacy (S&P), pp. 199–213. IEEE, Piscataway (2015)
90. Schäfer, M., Leu, P., Lenders, V., Schmitt, J.: Secure motion verification using the doppler effect. In: Proceedings of the 9th ACM Conference on Security & Privacy in Wireless and Mobile Networks, pp. 135–145. ACM, New York (2016)

91. Schäfer, M., Strohmeier, M., Smith, M., Fuchs, M., Pinheiro, R., Lenders, V., Martinovic, I.: OpenSky Report 2016: facts and figures on SSR mode S and ADS-B usage. In: 35th IEEE/AIAA Digital Avionics Systems Conference (DASC) (2016)
92. Sciancalepore, S., Di Pietro, R.: SOS - securing open skies. In: International Conference on Security, Privacy and Anonymity in Computation, Communication and Storage, pp. 15–32. Springer, Berlin (2018)
93. Selleck, D.: Iridium fault prompts ban by Oceanic ATC. Flight Service Bureau (2017). http://flightservicebureau.org/iridium-fault/
94. Shang, F., Wang, B., Yan, F., Li, T.: Multidevice false data injection attack models of ADS-B multilateration systems. Secur. Commun. Netw. **2019**, 1–11 (2019)
95. Smith, M., Strohmeier, M., Lenders, V., Martinovic, I.: On the security and privacy of ACARS. In: IEEE Integrated Communications, Navigation and Surveillance Conference (2016)
96. Smith, M., Moser, D., Strohmeier, M., Lenders, V., Martinovic, I.: Economy class crypto: exploring weak cipher usage in avionic communications via ACARS. In: International Conference on Financial Cryptography and Data Security (2017)
97. Smith, M., Moser, D., Strohmeier, M., Martinovic, I., Lenders, V.: Undermining privacy in the aircraft communications addressing and reporting system (ACARS). In: 18th Privacy Enhancing Technologies Symposium (PETS 2018) (2018)
98. Smith, M., Strohmeier, M., Harman, J., Lenders, V., Martinovic, I.: Safety vs. security: attacking avionic systems with humans in the loop. Preprint (2019). arXiv:1905.08039
99. Stavridou, V., Dutertre, B.: From security to safety and back. In: Computer Security, Dependability and Assurance: From Needs to Solutions, pp. 182–195. IEEE, Piscataway (1998)
100. Stelkens-Kobsch, T., Hasselberg, A., Mühlhausen, T., Carstengerdes, N.: Towards a more secure ATC voice communications system. In: Digital Avionics Systems Conference (2015)
101. Stewart, J.: Meet the NATS pirate hunters. NATS Blog (2015). https://nats.aero/blog/2015/05/meet-the-nats-pirate-hunters/
102. Storck, P.: Benefits of commercial data link security. In: IEEE Integrated Communications, Navigation and Surveillance Conference (ICNS) (2013)
103. Strand, D.A.: Automatic dependent surveillance - broadcast (ADS-B) vulnerabilities. Ph.D. thesis, Utica College (2017)
104. Strohmeier, M.: Security in next generation air traffic communication networks. Ph.D. thesis, University of Oxford (2016)
105. Strohmeier, M., Martinovic, I.: On passive data link layer fingerprinting of aircraft transponders. In: Proceedings of the First ACM Workshop on Cyber-Physical Systems-Security and/or PrivaCy (CPS-SPC), pp. 1–9. ACM, New York (2015)
106. Strohmeier, M., Lenders, V., Martinovic, I.: Intrusion detection for airborne communication using PHY-layer information. In: International Conference on Detection of Intrusions and Malware, and Vulnerability Assessment (DIMVA), pp. 67–77. Springer, Berlin (2015)
107. Strohmeier, M., Lenders, V., Martinovic, I.: Lightweight location verification in air traffic surveillance networks. In: Proceedings of the 1st ACM Workshop on Cyber-Physical System Security (CPSS), pp. 49–60. ACM, New York (2015)
108. Strohmeier, M., Lenders, V., Martinovic, I.: On the security of the automatic dependent surveillance-broadcast protocol. IEEE Commun. Surv. Tutorials **17**(2), 1066–1087 (2015)
109. Strohmeier, M., Smith, M., Schäfer, M., Lenders, V., Martinovic, I.: Assessing the impact of aviation security on cyber power. In: 8th International Conference on Cyber Conflict (CyCon), pp. 223–241 (2016)
110. Strohmeier, M., Schäfer, M., Pinheiro, R., Lenders, V., Martinovic, I.: On perception and reality in wireless air traffic communication security. IEEE Trans. Intell. Transp. Syst. **18**(6), 1338–1357 (2017)
111. Strohmeier, M., Smith, M., Schäfer, M., Lenders, V., Martinovic, I.: Crowdsourcing security for wireless air traffic communications. In: 9th International Conference on Cyber Conflict (CyCon), pp. 1–18 (2017)

112. Strohmeier, M., Lenders, V., Martinovic, I.: A k-NN-based localization approach for crowdsourced air traffic communication networks. IEEE Trans. Aerosp. Electron. Syst. **54**(3), 1519–1529 (2018)
113. Strohmeier, M., Niedbala, A.K., Schäfer, M., Lenders, V., Martinovic, I.: Surveying aviation professionals on the security of the air traffic control system. In: Security and Safety Interplay of Intelligent Software Systems, pp. 135–152. Springer, Berlin (2018)
114. Strohmeier, M., Smith, M., Lenders, V., Martinovic, I.: The real first class? Inferring confidential corporate mergers and government relations from air traffic communication. In: IEEE European Symposium on Security and Privacy (EuroS&P) (2018)
115. Strohmeier, M., Smith, M., Moser, D., Schäfer, M., Lenders, V., Martinovic, I.: Utilizing air traffic communications for OSINT on state and government aircraft. In: 10th International Conference on Cyber Conflict (CyCon) (2018)
116. Tamimi, A., Hahn, A., Roy, S.: Cyber threat impact analysis to air traffic flows through dynamic queue networks. Preprint (2018). arXiv:1810.07514
117. Tart, A., Trump, T.: Addressing security issues in ADS-B with robust two dimensional generalized sidelobe canceller. In: 2017 22nd International Conference on Digital Signal Processing (DSP), pp. 1–5. IEEE, Piscataway (2017)
118. Teso, H.: Aircraft hacking: Practical aero series. In: Fourth Annual Hack in the Box Security Conference (2013)
119. Thudimilla, A., McMillin, B.: Multiple security domain nondeducibility air traffic surveillance systems. In: 2017 IEEE 18th International Symposium on High Assurance Systems Engineering (HASE), pp. 136–139. IEEE, Piscataway (2017)
120. Thumbur, G., Gayathri, N., Reddy, P.V., Rahman, M.Z.U., Lay-Ekuakille, A.: Efficient pairing-free identity-based ADS-B authentication scheme with batch verification. IEEE Trans. Aerosp. Electron. Syst. (2019). https://doi.org/10.1109/TAES.2018.2890354
121. Tilly, P.: Die verpasste Chance. AEROPERS Rundschau (2013). https://www.aeropers.ch/index.php/der-verband/rundschau1/archiv/rundschau-archiv-rundschau-archiv-2013-1/638-rundschau-2-2013-1/file
122. Trautvetter, C.: FltPlan flight privacy program exposes tangled FAA policy. AIN Online (2011). https://www.ainonline.com/aviation-news/aviation-international-news/2011-08-31/fltplan-flight-privacy-program-exposes-tangled-faa-policy
123. Viveros, C.A.P.: Analysis of the cyber attacks against ADS-B perspective of aviation experts. Ph.D. thesis, Master's Thesis, University of Tartu, Institute of Computer Science (2016)
124. Wang, W., Chen, G., Wu, R., Lu, D., Wang, L.: A low-complexity spoofing detection and suppression approach for ADS-B. In: IEEE Integrated Communications, Navigation and Surveillance Conference (ICNS) (2015)
125. Wesson, K.D., Humphreys, T.E., Evans, B.L.: Can cryptography secure next generation air traffic surveillance? IEEE Security and Privacy Magazine (2014)
126. Wolper, J.: Security risks of laptops in airline cockpits (1998). http://catless.ncl.ac.uk/Risks/20/12
127. Wu, R., Chen, G., Wang, W., Lu, D., Wang, L.: Jamming suppression for ADS-B based on a cross-antenna array. In: IEEE Integrated Communications, Navigation and Surveillance Conference (ICNS) (2015)
128. Yang, H., Huang, R., Wang, X., Deng, J., Chen, R.: EBAA: an efficient broadcast authentication scheme for ADS-B communication based on IBS-MR. Elsevier Chin. J. Aeronaut. **27**(3), 688–696 (2014)
129. Yang, A., Tan, X., Baek, J., Wong, D.S.: A new ADS-B authentication framework based on efficient hierarchical identity-based signature with batch verification. IEEE Trans. Serv. Comput. **10**(2), 165–175 (2015)
130. Yang, H., Zhou, Q., Yao, M., Lu, R., Li, H., Zhang, X.: A practical and compatible cryptographic solution to ADS-B security. IEEE Internet Things J. (2018). https://doi.org/10.1109/JIOT.2018.2882633
131. Yermack, D.: Tailspotting: identifying and profiting from CEO vacation trips. J. Financ. Econ. **113**(2), 252–269 (2014)

132. Yeste-Ojeda, O., Landry, R.: ADS-B authentication compliant with Mode-S extended squitter using PSK modulation. In: IEEE 18th International Conference on Intelligent Transportation Systems (ITSC), pp. 1773–1778 (2015)
133. Ying, X., Mazer, J., Bernieri, G., Conti, M., Bushnell, L., Poovendran, R.: Detecting ADS-B spoofing attacks using deep neural networks. Preprint (2019). arXiv:1904.09969
134. Younger, E.: Melbourne Airport hoax caller Paul Sant pleads guilty to making fake flight calls, aborting Virgin landing. ABC News (2017). http://www.abc.net.au/news/2017-09-05/melbourne-airport-hoax-caller-paul-sant-pleads-guilty/8873984
135. Yue, M.: Security of VHF data link in ATM. In: Musa, M.S., Wu, Z. (eds.) Aeronautical Telecommunications Network: Advances, Challenges, and Modeling. CRC Press, Boca Raton (2015)
136. Yue, M., Wu, X.: The approach of ACARS data encryption and authentication. In: International Conference on Computational Intelligence and Security (CIS) (2010)
137. Zhang, R., Liu, G., Liu, J., Nees, J.P.: Analysis of message attacks in aviation data-link communication. IEEE Access **6**, 455–463 (2018)
138. Zhou, X., Song, L., Zhang, Y.: Physical Layer Security in Wireless Communications. CRC Press, Boca Raton (2014)

Part III
Defense

On Dependable Cyber-Physical Spaces of Critical Infrastructures

Timo Kehrer, Christos Tsigkanos, and Carlo Ghezzi

1 Introduction

More and more humans live in spaces that are populated by active entities which may be both physical and computational. Computational elements are an integral part of the physical space, and their operations can influence this space. They can react to sensory events occurring in a spatial environment and support advanced functionalities that affect physical entities. Spatial interactions between human movement and computational elements is commonplace in smart buildings, smart office spaces, airports and other public facilities, cyber-enabled transportation systems, traffic control, smart energy distribution, etc. Such systems in which humans and computational elements interact spatially may be collectively termed *cyber-physical spaces* (CPSp's).

Since many CPSp's are an integral part of critical infrastructures, they must be dependable. They do not only host and directly influence human behavior in safety-critical situations, but they also host processes and assets that need to be protected. In particular, CPSp's may be manipulated by agents who want to obtain access to the cyber-physical space. For example, attackers could manipulate building evacuation

T. Kehrer (✉)
Department of Computer Science, Humboldt-Universität zu Berlin, Berlin, Germany
e-mail: timo.kehrer@informatik.hu-berlin.de

C. Tsigkanos
Distributed Systems Group, Technical University of Vienna, Vienna, Austria
e-mail: christos.tsigkanos@tuwien.ac.at

C. Ghezzi
Dipartimento di Elettronica, Informazione e Bioingegneria, Politecnico di Milano, Milano, Italy
e-mail: carlo.ghezzi@polimi.it

M. M. Keupp (ed.), *The Security of Critical Infrastructures*, International Series in Operations Research & Management Science 288,
https://doi.org/10.1007/978-3-030-41826-7_10

procedures or exploit smart airport infrastructure in order to facilitate terrorist attacks.

Therefore, design methods should verify that CPSp's can satisfy mission-critical requirements. System compliance with critical requirements must be monitored and verified during operations, and counteractions must be deployed if violations are detected. In the context of CPSp's, these requirements typically pertain to a variety of complex spatio-temporal properties which originate from to the highly dynamic topology of a CPSp, and to which we refer to as the network of interrelated physical and digital entities. We argue that a holistic approach is needed which is based on a formal specification of the requirements in terms of spatio-temporal properties, on well-defined formal semantics that can capture system topology and dynamics, and on related automatic verification procedures which span the entire system lifecycle from design to run-time.

Extant approaches rarely take system topology and dynamics into account. While we will abstain from presenting theoretical and technical details as far as possible, we strive to demonstrate how our approach can be instantiated in the context of critical infrastructure defense. Therefore, we illustrate our approach by a case study that comprises two security scenarios which are relevant for the design and operation of the cyber-physical environment of a critical facility.

2 Case Study

In this section, we present a generalized operational environment of a critical facility which can be instantiated for a variety of mission-critical systems. We begin with a brief description of the static structure of the cyber-physical space. Then, we consider its dynamics, i.e., how this space may change over time. Subsequently, we introduce two scenarios in which the security of the facility is compromized. We suggest that the extent to which the security requirements are satisfied in each scenario can be evaluated at design-time or at run-time. The illustrative environment is presented in an informal manner; a concrete instance as well as its formalization will be presented in the following sections.

2.1 Cyber-Physical Space of a Critical Facility

We consider the physical structure of a public building that is partitioned into areas which may be connected through doors. Areas may contain various entities of computing equipment, and they may be populated by human agents. Certain areas may be classified depending on their purpose, such as secure data center areas or security checkpoint locations. Throughout the building, sensors record the presence of human agents. As it is common in contemporary environments, wireless connectivity is available throughout the facility. Assets, which may be digital or physical artefacts, may be stored in devices or located in protected areas.

We do not assume this environment to be static; on the contrary, we model human agents as operative entities who move and act in this cyber-physical space. Such actions may change both physical and computational aspects of the environment. In particular, we consider that humans may migrate between different areas by (unlocked) doors, and that they may connect to and disconnect from wireless networks.

2.2 *Security Scenarios*

We consider two key scenarios that capture generalized security concerns related to the cyber-physical environment of the critical facility:

- **Analysis scenario:** A rogue agent who has stolen an asset is attempting to exit the facility. Specifically, after extracting data from a secure data center, the agent is attempting to bypass security checkpoints, avoid CCTV surveillance and detection by roaming guards.
- **Operational scenario:** Cyber-physical access control to critical data assets requires constant monitoring of human agents across networked data center facilities. Specifically, in order to avoid information leaks, a human agent connected to a digital asset by a mobile device must not physically access unsecured areas of the facility, e.g., exit corridors.

Both scenarios require an analysis of the security infrastructure of the critical facility. As security checkpoints may fail, CCTV infrastructure may malfunction or roaming guards may not succeed in detecting malicious behavior, a rogue agent may take advantage of these vulnerabilities. Such vulnerabilities arising from failures in certain system components may be probabilistic. We assume that the probabilities of equipment failures or guard detection can be obtained from prior research.[1] Hence, security engineers can use the analytic scenario we propose as they scan the design of the CPSp for weaknesses.

They can use the operational scenario to assess which properties of the CPSp must be constantly monitored and assessed, and which reactions are appropriate in the case of a security breach. They can use the results of this analysis to propose measures for physical access control that prevent future entries into unsecured areas.

---

[1] We acknowledge that the construction of such a probabilistic model constitutes a separate and significant research problem [4]

3 Modeling and Early Design Validation

In this section, we will first introduce the concept of bigraphs [24], which we use to model the topology of a CPSp. We then discuss the properties of bigraphical reactive systems which we use to model bigraph dynamics. This formalization is not only concise, but it also allows us to analyze the spatio-temporal properties of a CPSp. The bigraphical description of the static and dynamic aspects of a CPSp topology may be translated into a variety of quality evaluation models for different purposes. In the remainder of this section, we will focus on the development of formal analyses for our two scenarios.

3.1 Modeling Space with Bigraphs

Graphs facilitate the analysis of the topology of a CPSp since entities are represented by nodes, while relations between entities are represented by edges. We distinguish two fundamental kinds of relations between entities to which we refer to as *containment* and *linking*. Containment signifies that an entity is located within another, while linking expresses the fact that two entities are connected in some way. Bigraphs [24], an emerging formalism for structures in ubiquitous computing, can handle both containment and linking among entities. We use the basic notion of a *bigraph* which consists of two superimposed yet orthogonal graphs: a *place graph* is a forest—a set of trees defined over a set of nodes—and a *link graph* is a hypergraph over the same set of nodes, where edges between nodes can cross locality boundaries. Nodes are typed, and the node types are called *controls* in bigraphical terminology. A formal treatment of this basic form of bigraphs is given in Definition 1.

Definition 1 (Bigraph) A bigraph is a tuple $\mathsf{B} = (\mathsf{K}, \mathsf{V}, \mathsf{E}, \mathsf{ctrl}, \mathsf{prnt}, \mathsf{link})$ where:

- K is a set of node types, called controls,
- V is a set of nodes,
- E is a set of edges,
- $\mathsf{ctrl} : \mathsf{V} \rightarrow \mathsf{K}$ is a typing function, called control map,
- $\mathsf{prnt} : \mathsf{V} \rightarrow \mathsf{V}$ is an acyclic parent mapping which models containment, and
- $\mathsf{link} : \mathsf{E} \rightarrow 2^{\mathsf{V}}$ is a link mapping which assigns to each edge the set of nodes which are connected by that edge.

Bigraphs can be described in algebraic terms according to the following Formulae 1a–1e. Basically, nodes are written in terms of their controls, i.e., names that define a node's type, such as P, Q, and U. The hierarchical structure of nodes through containment relationships is expressed according to Formula 1a, while the notation in Formula 1b is used to indicate that two nodes are placed at the same hierarchical level. Bigraphs form rooted hierarchies; in Formula 1c, W and R indicate different roots. Finally, we extend our basic definition of a bigraph in two ways: first, bigraphs can contain *sites*, a special kind of node that denotes a placeholder, indicating the presence of unspecified nodes. A node may contain any number of sites, which are simply indexed in the context of their defining bigraph, as expressed in Formula 1d. Second, connections of an edge with its node are treated as separate elements of a bigraph, referred to as *ports*. Port names appear in the algebraic notation; in Formula 1e, the node of control K has port names in w. These port names are used to identify nodes, which may be omitted if a single instance node of a given type exists in the bigraph, and to express the linking structure: ports with the same name are connected forming a hyper-edge in the link graph. By convention, we use uppercase letters for controls (e.g. AG) and lowercase letters for port names (e.g., net). Port names comprising a single character are variables that range over the names of a bigraph, while we use the wildcard? to denote any port name(s).

$$\mathsf{P.Q} \qquad \textit{Nesting } (\mathsf{P} \textit{ contains } \mathsf{Q}) \tag{1a}$$

$$\mathsf{P} \mid \mathsf{Q} \qquad \textit{Juxtaposition of nodes} \tag{1b}$$

$$\mathsf{W} \parallel \mathsf{R} \qquad \textit{Juxtaposition of bigraphs} \tag{1c}$$

$$-_{\mathsf{i}} \qquad \textit{Site numbered } \mathsf{i} \tag{1d}$$

$$\mathsf{K}_{\mathsf{w}} \qquad \textit{Node with control } \mathsf{K} \textit{ having ports } \mathsf{w} \tag{1e}$$

In addition to the algebraic notation introduced in Formulae 1a–1e, bigraphs may be described by using an equivalently expressive and rigorous graphical representation. Figure 1 shows a graphical representation of a bigraph that models the space of a critical facility environment as introduced in Sect. 2. A and AG are examples of node controls signifying a node type; A represents an area of the critical facility, while AG represents a human agent. Containment is represented graphically by nesting one node inside another; the AG to the upper righthand corner of Fig. 1 contains a node CN, which signifies that the agent is connected to the wireless network. Sites, which are graphically represented as shaded boxes, denote the presence of unspecified nodes. For example, the cloud node CLD may contain an arbitrary number of INF nodes which denote information quanta. Black dots attached to nodes represent ports. These may be linked to names in order to identify nodes of a certain type, e.g., isolde as an agent AG. In addition, ports may be linked to shared names in order to form edges, e.g., the edge net between the server node of type SRV and the access points of type WN represents network connectivity between them. Moreover, the reception area is connected by a door D to the lab area, which in turn is connected to the elevator and the data center area, and both of these are connected to the secure area. Finally, the dotted outer box graphically represents a root.

In algebraic notation, the bigraph in Fig. 1 is partially represented by Formula 2. It represents both the reception and the lab area and their connecting door.. We abstract from all other components by using the juxtaposed site $-_5$ (note that, instead of numbering sites in sequential order starting from 0, we keep the site

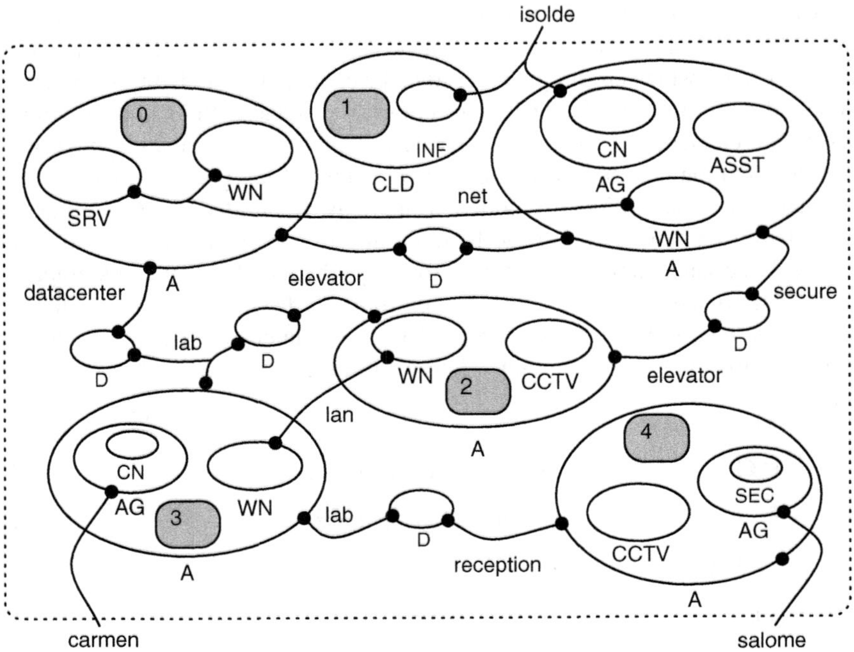

Fig. 1 Bigraphical model of a critical facility

numbering of Fig. 1 in order to facilitate orientation).

$$\begin{aligned} & \mathsf{A}_{\mathsf{reception}}.(\mathsf{AG}_{\mathsf{salome}} \mid \mathsf{CCTV} \mid -_4) \mid \mathsf{D}_{\mathsf{reception,lab}} \mid \\ & \qquad \mathsf{A}_{\mathsf{lab}}.(\mathsf{AG}_{\mathsf{carmen}}.(\mathsf{CN}_{\mathsf{net}}) \mid \mathsf{WN}_{\mathsf{net}} \mid -_3) \mid -_5 \end{aligned} \tag{2}$$

We now consider the dynamics of this representation by using bigraphical reactive systems (BRS). These specify how a bigraph can be modified by selectively rewriting some of its portions. Reaction rules have the general form of $\mathsf{R} \rightarrow \mathsf{R}'$; both R and R' are bigraphs, called *redex* and *reactum* in the bigraphical terminology. The intuition is that if an occurrence of the redex is found in a larger "host bigraph", the redex can be replaced by the reactum, in a fashion similar to graph rewriting [10]. BRS allow the analyst to describe possible ways in which cyber and physical spaces can evolve through reaction rules. Such rules need to be specified in order to reflect the change primitives required for the intended analysis. In the case presented in Sect. 2, this includes human agents who establish network connections with their mobile devices and move inside the physical space by entering areas connected through doors.

Formula 3 illustrates a rule which specifies how an agent may move from one area to another. The bigraphical linking structure is used to capture the identifier of the agent (n), and those of the areas (r and v) through named ports. The two areas are connected since a door node D exists with port names that correspond to the two room identifiers. Such port name variables in reaction formulae can be instantiated and bound to specific ports in a given bigraphical model to which the reaction rules are applied. Areas adjacent to the connected areas (r and v) as well as other entities which may be contained by the moving agent (v) are not modified if the reaction takes place. This is indicated by sites which appear both in the redex and the reactum of the rule In our scenario, human security guards patrol the critical facility by moving inside it, so Formula 3 applies both to rogue agents and security guards.

$$\begin{aligned} &\mathsf{A_r}.(\mathsf{AG_n}.(-_0) \mid -_1) \mid \mathsf{A_v}.(-_2) \mid \mathsf{D_{r,v}} \mid -_3 \;\rightarrow \\ &\qquad \mathsf{A_r}.(-_1) \mid \mathsf{A_v}.(\mathsf{AG_n}.(-_0) \mid -_2) \mid \mathsf{D_{r,v}} \mid -_3 \end{aligned} \tag{3}$$

In the same way, Formula 4 specifies a reaction rule that models an agent (AG) who connects to a network access point (WN) located in the same. This set-up yields a configuration where a token signifying connection (CN) is contained in the agent node and the bigraphical linking structure is used to capture the connection to the network (through the port named net). The redex of this reaction rule applies, e.g., to agent isolde who is located in the secure area which contains a network-connected access point $\mathsf{WN_{net}}$. The reaction induced by applying the rule would result in isolde being connected to the network.

$$\mathsf{A_r}.(\mathsf{AG_n}.(\mathsf{CN}) \mid \mathsf{WN_{net}} \mid -_0) \mid -_1 \;\rightarrow\; \mathsf{A_r}.(\mathsf{AG_n}.(\mathsf{CN_{net}}) \mid \mathsf{W_{net}} \mid -_0) \mid -_1 \tag{4}$$

We additionally consider reactions which model detection by a security guard or a CCTV camera as specified in Formulae 5 and 6. Successful detection is modeled by a token DCT placed inside an AG node representing the rogue agent if an agent marked with SEC is located in the same area (Formula 5) or if the rogue agent is located in a room which contains a CCTV camera (Formula 6).

$$\begin{aligned} &\mathsf{A_r}.(\mathsf{AG_n}.(-_0) \mid \mathsf{AG_n}.(\mathsf{SEC}) \mid -_1) \mid -_2 \;\rightarrow \\ &\qquad \mathsf{A_r}.(\mathsf{AG_n}.(\mathsf{DCT} \mid -_0) \mid \mathsf{AG_n}.(\mathsf{SEC}) \mid -_1) \mid -_2 \end{aligned} \tag{5}$$

$$\begin{aligned} &\mathsf{A_r}.(\mathsf{AG_n}.(-_0) \mid \mathsf{CCTV} \mid -_1) \mid -_2 \;\rightarrow \\ &\qquad \mathsf{A_r}.(\mathsf{AG_n}.(\mathsf{DCT} \mid -_0) \mid \mathsf{CCTV} \mid -_1) \mid -_3 \end{aligned} \tag{6}$$

3.2 *Enabling Automated Analysis*

While bigraphs and bigraphical reaction rules are adequate for describing the topology of a CPSp and its inherent dynamics, a quality evaluation model that supports systematic analyses of the behavior of the changing system is required.

We assume that a CPSp is specified by a BRS as in the previous section. To enable automated analysis, we transform this specification into an equivalent transition system generally known as a (Doubly) *Labelled Transition System* (dLTS) [8] as specified in Definition 2.

Definition 2 ((Doubly) ***Labelled Transition System*****)** A doubly Labelled Transition System, for short dLTS, is a tuple $\mathsf{K} = (\mathsf{S}, \Lambda, \mathsf{R}, \mathsf{I}, \mathsf{BP}, \mathsf{L})$ where:

- S is a set of states that describe configurations of space,
- Λ is a set of transition labels,
- $\mathsf{R} \subseteq \mathsf{S} \times \Lambda \times \mathsf{S}$ is a 3-adic accessibility relation. If $p, q \in \mathsf{S}$ and $\alpha \in \Lambda$, then $(p, \alpha, q) \in \mathsf{R}$ is written as $p \overset{\alpha}{\to} q$,
- $\mathsf{I} \subseteq \mathsf{S}$ is a set of initial states,
- BP is a set of atomic propositions,
- $\mathsf{L} : \mathsf{S} \to 2^{\mathsf{BP}}$ is a function that labels each state with the set of propositions that are true in that state.

States of K describe bigraphical configurations of space, while transitions describe how the configuration of the system can change by moving from one state to its successors. Interpreting a BRS specification as a dLTS entails describing its possible evolution based on the application of reaction rules. Each bigraph configuration is represented by a state $s \in \mathsf{S}$ in K, and each state declaratively represents a bigraphical structure. The set BP of atomic propositions that label (L) the state can be systematically generated since a set of propositions declaratively represents the corresponding bigraph configuration by reflecting the elementary relations and entities involved in the space. The accessibility relation R between states shows how configurations change as a state s is transformed to a state s'; it corresponds to the transitions in the transition system. Starting from an initial state ($i \in \mathsf{I}$) of the system which represents an initial configuration, the BRS-based specification is interpreted by generating states according to reaction rules. BRS interpretation entails bigraph matching [2, 24] and can be automated by, e.g., configuring existing tool suites [25, 27, 29].

Figure 2 shows a fragment of the dLTS which is generated according to the possible movements of human agents (rogue agents and security guards) and the possible ways of how rogue agents may be detected. State a represents the bigraphical configuration of Fig. 1 as the initial state. From state a, if the reaction illustrated occurs, the CPSp is found in state b, where isolde is now located in the datacenter area which she has entered from the secure area. The same basic principle applies to all other transitions for which formal representations of the reactions are omitted in Fig. 2: From state a, isolde may also move to the elevator area; there, she may be either detected by the CCTV in place, or move to the lab area undetected, etc.

Labelled transition systems are amenable to formal verification by model checking. Model checking performs an exhaustive analysis of the state space to check the validity of a property. Properties define constraints on execution traces and are expressed in languages based on different kinds of temporal logic [8].

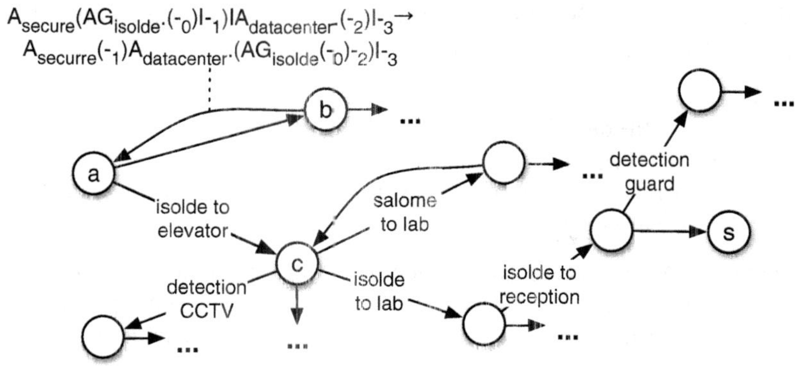

Fig. 2 dLTS showing the evolution of the critical facility CPSp

The kinds of properties we can reason about are qualitative. For example, they can express the requirement that for all execution traces, if a certain state $S1$ is entered then another state $S2$ is also entered. Such qualitative verification, however, does not provide the required level of assurances needed for critical infrastructures which exhibit stochastic behavior; in this case, quantitative verification is required to support the analysis of dependability properties [5]. In the next section, options for such quantitative analysis are discussed.

3.3 Design-Time Probabilistic Analysis

In this section, we attempt to sketch a formal reasoning strategy that addresses the analysis scenario outlined in Sect. 2. We propose an interpretation of the BRS description over a state-transition structure with probabilities on transitions, such that quantitative modeling and verification is possible. We propose that any agent actions in a given state of the dLTS generated from a BRS description may occur with different probabilities. Our strategy entails to superimpose a probability distribution onto the set of possible actions performed by each agent in every state. It thus transforms the dLTS into a Markov Decision Process, which is amenable to formal verification via probabilistic model checking.

A Markov Decision Process (MDP) is essentially a state-transition system where in each state a non-deterministic choice occurs between several discrete probability distributions of an agent's transitions to successor states.[2] The following Definition 3 reflects these considerations.

[2]For convenience, the formal definition of an MDP is applied to the context of our problem setting, ignoring rewards and the discount factor. We assume that the effects of any action taken in a particular state depend only on that state and not on the prior history.

Definition 3 (Markov Decision Process) A Markov Decision Process (MDP) is defined as a 4-tuple $\mathsf{M} = (\mathsf{S}, \mathsf{S_0}, \mathsf{A}, \mathsf{P_a})$ where:

- S is a finite set of states;
- S_0 is a subset of S denoting the set of initial states;
- A is a finite set of agents;
- $\mathsf{P_a(s, s') = Pr(s_{t+1} | s_t = s, a_t = a)}$ is the probability that agent a in state s at time t will reach state s' at time $t + 1$.

Note that an MDP process exhibits non-determinism that describes the freedom of choice the entities enjoy in every state. Several logics can subsequently express properties on probabilistic structures [15]. Probabilistic Computation Tree Logic (PCTL) [20] is such a branching time logic which extends classical Computation Tree Logic (CTL) [8] by a probabilistic operator that manifests as quantitative extensions of CTL's *all* (A) and *exists* (E) operators. Model checking for PCTL involves to identify those states of an MDP that satisfy a PCTL formula.

We do not go here into the very details of the syntax and semantics of PCTL, but rather illustrate its expressive power by means of our analysis scenario. Formula 7 specifies a property that is evaluated over MDP M which describes the probabilistic evolution of the CPSp, where elementary predicates are expressed in terms of bigraphical patterns. In this case, we have a single predicate, namely the bigraphical pattern $\mathsf{A_{rec}}.(\mathsf{AG_n}.-_0) \mid -_1$, which denotes a situation in which a rogue agent is located within the reception area. The *exists* operator states that, starting from the initial state of the MDP, there exists a path in the MDP such that a state is reached in which the above predicate holds (states in our MDP represent bigraphical configurations of the entire space). Finally, existence is quantified by the probabilistic operator P which specifies a probability threshold. Therefore, the PCTL property shown in Formula 7 expresses the fact that the rogue agent may successfully reach the unsecured reception area of the critical facility with a probability of 5% or less.

$$P_{\leq 0.05}\, E\big(\mathsf{A_{rec}}.(\mathsf{AG_n}.-_0) \mid -_1\big) \tag{7}$$

The evaluation of Formula 7 over MDP M through explicit-state model checking provides the security engineer with a quantitative assessment of the critical facility's security level if the property is satisfied. Otherwise, a model checker would generate a set of paths by which the rogue agent may reach the unsecured reception area in an undesired way. Such counter-examples thus provide the security engineer with valuable information about how the facility's cyber-physical spatial design could be improved.

4 Spatial Verification of Cyber-Physical Spaces at Runtime

In order to prevent the extraction of information by unauthorized agents, any human agent connected to a digital asset inside the facility must not be allowed to physically access unsecured areas of the facility (e.g., the exit corridor). Hence, the presence of connected agents in secured areas must be continuously monitored and evaluated. Verification of this property takes place at run-time over the current state of the environment. The agent might access a digital asset which may be located in any networked facility other than the one she is located in. This possibility implies challenges for both the specification and the verification of the property, as such a predicate cannot be encoded in a static manner; the model is unknown (or underspecified) at design time, and it is only built or updated at run-time through monitoring. We therefore propose to use a spatial logic by which we can capture and verify the property at hand. The logic will be evaluated accordingly upon updated static models of the CPSp obtained at run-time, assuming there is no information about the structure of the model at design-time beyond the actual property specification.

4.1 Bigraphical Closure Models at Runtime

Similar to the probabilistic analysis presented in Sect. 3, a basic prerequisite for the analysis of any spatial properties of a CPSp is to develop a suitable evaluation model that has well-defined spatial semantics. Our spatial reasoning approach is based on SLCS [6], a formalism for specifying and verifying properties of space which is based on an evaluation model referred to as *closure model*. We will first clarify this important term and then suggest an approach to systematically derive a bigraphical closure model from (1) a structural description of a CPSp as presented in Sect. 3.1 and (2) a set of atomic propositions of interest specified as bigraphical patterns. In contrast to the design-time probabilistic analysis presented in the previous section, which exhaustively analyses topological evolution by considering all possible changes specified by reaction rules, the derivation of a bigraphical closure model only requires a single discrete specification of the bigraphical model. The idea is that an updated bigraphical model and thus an updated bigraphical closure model is obtained through run-time monitoring of the CPSp when it is operational.

To introduce the concept of a closure model as the underlying evaluation model of SLCS, we first introduce the central term *closure space* as it is used in mathematical topology.

Definition 4 (Closure Space) A closure space is a pair $\mathsf{CS} = (\mathsf{X}, \mathsf{C})$ where:

- X is a set whose elements are called points,

- $C : 2^X \to 2^X$ is a function, called the closure operator, which assigns to each subset A of X its closure, such that for all $A, B \subseteq X$:
  - $C(\emptyset) = \emptyset$;
  - $A \subseteq C(A)$;
  - $C(A \cup B) = C(A) \cup C(B)$.

A *closure model* is an extension of a closure space whereupon truth values can be evaluated. To this end each point $x \in X$ of a closure space (X, C) is associated with a set of atomic propositions that hold for that point.

Definition 5 (Closure Model) A closure model is a tuple $M = \big((X, C), P, v\big)$ where:

- (X, C) is a closure space,
- P is a set of atomic propositions,
- $v : P \to 2^X$ is a valuation function that assigns to each atomic proposition in P the set of points in X for which the proposition holds.

To make SLCS accessible for the analysis of structural descriptions of cyber-physical environments, we need to adapt the key concepts of a closure space and closure model to bigraphs. We refer to these adapted concepts as *bigraphical closure space* and *bigraphical closure model*, respectively [31]. We exploit the fact that every graph for which the set of edges forms a binary relation induces a closure space, called quasi-discrete closure space. We therefore interpret closure as the adjacency of nodes [6]. Thus, the idea of obtaining a closure space over bigraphs is to transform a bigraph into a simple graph. This transformation comprises three steps [31]. First, the nodes of a bigraph are mapped onto the nodes of the corresponding simple graph. Second, the hyperlink structure is flattened such that bigraphical links are represented by dedicated simple graph nodes, where every simple graph node representing a link is adjacent to the simple graph nodes corresponding to the bigraphical nodes which are connected by the link. Third, bigraphical nesting relationships are also represented by nodes in a simple graph, in order to treat containment and linking in a uniform way. The resulting simple graph may be interpreted as a bigraphical closure space whose nodes represent the points of the closure space and whose edges induce a closure operator, according to Definition 6.

Definition 6 (Closure Space Over Bigraphs) Let B be a bigraph according to Definition 1, and $G = V, E$ be a simple graph consisting of a set V of nodes and a set $E \subseteq \big\{\{x, y\} \mid x, y \in V\big\}$ of edges; G is obtained from B according to [31]. A closure space is a tuple $CS_B = (V, C_E)$ where:

- V constitutes the set of points of the closure space,
- C_E is obtained from E such that for all $A \in V$:
  - $C_E(A) = A \cup \{x \in V \mid \exists\, a \in A : \{a, x\} \in E\}$.

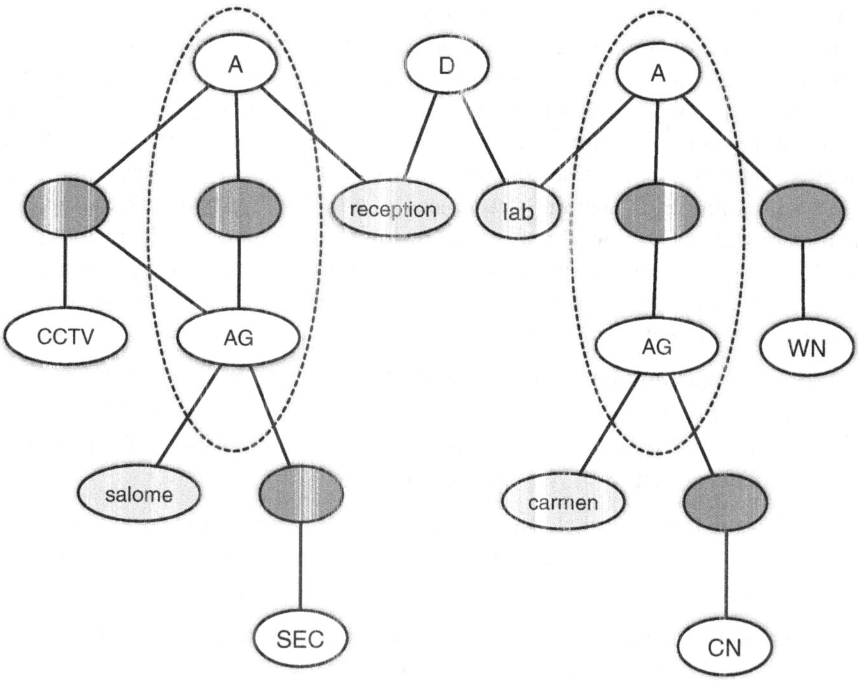

Fig. 3 Bigraphical closure space obtained from parts of the bigraph of Fig. 1, with occurrences of pattern $p_1 = A_?.(AG_?.(-_1)) \mid -_0$

Figure 3 illustrates this definition, using the partial bigraph as described by Formula 2. It shows the reception and lab areas, the entities these areas contain, and the door that connects them. Nodes derived from bigraphical nodes are rendered in white, labelled by their node types (A, D, CCTV, etc.). Nodes representing bigraphical linking are rendered in light gray, labelled by the name of the link (reception, lab, salome and carmen). Nodes representing bigraphical nesting relationships are unlabelled and rendered in dark grey (e.g., relationship between nodes of type A and CCTV). The simple graph presented in Fig. 3 may be interpreted as a bigraphical closure space, its nodes representing the points of the closure space. The closure of a set of points can be intuitively obtained based on adjacency relationships. For example, the closure of the D node would include itself, the reception node as well as the lab node, i.e., $C(\{D\}) = \{D, \text{reception}, \text{lab}\}$.

The next step is to associate each point $x \in V$ of a bigraphical closure space (V, C_E) with a set of atomic propositions that hold for that point. We suggest that properties arising from critical requirements often need to be predicated on complex entities, i.e., locally bounded spatial structures of interest that the system developer must specify. She must consider an agent with a network connection token, an area in which a certain valuable asset or some other entities of interest such as a CCTV camera or a network access point is located, etc. Such complex entities may be conveniently specified through bigraphical patterns, occurrences of which can be found in a bigraph through bigraph matching, analogously to finding occurrences of a redex of a reaction rule (see Sect. 3.1). To make the complex entities of interest accessible to our spatial reasoning approach based on SLCS, we propose that the atomic propositions of a bigraphical closure model are given in terms of bigraphical patterns. Then, the set of atomic propositions that hold for a particular point $x \in V$ is defined as the set of pattern occurrences of which x is a part. For example, in the bigraphical closure space represented by Fig. 3, occurrences of the pattern $p_1 = A_?.(AG_?.(-_1)) \mid -_0$ in the bigraphical closure space are enclosed by dotted lines. Thus, p_1 holds for every point which is part of an occurrence of this pattern. We formalize the concept of a bigraphical closure model in Definition 7.

Definition 7 (Bigraphical Closure Model) Let B be a bigraph and G be a simple graph obtained from B as in Definition 6, and P be the overall set of bigraphical patterns specified by the developer serving as atomic propositions. A bigraphical closure model is a pair $M = \big((V, C), v\big)$ where:

- (V, C) is the bigraphical closure space induced by graph G obtained from B,
- $v : P \rightarrow 2^V$ is a valuation function assigning to each bigraphical pattern $p \in P$ the set of points in V which are part of an occurrence of p in B mapped to G.

A bigraphical closure model is derived from a dedicated configuration; in our case, the configuration which represents the current state of the cyber-physical environment as it is being operated. We assume that all actions occurring in the environment are adequately monitored. During monitoring, events generated in the CPSp indicating changes are received. These are all change events in the CPSp that are relevant for the system. The model of the cyber-physical space maintained at run time is updated accordingly. We note that if events are modeled as bigraphical reactions, model updates are precisely defined [29].

4.2 Run-Time Verification of Spatial Properties

In this section, we outline the syntax and semantics of a slightly extended form of SLCS [6], a spatial logic for closure spaces that we use in our subsequent analysis of the topological properties of a CPSp. A formula, in our case, consists of propositions that represent bigraphical patterns along with SLCS operators. The logic features boolean operators, a "one step" modality that transforms closure into a logical operator, and a surrounds operator [31]. Given that p is drawn from a set of bigraph patterns P, the syntax of SLCS is defined by the following grammar:

$$\phi ::= p \mid \top \mid \neg\phi \mid \phi \wedge \psi \mid C\,\phi \mid \phi\, S\, \psi. \tag{8}$$

In Formula 8, $\top$ denotes true, $\neg$ is negation, $\wedge$ is conjunction, C is the closure operator, and S is the spatial surrounds operator. When used for the sake of spatial model checking, SLCS formulae are evaluated with bigraphical closure models. Initially, following the procedure presented in [7], such an evaluation yields the set of points of the bigraphical closure space where the formula is true; the satisfaction $\mathsf{M}, \mathsf{x} \models \phi$ of formula ϕ is defined by induction on terms. For the sake of verification, however, we rather return a truth value which indicates the existence of (any) points in the bigraphical closure space for which the evaluated formula is true. In other words, the SLCS property is considered to be fulfilled on a bigraphical closure model if the set of points returned by the initial model checking procedure presented in [7] is not empty. While the elementary syntax presented in Formula 8 features the two fundamental spatial operators of closure and surrounds, a set of more complex operators may be derived from them. In [7, 31], for instance, complex operators reflecting the notions of nearness and reachability have been derived. In particular, the so-called "reach through" operator is defined as $\phi\ \Re(\psi)\ \zeta$. Informally, it is satisfied for a point x, if x satisfies ϕ and there is a sequence of points starting from x, all satisfying ψ, that reaches a target point satisfying ζ.

Formula 9 below formally encodes a property which needs to be verified for the operational scenario we introduced in Sect. 2. The premise of the implication states that an agent ($\mathsf{AG_n}.(-_1)$) is able to reach a sensitive file ($\mathsf{FILE_n}$) through network entities like a network access point or the cloud ($WN_? \wedge CLD$). If this is the case, this agent must not be located in the reception area, which is an unsecured area in our critical facility ($\neg \mathsf{A_{reception}}.(\mathsf{AG_n}.(-_1) \mid -_0)$). This property encodes that points belonging to a bigraphical pattern that captures an agent n, ($\mathsf{AG_n}.(-_1)$) are able to reach points of a file node with the same port name of the agent ($\mathsf{FILE_n}$) through network entities ($\mathsf{WN_?}$ or CLD). Note that there is no information encoded on *how* the file should be reachable through the network, and the specification is able to capture every possible instance of a reachability realization that may appear on a model.

$$\left(\mathsf{AG_n}.(-_1)\ \Re(\mathsf{WN_?} \vee \mathsf{CLD})\ \mathsf{INF_n}\right) \Rightarrow \neg A_{reception}.(AG_n.(-_1) \mid -_0). \tag{9}$$

To support run-time verification of the CPSp in our operational scenario, properties like the one presented in Formula 9 will be evaluated whenever the monitoring indicates a change in the CPSp's toplogy, which is reflected in the bigraphical closure model. In the simplest case, an alarm may be generated if a critical property is violated. More advanced systems could be self-adaptive, counteracting property violations by triggering measures that ensure that all security requirements are satisfied. While the specification of such systems is beyond the scope of our contribution, related research has proposed a number of modeling strategies [29, 30]. Although self-adaptation has been studied for temporal properties in this work, we believe that the basic ideas may be adopted for the spatial domain.

5 Related Work and Further Reading

In this chapter, we have illustrated how formal methods from various areas of computer science may be applied to the design and operation of cyber-physical spaces for which dependability is of utmost importance, notably spatial environments with smart functionalities which exist within critical infrastructures. Consequently, related work may be considered from two different perspectives. From an application-oriented perspective, contemporary design practices for spatial environments, their limitations as regards smart CPSp's, and alternative approaches which propose to overcome these limitations should all be evaluated. From a theoretical perspective, our work contributes to the understanding of how spatial environments and their dynamics can be formally modeled. Specifically, we emphasize topology-centric approaches and formalisms that support temporal and spatial analysis. While we do not claim that our work is exhaustive, we do believe it points the reader's attention to a number of related research areas as well as to opportunities for practical application.

5.1 Application-Oriented Perspective

Computer-Aided Design (CAD) tools have been used in the Architecture-Engineering-Construction (AEC) industry for several decades, and Building Information Modeling (BIM) emerged as a more recent paradigm to support various engineering and maintenance tasks throughout a building's lifecycle [11, 12]. To support interoperability, the BIM principles are reflected in the Industry Foundation Classes (IFC) format, which has become the de-facto standard for BIM models [22]. However, extant quality evaluation procedures for spatial designs fail to construct dependable CPSp's. Dynamic aspects, cyber-physical, and human-spatial interactions are hardly taken into account. As discussed in more detail in [30], existing techniques mostly revolve around rather simple rule-based checks that intend to assure compliance with legal requirements.

Some of the above mentioned limitations have been partially addressed in the literature. Model-based reasoning techniques have been applied to the simulation of certain dynamic aspects of building information models, such as for the evacuation of buildings [17, 19] or fire response management processes [21]. While the approach presented in [26] proposes a heuristic method which utilizes BIM to discover security threats by way of simulation, it does not address threats that arise from cyber-physical interaction. An approach for extending BIM by smart objects has been proposed in [32], yet without the proposition of a generalizable method.

Further work on computational methods for spatial environments and systems is discussed extensively in [30, 31]. In the context of our approach, two lines of work seem particularly promising. First, spatial assistance systems as developed in a larger research project on spatial cognition [1] discuss sophisticated services that may enhance a user's visuo-spatial and navigational experience. These services largely complementary to the security requirements and quality attributes that our understanding of dependability subsumes. Second, the research collaborators of the ScenarioTools project [18] are currently developing a methodology and supporting tool suite for the scenario-based modeling and analysis of reactive systems with dynamic topologies. They emphasize the communication of autonomously driving cars whose interaction is influenced by their movements. This approach may be adopted for the modeling and analysis of CPSp's since formal analysis mostly concerns the detection of inconsistencies among scenarios that represent different states of the system.

5.2 Theoretical Perspective

The formalism we have proposed in this chapter constitues a design decision. Future work may elaborate on this formalism. For example, a more conventional notion of a graph and its transformations such as [10] could be used to precisely model dynamic topologies. This approach would also allow researchers to deploy established techniques that use models derived from graph transformation systems [16]. However, we propose that bigraphs are a natural choice here since they natively support the concepts of locality and linking which play a fundamental role in our notion of the topology of a CPSp. An alternative to transforming bigraphical models into traditional quality evaluation models is BiLog [9] which supports formal reasoning directly on the bigraphical level. However, the development of BiLog is still in its infancy, and only a subset has been implemented in [28]. Thus, we decided to resort to more established approaches, following classical research on temporal model checking [8]. In fact, our approach is open to a family of temporal logics such as Linear Temporal Logic (LTL) or Computation Tree Logic (CTL), and it is compatible with their probabilistic extensions and related evaluation models. As regards spatial reasoning support, topological relations have been traditionally considered in the context of database systems, query languages [23] and logics for spatial data analysis in Geographical Information Systems [3]. These contexts emphasize the significance of geometric model elements [13, 14] such as regions, lines, and points. However, we prefer a spatial logic over closure spaces for two reasons. First, closure spaces are a generic mathematical concept which constitutes an interface between arbitrary binary relations and our structural modeling formalism. Second, choosing a spatial logic which is a specific kind of modal logic is in line with our choice of using other kinds of modal logics in the temporal domain. In fact, SLCS can even be integrated with such a temporal logic to provide a powerful formalism for expressing spatio-temporal properties; integrations of SLCS with CTL and LTL have been presented in [7] and [31], respectively. All in all, the intercompatibility of the techniques we use allow both us and future work to construct versatile, flexible and extendible frameworks.

6 Summary and Concluding Remarks

Contemporary spatial environments are increasingly evolving into dynamic cyber-physical spaces in which the physical world and the digital world interact significantly. Thus, designing and operating dependable CPSp's becomes increasingly challenging, and future strategies for defending critical infrastructures, which are to a large extent comprised of CPSp's, need to tackle these challenges by taking a multitude of novel risks and threat scenarios into account. In particular, cyber-enabled physical attacks can occur whenever access control systems that protect valuable assets are cyber-manipulated by intruders, or when the system fails due to technical, design or operational defects. Conversely, physically-enabled cyber attacks can occur when physical access to assets such as networks or other computational infrastructure enables attackers to enter and cyber-control the CPSp.

We argue that rethinking the design and operation of spatial environments from a software and systems engineering perspective may allow operators to respond more effectively to such challenges. To that end, we have started to develop a conceptual framework for formally modeling and reasoning about CPSp's on a topological level, supporting automatic verification procedures which span the entire lifecycle from design to run-time. In this chapter, we have illustrated how this general framework can be instantiated in two security scenarios that model malicious human action. We illustrated how our bigraphical modeling approach can be used to concisely describe the topology of the critical facility as well as its inherent dynamics and interactions with human agents. In the first scenario, we have shown how to adopt and integrate classical probabilistic model checking techniques for the quantitative validation of temporal properties in early design stages. In the second scenario, explained how to monitor and verify an actively operated CPSp with spatial properties which cannot be checked at design time due to unforeseeable topology evolution.

While the main goal of this chapter is to present our ideas on a conceptual level, recent experimental results suggest that our approach is also technologically feasible. In particular, the results of stress-testing a non-optimized prototypical implementation in a trace checking scenario [31] suggest that the run-time verification approach can also be applied to larger and fast-evolving spatial environments. Nonetheless, further research is needed to fully realize our vision of a holistic approach to the modeling, analysis, and operation of cyber-physical spaces. Further, our approach makes a number of assumptions that future research could relax. For example, agent behaviors are assumed to be mutually independent, access points are assumed to be only reachable within the areas in which they are located, and time is considered in terms of discrete ticks which correspond to the primitive changes in the spatial topology. However, we have deliberately chosen an incremental research process to enrich our reasoning techniques and their underlying quality evaluation models in a stepwise manner. From a technical point of view, our prototypical implementation needs to be significantly extended in order to be deployed on modern clusters or high-performance computers to ensure its scalability and to guarantee sufficient response times. For example, algorithmic designs of model transformations, adaptations and reasoning procedures should function incrementally and in parallel as far as possible. Finally, from an operationalization point of view, our solutions need to be integrated into state-of-the-art toolchains in order to make them accessible to domain experts. Such an integration would allow us to test and further develop our approach in diverse industry contexts.

References

1. Barkowsky, T., Bateman, J.A., Freksa, C., Burgard, W., Knauff, M.: Transregional collaborative research center SFB/TR 8 spatial cognition: reasoning, action, interaction. it–Inf. Technol. **47**(3), 163–171 (2005)
2. Birkedal, L., Damgaard, T.C., Glenstrup, A.J., Milner, R.: Matching of bigraphs. Electron. Notes Theor. Comput. Sci. **175**(4), 3–19 (2007)
3. Bivand, R.S., Pebesma, E., Gómez-Rubio, V.: Spatial Data Import and Export. Springer, Berlin (2013)
4. Busari, S.A., Letier, E.: Radar: A lightweight tool for requirements and architecture decision analysis. In: Proceedings of the 39th International Conference on Software Engineering, pp. 552–562. IEEE Press, Piscataway (2017)
5. Calinescu, R., Ghezzi, C., Kwiatkowska, M.Z., Mirandola, R.: Self-adaptive software needs quantitative verification at runtime. Commun. ACM **55**(9), 69–77 (2012)
6. Ciancia, V., Latella, D., Loreti, M., Massink, M.: Specifying and verifying properties of space. In: Theoretical Computer Science, pp. 222–235. Springer, Berlin (2014)
7. Ciancia, V., Grilletti, G., Latella, D., Loreti, M., Massink, M.: An experimental spatio-temporal model checker. In: International Conference on Software Engineering and Formal Methods, pp. 297–311. Springer, Berlin (2015)
8. Clarke, E.M., Grumberg, O., Peled, D.A.: Model Checking. MIT Press, Cambridge (1999)
9. Conforti, G., Macedonio, D., Sassone, V.: Spatial Logics for Bigraphs. Springer, Berlin (2005)
10. Corradini, A., Montanari, U., Rossi, F., Ehrig, H., Heckel, R., Löwe, M.: Algebraic approaches to graph transformation-part I: Basic concepts and double pushout approach. In: Handbook of Graph Grammars, pp. 163–246. University of Pisa, Pisa (1997)
11. Day, M.: The move to BIM with archicad 12. In: AEC Magazine. August 23, 2008
12. Eastman, C., Eastman, C.M., Teicholz, P., Sacks, R.: BIM Handbook: A Guide to Building Information Modeling for Owners, Managers, Designers, Engineers and Contractors. Wiley, Hoboken (2011)
13. Egenhofer, M.J., Frank, A.U., Jackson, J.P.: A Topological Data Model for Spatial Databases. Springer, Berlin (1989)
14. Egenhofer, M.J., Herring, J. Categorizing binary topological relations between regions, lines, and points in geographic databases. The **9**, 94–1 (1990)
15. Forejt, V., Kwiatkowska, M., Norman, G., Parker, D.: Automated verification techniques for probabilistic systems. In: Formal Methods for Eternal Networked Software Systems, pp. 53–113. Springer, Berlin (2011)
16. Gadducci, F., Heckel, R., Koch, M.: A fully abstract model for graph-interpreted temporal logic. In: International Workshop on Theory and Application of Graph Transformations, pp. 310–322. Springer, Berlin (1998)
17. Gianni, D., Bocciarelli, P., D'Ambrogio, A., Iazeolla, G.: A model-driven and simulation-based method to analyze building evacuation plans. In: Proceedings of the 2015 Winter Simulation Conference, pp. 2644–2655. IEEE Press, Piscataway (2015)
18. Greenyer, J., Gritzner, D., Gutjahr, T., König, F., Glade, N., Marron, A., Katz, G.: Scenariotools–a tool suite for the scenario-based modeling and analysis of reactive systems. Sci. Comput. Program. **149**, 15–27 (2017)

19. Hamacher, H.W., Tjandra, S.A.: Mathematical Modelling of Evacuation Problems: A State of Art. Fraunhofer-Institut (ITWM), Munich (2001)
20. Hansson, H., Jonsson, B.: A logic for reasoning about time and reliability. Form. Asp. Comput. **6**(5), 512–535 (1994)
21. Isikdag, U., Underwood, J., Aouad, G.: An investigation into the applicability of building information models in geospatial environment in support of site selection and fire response management processes. Adv. Eng. Inform. **22**(4), 504–519 (2008)
22. ISO 16739: Industry Foundation Classes (IFC): Data Sharing in the Construction and Facility Management Industries (2013)
23. Aufaure-Portier, M.-A., Trépied, C.: A survey of query languages for geographic information systems. In: Proceedings of the 3rd International Workshop on Interfaces to Databases, pp. 1–14, Napier University, Edinburgh (1996)
24. Milner, R.: The Space and Motion of Communicating Agents. Cambridge University Press, Cambridge (2009)
25. Perrone, G., Debois, S., Hildebrandt, T.T.: A Verification Environment for Bigraphs. Innov. Syst. Softw. Eng. **9**(2), 95–104 (2013)
26. Porter, S., Tan, T., Tan, T., West, G.: Breaking into BIM: Performing static and dynamic security analysis with the aid of BIM. Autom. Constr. **40**, 84–95 (2014)
27. Sevegnani, M., Calder, M.: Bigraphs with sharing. Theor. Comput. Sci. **577**, 43–73 (2015)
28. Sevegnani, M., Unsworth, C., Calder, M.: A SAT Based Algorithm for the Matching Problem in Bigraphs with Sharing. Technical Report, University of Glasgow (2010)
29. Tsigkanos, C., Pasquale, L., Ghezzi, C., Nuseibeh, B.: On the interplay between cyber and physical spaces for adaptive security. IEEE Trans. Dependable Secure Computing **PP**(99), 1–1 (2016)
30. Tsigkanos, C., Kehrer, T., Ghezzi, C.: Architecting dynamic cyber-physical spaces. Computing **98**(10), 1011–1040 (2016)
31. Tsigkanos, C., Kehrer, T., Ghezzi, C.: Modeling and verification of evolving cyber-physical spaces. In: Proceedings of the 2017 11th Joint Meeting on Foundations of Software Engineering, ESEC/FSE 2017, pp. 38–48 (2017)
32. Zhang, S., Teizer, J., Lee, J.K., Eastman, C.M., Venugopal, M.: Building information modeling (BIM) and safety: automatic safety checking of construction models and schedules. Autom. Constr. **29**, 183–195 (2013)

Forensic Analysis as Iterative Learning

Eoghan Casey and Bruce Nikkel

1 Introduction

Protecting critical infrastructure requires up-to-date understanding of cyberattacker behavior, including their methods of approach, attack, concealment and control. Forensic analysis plays a central role in the readiness and resilience of an organization against cyberattacks; helping reduce disruption of service, data theft, financial loss, manipulation of data integrity, reputational harm, privacy violations, physical damage, and reduction of public trust. Crucially, insights gathered from forensic analysis of intrusions targeting specific organizations or an entire industry sector are invaluable for detecting and disrupting cyberattacks, and for strengthening the overall security of critical infrastructure.

Cyberattackers can compromise critical infrastructure in a number of ways, many of which are difficult to detect. In the technical domain, attackers can exploit compromised applications, rogue devices, remote access gateways, un-trusted bring your own devices (BYODs), third party outsourcing contractors, software updates and telemetry mechanisms (e.g., by modifying code on update servers of popular software products), unencrypted information in cloud environments, and weak credential management. Additionally, attackers may deploy social engineering techniques as stronger security measures strengthen the resilience of hardware and software systems. There has been a significant increase in social engineering of staff and clients of target organizations [16]. Phishing attacks can be broadly or

E. Casey (✉)
School of Criminal Sciences, University of Lausanne, Lausanne, Switzerland
e-mail: eoghan.casey@unil.ch

B. Nikkel
Bern University of Applied Sciences, Bern, Biel, Switzerland
e-mail: bruce.nikkel@bfh.ch

M. M. Keupp (ed.), *The Security of Critical Infrastructures*, International Series in Operations Research & Management Science 288,
https://doi.org/10.1007/978-3-030-41826-7_11

narrowly targeted, and implemented in different forms (e.g., email, social networks or telephone), depending on the objectives of the threat actors. The most narrowly targeted phishing attacks select particular individuals or departments within a target organization and can be crafted with personal details gathered from open sources on the Internet. With social media and open source intelligence, it is easier to prepare plausible social engineering attack scenarios. In some cases, cyberattackers hacked personal email accounts of individuals in target organizations and masqueraded as the person in order to create more convincing social engineering attacks. In other cases, cyberattackers created email filters to block or redirect responses from people attempting to check the legitimacy of the email they received. When cybercriminals use such subtle, targeted social engineering approaches, the infiltration is difficult to detect.

Case Example: Operation Sharpshooter
In late 2018, a phishing campaign called Operation Sharpshooter targeted critical infrastructure by contacting individuals under the pretext of job recruitment in order to entice them to open malicious documents that installed malware on their computers. Forensic analysis of the malicious code revealed similarities with malware used by the Lazarus (a.k.a. Hidden Cobra) group that targeted energy sectors the year before. However, forensic analysts must be careful not to jump to conclusions because different groups can reuse the same tools, and threat actors can employ misdirection. In this case, the numerous technical links to the Lazarus Group seem too obvious, and they indicate a potential for digital deception [31].

System operators should be aware that forensic analysis techniques can help neutralize these threats. Forensic analysis involves in-depth study of available evidence in a systematic and coherent manner. Employing critical thinking and bias mitigation strategies, allows analysts to gain insights into events and activities under investigation. Although incident response processes often uncover useful information, forensic analysis of the same event can yield more detailed descriptions of adversary methods and associated digital evidence that enable more effective detection of related activities. For example, a system operator or incident responder might observe that an adversary has made unauthorized use of Remote Desktop Protocol (RDP), whereas in-depth forensic analysis might find additional anomalies about that behavior that subsequently enable the victim organization to differentiate between authorized and unauthorized RDP connections.

The primary purpose of forensic analysis is to provide reliable information to support decision making. Forensic analysis is a central part of digital forensics, which is the general term used to describe the application of scientific principles and processes to recognition, preservation, examination, documentation, analysis, integration and interpretation of digital evidence for a legal context [28]. Digital evidence is any information of probative value that is stored or transmitted in binary form [33]. Key aspects of managing digital evidence include forensically sound preservation of evidence, and maintaining chain of custody and integrity information using cryptography [25]. Examples of digital evidence may include computer drive images and other storage media, volatile memory, server log files, cloud artifacts, or other extracted digital traces.

Forensic analysis can often reveal the root causes of a cyberattack to system operators, such that insights gathered from past attacks can be used to prevent similar attacks from reoccurring. Forensic analysis also employs scientific interpretation of evidence to support important decisions such as attack attribution and public notification. Formal evaluation of the relative strength of evidence in light of alternative hypotheses is invaluable when making risk-based decisions [5]. Nonetheless, digital forensics is underutilized for securing critical infrastructures. Preparing systems from a forensic perspective can significantly enhance an organization's resilience to cyberattacks.

Digital evidence can be useful for reconstructing and understanding complex cyberattacks, including the temporal sequence of the attack, the extent to which malicious code was introduced, and the number of user accounts compromised. Further, the study of adversary techniques and objectives can help build more effective cybersecurity defenses [32]. Forensic analysis also enables intelligence-driven approaches to cyberdefense by capturing knowledge and insights gathered from past incidents to support detection, scope assessment and strategic capability enhancement [29]. Curating and sharing such forensic intelligence can help organizations enhance cybersecurity and disrupt future cyberattacks [1].

2 Forensic Defense as an Iterative Learning Cycle

To date, much past work has seen forensics as a passive and responsive tool that is deployed only after an attack has occurred. We propose an alternative view, suggesting that forensics should be seen as a process of iterative learning whose goal is to continuously advance the defensive capabilities of the organization.

Traditionally, conceptualizations of forensic analysis concentrated on reducing the business impact and recovery time of incidents [30]. For example, guidelines developed by the US National Institute of Standards and Technology (NIST) focus on incident response, with forensic analysis in a supportive capacity. The NIST document SP 800-86 *(Guide to Integrating Forensic Techniques into Incident Response)* highlights the importance of investigating security incidents in the context of incident response, but does not address the role of forensic analysis in overall cybersecurity improvement. The NIST Cybersecurity Framework defines the main functional areas of Identify, Protect, Detect, Respond, and Recover [27]. As part of risk assessment, the framework emphasizes the need to take into account current knowledge of cyberattacks, but it is not made clear that forensic analysis of security breaches is necessary to learn from past mistakes and ameliorate security weaknesses. The framework constrains forensic analysis under response activities, with the limited objective of ensuring effective response and supporting recovery activities.

It is important not to conflate forensic analysis and incident response—they are interdependent processes that serve different purposes. The purpose of incident response is to contain and recover from a cyberattack, whereas the purpose of forensic analysis is to understand what happened [6]. There is much to be gained by realizing the crucial role of forensic analysis throughout the cybersecurity risk management lifecycle. When an attack is detected, forensic analysis helps extract information that can be used to search for additional digital evidence and exposures such as compromised accounts in order to assess the scale and severity of the breach (a.k.a. scope assessment). A victim organization that favors quick reaction and containment over thorough scope assessment misses an opportunity to observe the attack in progress and understand what is happening in more detail, and potentially loses the ability to collect ephemeral digital evidence. Before attempting to clean up and carry on with normal business, performing a thorough forensic analysis of cyberattacks can uncover additional problems, can shed light on security weaknesses that need to be addressed, and can increase chances of detecting future cyberattacks more quickly. Ultimately, findings from forensic analysis feed into detection, forensic preparedness, scope assessment, cyberthreat information, and enhanced security. In the following subsections, we explain the elements of this iterative learning cycle.

2.1 *Forensic Preparedness*

Forensic preparedness is an organizational strategy for managing risks associated with computer misuse. Fundamentally, this involves specification of a policy that lays down a consistent approach, detailed planning against typical (and actual) case scenarios that an organization faces, identification of (internal or external) resources that can be deployed as part of those plans, identification of where and how the associated digital evidence can be gathered that will support case investigation and a process of continuous improvement that learns from experience [17]. Lack of forensic preparedness increases the risks of cyberattacks going undetected and will impair the effectiveness of response activities after a cyberattack is detected. This reactive approach is also costly as it involves the hiring of external consultants. In contrast, organizations that are prepared to gather digital evidence and employ forensic analysis in anticipation of cyberattacks put themselves in a better position to detect, investigate and neutralize attacks [15, 20]. Forensic preparedness includes producing an inventory of IT assets, prioritizing systems according to criticality, maintaining a digital evidence map [4] and developing the capability to take evasive action (e.g., changing critical account names, adding decoys). Further, it comprises the ability for intelligent logging, whereby critical systems enjoy a heightened level of monitoring, strategic ingress and egress filtering, norm deviation detection, and the capability to establish internal defense perimeters, specifically, secure communication channels which are not accessible to network intruders. These channels serve to collect and document forensic evidence and case details during an intrusion investigation. Forensic preparedness involves having predefined processes for incident response and forensic analysis that are regularly tested and updated by a properly trained and resourced response team. Finally, forensic preparedness in organizations that operate ICS/SCADA equipment can be more challenging because these systems often use specialized data formats and network protocols. For instance, Triton malware specifically targets Safety Instrumented System controllers [21]. Such organizations may require specialized forensic acquisition and analysis methods to support their ICT/SCADA systems, and may require additional procedures to mitigate negative physical consequences resulting from cyberattacks against these systems.

2.2 *Instrumenting Networks to Increase Visibility Over Cyberattacks*

Two excellent data sources for detection and investigation are internal sinkholes and Netflow collectors. These mechanisms for capturing digital evidence give the greatest visibility on infections, breaches, and unauthorized activity. A private network separated from the Internet by a proxy architecture provides a higher level of security than a simple packet filtered or netted perimeter. Proxy technologies offer more possibilities for control and authentication at the application layer, and prevent any traffic from routing directly to the Internet. A proxied architecture also allows the internal propagation of a default route that ends at a special router called a sinkhole. A sinkhole will receive all internal network layer traffic destined for the Internet (something which should never happen in a proxied environment). This sinkhole traffic can be logged or monitored for possible malicious activity (e.g., malware that attempts to establish direct connections to command and control servers).

Case Example: Sinkhole

A large multinational firm implemented an internal sinkhole infrastructure. When analyzing the network traffic, they found IP packets arriving at the sinkhole destined for external Internet IP addresses. The origin of the packets was the company's perimeter infrastructure security systems (firewall/proxy). An investigation determined that the perimeter infrastructure was misconfigured to forward external packets to internal systems. The internal sinkholes enabled network level detection of a vulnerable control configuration, thus posing a risk to the firm. This misconfiguration was not detected by perimeter NIDS systems or other security detection systems.

Netflow is a standard (RFC 3954) that allows routers to collect information about network traffic. Collecting Netflow data on perimeter routers provides an historic log of all network activity, including connections to and from a network, connection time and duration, bytes transferred, IP addresses and ports, and both failed and successful connection attempts. Netflow data provides useful evidence for investigations, checking against cyberthreat information feeds, and for hunt teams looking for suspicious activity [3, 20]. Forensic analysis is empowered most when data from NetFlow and sinkhole infrastructures are correlated to gain detailed insights into cyberattacks.

Honey pots and honey tokens provide another form of visibility over cyberattacks. Honey pots can be used to redirect cyberattackers to a staged system, observe their actions, and feed them deceptive information. A honey token is a planted piece of information or fake user account that should be invisible under normal operations, but used to collect information about adversary behavior.

Organizations should use these tools to continuously improve their forensic preparedness, applying lessons learning from past security breaches. Without the productive use of insights from past breaches, defenders will not be able to avoid and prevent future similar attacks [22].

2.3 Cyberattack Detection

Detection is the use of information uncovered through forensic analysis to sweep the target network for any additional compromised systems, network segments, credentials or other IT assets [6]. Successful cyberattackers understand commonly used security systems well enough to undermine them and avoid detection. In addition, sophisticated intruders take full advantage of the lack of forensic preparedness [4]. The skill level and motivation of intruders targeting critical infrastructure has evolved to the point where gaining broad access to the target network in order to maintain unauthorized access for as long as possible without detection has become a common occurrence.

Case Example: RUAG

The Swiss company RUAG was compromised and intruders had access to internal systems for several years before being detected. The intruders used various concealment techniques on compromised systems and the network to avoid detection, and used their access to explore the RUAG network and steal substantial amounts of data. The technical report of Switzerland's Information and Security Analysis Center (MELANI) noted that 'one of the most effective countermeasures from a victim's perspective is the sharing of information about such attacks with other organizations, also crossing national borders' [18]. Several security recommendations emerged from the forensic analysis

(continued)

of this incident: to use multi-factor authentication, to implement a proxy architecture, to restrict administrator accounts and outbound connections from internal servers, to block internal direct client-to-client communication, to segment critical networks, to write-protect USB/Firewire devices, to restrict the execution of macros and unnecessary applications, and to prevent the execution of unauthorized binaries.

Results of forensic analysis can be used to detect related attacks, including static indicators such as MD5 hashes, IP addresses and domain names. Looking for static indicators of known attacks is necessary, but not sufficient for effective cybersecurity. Such static indicators are narrow and easily changed, whereas the repeated behavior patterns across related cyberattacks are more stable and difficult to change [32]. Therefore, it is also important to look for similar patterns, behaviors and anomalous activities.

The potential value of various forensic analysis results includes:

- Contextual information related to static indicators, including the location and nature of supporting digital evidence and artifacts;
- Recovered information that cyberattackers try to conceal, including deleted files, hidden processes, and encrypted data on storage media and in network traffic;
- Comprehensive event reconstruction enabling broader visibility over cyber-attacks, including correlation across data sources (e.g., file systems, volatile memory, system logs, router/firewall configuration, network traffic, backup tapes);
- Modus operandi information and behavior signature characteristics that can be used to recognize repetitions of malicious actions across different incidents, various technologies, and multiple adversary groups over prolonged time periods.

Such forensic findings can be useful for developing new and improved detection measures and defensive countermeasures.

Case Example: JSSD

A distinctive characteristic of the modus operandi of members of the JSSD (Jiangsu Province Ministry of State Security) was the use of doppelganger domain names, which involve registering and using domain names that closely resemble legitimate domain names to trick unwitting recipients of spear phishing emails. For instance, the cyberattackers registered the doppelganger domain name http://capstonetrubine.com which closely resembles the legitimate domain name of one organization that was targeted (Capstone Turbine). They also registered the domain name capstoneturbine.cechire.com to receive

(continued)

beacons from malware installed on compromised systems. An insight gathered from the forensic analysis of these cyberattacks was to monitor DNS registrations for doppelganger websites targeting specific organizations or sectors in critical infrastructure. The cyberattackers also manipulated domain registrars in order to hijack legitimate domains. After compromising the targeted organizations, the cyberattackers installed malware on some of the victimized organization's websites in order to infect computers of other organizations and thus gain unauthorized access to their systems [34]. The cyberattackers who gained unauthorized access to the Office of Personnel Management (OPM) in 2016 also used doppelganger domain names [10].

To protect an organization, it is necessary to study emerging cyberattacks, combine information and knowledge about current cyberattacks from multiple sources, and use the insights gathered to predict and prevent future attacks. The ability to find such patterns depends heavily on iterative learning using forensic analysis of digital evidence associated with cyberattacks. Victim organizations that lack visibility into cyberattacks and do not detect an intrusion for months or years have limited opportunities to learn from the situation, particularly so if digital evidence of the original attack was not forensically preserved.

2.4 Scope Assessment and Eradication

Scope assessment builds on information collected during the detection phase, and typically expands as forensic analysis uncovers additional details of a cyberattack, such as the number of systems attacked and the depth of intrusion into each system. It specifies the actually and potentially compromised systems, network segments, and credentials at a given point in time during the investigation [6]. In this context, a potentially compromised system is any device for which a cyberattacker has network access and valid credentials or remote access via installed malware.

The ultimate goal of scope assessment is to assess the scale of the attack, to determine damages and losses, and to provide information concerning the intrusion and the adversary to prepare the remediation plan of action. In addition, the scope assessment can help identify potential locations to collect digital evidence. Scope assessment requires visibility on the network, a response plan and associated personnel who have the broadest possible visibility across the cyberattack landscape. Scope assessment can also include studying related attacks or repetitive activities beyond the confines of a single organization or infrastructure. Without full knowledge about these issues, any response or containment efforts will be incomplete and not fully effective. It is worthwhile to note that existing guidelines such as NIST incident response documents do not specifically address scope assessment and coordinated or orchestrated response. The challenge of keeping pace with evolving capabilities emphasizes the importance of using all available forensic information to understand cyberattacks and enhance cybersecurity.

As the necessary steps are taken to eradicate the attack, organizations must be careful not to disclose information to the attacker. Eradication needs to be a carefully planned and tailored operation. Modern adversaries and malwares are adept at maintaining a foothold on compromised networks, hence, quick and direct responses that attempt to block access or patch systems are unlikely to be successful. Instead, insights gained from forensic analysis should guide the eradication process. Forensic analysis is central to assessing the full scope of a cyberattack since it systematically uncovers clues that can be used to follow the cybertrail left by the attackers.

Therefore, digital forensic experts should work closely with a network of stakeholders (internal and external to an organization), correlating data from diverse sources to assess the scope of the breach [4]. Compromised systems should not always be immediately cleaned or patched, but forensically preserved and analyzed (live or offline) where feasible, followed by carefully coordinated remediation of the compromised systems. In some cases, it makes sense to delay eradication until enough evidence can be collected (traffic captures, memory dumps) and the attack and its scope can be understood more fully. Hence, the victim organization must weigh the risks of reinstalling or replacing compromised systems before understanding the scope of the problem. This is balanced against allowing the attackers to remain on the network for some time before attempting to expunge their intrusion on the network. If an intruder has already been in a network for several months or more, the organization takes on little additional risk if the malicious activity is allowed to continue for an additional few days. Taking this time between detection and eradication gives the organization an opportunity to forensically preserve and analyze sources of evidence, and to study the extent to which the attackers can access and exploit the network. This information should be the basis of a thorough, orchestrated eradication strategy.

Case Example: Financial Industry
A large financial firm was experiencing malware attacks against retail clients using the online banking portal. Forensic analysis of the attacks determined that the malware was easily scraping credential information from the HTML code and performing automated login interception. The forensic team passed this information on to the banking platform developers with a suggestion to use graphical images instead of HTML text to display credential information. Implementing this suggestion stopped an entire class of banking malware from functioning, preventing significant amounts of fraud.

In some situations, it might be more advantageous to reroute malicious activity to honey pots instead of attempting to block or disrupt the attack. Sophisticated infections are often very resilient and difficult to clean by simple file deletion or antivirus cleaning kits. Sophisticated cyberattackers take precautions to obfuscate distinctive characteristics in their tools or execute malicious code in ways that make only minimal modifications to the compromised system, creating a need for enhanced methods and tools to search for digital evidence with minimal false positives.

Historically, it was necessary to develop customized 'antidote' tools to scan a compromised network for various versions of customized, packed malware [23]. Today, open source mechanisms such as YARA can search a network for specific digital evidence. To facilitate the use of these open source capabilities, some detailed reports of cyberattacks against critical infrastructure codify forensic findings in YARA such that organizations can automatically scan for distinctive characteristics on compromised systems. A similar capability for custom detection methods in network traffic is provided by Snort signatures.

2.5 Capability Development

Forensic insights from scrutinizing past attacks should be used to continuously develop the organization's defensive skills. Defenders should, therefore, promote prompt adoption of lessons learned from forensic analysis, through a combination of cyberrisk management processes and knowledge exchange mechanisms.

Applying insights gathered from past incidents is important since the effectiveness of defense improves with the integration of agile retrospectives [19]. In this context, lightweight agile retrospectives refer to an efficient collaborative approach to problem-solving that takes into account all stakeholder perspectives in an organization, enabling rapid improvements. A rapid reflection on the outcomes of a cyberattack can provide significant and actionable cybersecurity improvements. In some incidents, one or two security controls could have prevented a security breach from occurring. Some retrospectives revealed needed process changes or new processes to be better able to handle future cyberattacks. Senior management is crucial to implement actionable responses on the basis of such retrospection.

Case Example: The Dragonfly Attack
The Dragonfly group attacked industrial control systems through compromised computers. Although specific indicators of compromise such as IP addresses, domain names and MD5 hash values may only be useful for a limited time, forensic analysis of their activities on the targeted systems provided substantial insights into their tactics, techniques, and procedures. Defenders also learned that the group tried to conceal their activity by deleting Windows event logs. Additional concealment actions included deleting the registry key associated with terminal server client that tracks connections made to remote

(continued)

systems. After the attack was eradicated, several recommendations suggested that this forensic evidence be used to prevent future attacks. For example, one specific recommendation in the DHS/FBI report [14] is to look for this specific concealment activity by searching for event 104 on Windows system logs. Moreover, defenders learned that the attacks were facilitated by users opening malicious emails or entering their passwords on malicious websites, the absence of multi-factor authentication within the victim organizations, insufficient restrictions of administrator accounts and inadequate network segmentation of critical networks or control systems. Dragonfly also benefited from weak ingress/egress filtering, which could have detected or blocked malicious traffic. The DHS/FBI report concludes with a list of twenty-eight security measures for organizations to implement in order to prevent or disrupt similar attacks in the future.

Further, the realization of insights gathered from past incidents is facilitated by the creation of logs and databases such that one may detect commonalities across different attacks and identify patterns. When dealing with a cyberattack, it is necessary to pull together disparate data sources needed to perform forensic analysis, including timelines and link analysis. Internally, organizations can generate significant amounts of data that is useful for forensic analysis, e.g., system and application logs, perimeter NetFlow data, internal router/DNS sinkhole data, and data collected intrusion detection systems (IDS), firewalls, and anomaly detection systems (ADS). Externally, data sources may be purchased from commercial providers, collected via open source data feeds, or obtained from peer organizations facing similar threats. In many cases such external information is shared via connected software systems.

Curating such a repository of knowledge about past incidents (memory) is a crucial component of forensic intelligence. This memory is an accumulation of information, repetitions and insights gathered from past cases, which can be applied to new cases. For example, information about distinctive patterns and sequences of command line execution should be stored as it allows defenders to fingerprint attackers and to prevent future attacks.

However, any attempt to manually integrate and correlate separate data sources from various systems and formats is labor intensive, time consuming, and error-prone. Specifically, using a non-standardized system to import and format data from various sources can result in items such as date time stamps being altered, entries not being imported properly, and other errors or omissions that negatively impact forensic analysis [7]. The more time analysts spend extracting and correlating information from different sources, the less time they have left to analyze it, resulting in fewer opportunities to detect problems. These challenges are amplified when an incident spans multiple networks, and sharing of information between organizations is crucial for a successful resolution. Furthermore, without a standardized approach to representing and sharing digital forensic information, defenders might never realize that they are investigating cyberattacks committed by the same threat actors.

As a result, the creation of useful and necessary threat information requires the ability to analyze big data effectively and efficiently. This is achieved through data analytics, which is the compilation and analysis of various types of information with the goal of using this information to drive decision-making. The analysis of complex behaviors in large scale-systems can begin to address issues of provenance, attribution, and discernment of attack patterns. Possible applications of data analytics in this field include integration of threat feeds from varying sources, automated triage, data filtering, indicator tracking, visualization, and reporting [26]. There are multiple approaches to this type of memory curation, including unstructured data to support machine learning and structured data and support for linked data analysis.

For example, the U.S. Department of Defense Cyber Crime Center (DC3) captures and reuses knowledge in intrusion-malware investigations to provide timely results and feed forensic intelligence [11]. When digital data are submitted, they are processed using automated systems that contain codified forensic knowledge accumulated from prior casework and research. Specifically, a database is maintained with the forensic analysis results from all past malware samples for future reference, functioning as institutional memory of past forensic analysis. In this way, when malware in a new case has commonality with malware that has already been encountered and processed in a previous case, the results from the prior file instances can be reused, saving time on both processing and forensic analysis. In addition, customized methods for extracting encoded information from malware samples are codified and reused to extract additional details that are not obtainable using commercial systems [12].

Further, the Malware Information Sharing Platform (MISP) is an open source threat information sharing platform that has support from the European Union. This system is growing in popularity due to the ease of use and possibilities for connecting and sharing cyberthreat information with multiple communities [24].

The Cyber-investigation Analysis Standard Expression (CASE) contributes to harmonizing disparate data sources and exchanging of cyberinvestigation in a standardized form, and maintaining provenance throughout the cyberinvestigation lifecycle, including incident response and forensic analysis [8]. The primary motivation for CASE is interoperability—to advance the exchange of cyberinvestigation information between systems, tools and countries. Such interoperability, data fusion, and information sharing can be invaluable when dealing with a single incident involving multiple data sources, and when dealing with cyberattacks against multiple organizations. CASE supports automated normalization, combination, correlation, and validation of information, which means less time extracting and combining data, and more time analyzing information [2].

For example, the DCISE (*Defense Industrial Base Collaborative Information Sharing Environment*), enables specialized analysts to find linkages between related offenses and to observe patterns across all investigations. The aim of such intelligence is to provide stakeholders with knowledge that can be useful for detecting and disrupting future attacks at both an operational and strategic level. The success of this approach led to the development of standardized, federated computer systems that enable sharing of actionable intelligence about malware and network intrusions at machine speed. The Automated Indicator Sharing (AIS) capability maintained by the U.S. Department of Homeland Security (DHS) extended this approach, in 2015, to encompass a growing number of organizations in the private and public sector [9, 13].

Finally, this automated exchange of forensic information can be complemented by higher level organizational information exchange. For example, collaboration among banks and law enforcement is common in the fight against cybercrime activity. Modern banking malware is designed using a modular architecture allowing criminals to simultaneously target account logins at multiple banks. A single malware infection will give attackers access to bank accounts without knowing which bank the victim is using. When banks collaborate and share intelligence information about attackers, infections, and money flows, they are able to find common ways to detect attacks, block fraudulent payments, or disrupt criminal operations. Law enforcement is also involved with the banks, and intelligence sharing helps ongoing investigations and leads to additional sources of digital evidence.

While most cyberthreat information shared is sector-independent, and useful for any organization, including common infrastructure indicators of compromise (IOCs) such as hashes of malware files, botnet command and control IPs, and malicious URLs or domain names. However, some of the cyberthreat information shared is sector-specific and hence only of interest to a particular industry. For example, finance industry stakeholders share fraud indicators and information about criminal money mules, and other threat information directly relevant to their business. The automotive industry shares information specific to automotive electronics (e.g., CAN bus vulnerabilities.), and the entertainment industry focuses more on cyberthreat information related to copyright violations (e.g., peer-to-peer file sharing, DRM vulnerabilities). Managers and stakeholders must, therefore, tailor their efforts, such as ISAC memberships, to the extent to which the attacks they face are more of a general or more of a sector-specific nature.

3 Illustrative Example

The following scenario illustrates the iterative forensic learning cycle we have described in the preceding subsections. It is not intended to represent all possible steps that an organization can take when faced with a targeted cyberattack. Instead, we aim to illustrate how forensic preparedness, detection, scope assessment, agile cybersecurity retrospectives, forensic intelligence and information sharing can interact.

An organization was alerted by a government organization that known threat actors were observed accessing the organization's network. As part of its forensic preparations years before, the organization had segmented critical IT assets onto a secured network with full network level logging/monitoring that was only accessible from certain systems within their network. However, the victim organization did not have centralized logging infrastructure, making it necessary to search logs stored on potentially compromised systems. In addition, they did not have all of their system clocks synchronized, creating added work when correlating logs. Indications of compromise were found in some logs but the organization did not have an archive of old logs, and the root cause and original date of compromise could not be determined. While assessing the scope of the intrusion, the victim organization held daily calls for members of the cyberdefense team to exchange forensic findings from compromised hosts, logs, network traffic and backups.

The team used a shared spreadsheet to track tasks as well as significant forensic analysis findings (e.g., compromised systems, accounts, external IP addresses, domains). They used a separate secure system for all electronic communications. When the cyberdefense team was satisfied that they had performed a comprehensive scope assessment, the organization executed a coordinated containment and eradication plan that removed all known compromised assets. The team maintained a heightened level of monitoring across the organization to determine whether the cyberattackers still had unauthorized access. Applying the lessons learned from the cyberattack, the organization reduced its number of Internet gateways and implemented full packet network monitoring and NetFlow at strategic points throughout the network. Realizing the value of having a mechanism to keep track of forensic analysis tasks and findings, the organization implemented a system for managing incidents to observe trends and potential links between incidents, rather than relying on a shared spreadsheet to track details of cyberattacks. This system was developed into a Forensic Intelligence platform that served internal cybersecurity operations. The organization also shared cyberthreat information with others in the industry sector to determine the full scope of the cyberattack. Industry partners used this cyberthreat information to gain more insight into cyberattacks on their networks, and developed YARA signatures that were shared back with the original organization to enable detection at all phases of the defense process.

4 Conclusion

Effective detection of cyberattacks depends on forensic findings and fuels scope assessment and forensic intelligence. Forensic preparedness, in turn, reinforces scope assessment and increases the cyberresilience critical infrastructure. It also enables rapid cyberdefense decision-making. Effective scope assessment requires organizations to resist the impulse to block or eradicate longstanding attacks until they have been more fully understood with the support of forensic analysis. An agile cycle of implementing insights gathered from forensic analysis of cyberattacks facilitates the continuous improvement of security measures. Forensic intelligence systematically keeps track of evidence and defensive measures from past cyberattacks. This repository of past knowledge (memory) is a crucial component of forensic intelligence. Building and querying this memory must be continuous, iterative and integrated in overall cybersecurity operations. The resulting insights into threat actor Tactics, Techniques and Procedures (TTPs) and generalized behaviors provide actionable intelligence to counter targeted cyberattacks.

All in all, the iterative learning cycle proposed in this chapter should help organizations to establish a resilient and rapid cyberdefense capability. Forensic preparedness, a robust scope assessment process, an agile improvement cycle, and a strong forensic intelligence feedback loop are the tools by which this capability is created in organizational practice. This capability does not only improve the cybersecurity of the focal organization, but also contributes to a better industry-wide protection once forensic knowledge is systematically integrated and shared. For example, the particular experience of a single organization can aid law enforcement as they conduct inquiries into similar attacks.

Acknowledgement Thanks to Christopher Daywalt for his collaboration and talents investigating sophisticated network intrusions and malware.

References

1. Barnum, S.: Enabling effective cyber threat intelligence and information sharing. In: Proceedings of the International Conference on Cyber Security. Fordham University, New York (2013)
2. CASE: An international standard for sharing cyber-investigation traces. Cyber-Investigation Analysis Standard Expression (2019). https://caseontology.org/
3. Casey, E.: Digital Evidence and Computer Crime: Forensic Science, Computers and the Internet. Academic, Waltham (2004)
4. Casey, E.: Investigating sophisticated security breaches. Commun. ACM **49**(2), 48–55 (2006)
5. Casey, E.: Standarization of forming and expressing preliminary evaluative opinions on digital evidence. Digital Investigation **32** (2020)
6. Casey, E., Daywalt, C., Johnston, A.: Chapter 4 - Intrusion investigation. In: Casey, E., et al. (eds.) Handbook of Digital Forensics and Investigation, pp. 135–206. Academic Press, San Diego (2010)
7. Casey, E., Back, G., Barnum, S.: Leveraging cybox to standardize representation and exchange of digital forensic information. Digit. Investig. **12**, 102–110 (2015)
8. Casey, E., Barnum, S., Griffith, R., Snyder, J., van Beek, H., Nelson, A.: Advancing coordinated cyber-investigations and tool interoperability using a community developed specification language. J. Digit. Investig. **22**, 14–45 (2017)
9. Casey, E., Ribaux, O., Roux, C.: The kodak syndrome: risks and opportunities created by decentralization of forensic capabilities. J. Forensic Sci. **64**(1), 127–136 (2019)
10. Chaffetz, J., Meadows, M., Hurd, W.: The OPM Data Breach: How the Government Jeopardized Our National Security for More than a Generation. Committee on Oversight and Government Reform, U.S. House of Representatives, 114th Congress (2016)
11. CHDS: Department of Defense Cyber Crime Center. Center for Homeland Defense and Security (2019). https://www.hsdl.org/?abstract&did=690826
12. DC3 Malware Configuration Parser (DC3-MWCP) (2020). https://github.com/Defense-Cyber-Crime-Center/DC3-MWCP
13. DHS: Automated Indicator Sharing (AIS). U.S. Department of Homeland Security, CISA (2019). https://www.us-cert.gov/ais

14. DHS/FBI: Alert (TA18-074A): Russian Government Cyber Activity Targeting Energy and Other Critical Infrastructures Sectors. U.S. Department of Homeland Security, CISA (2018). https://www.us-cert.gov/ncas/alerts/TA18-074A
15. Elyas, M., Ahmad, A., Maynard, S., Lonie, A.: Digital forensic readiness: expert perspectives on a theoretical framework. Comput. Secur. **52**, 70–89 (2015)
16. Europol: Internet Organized Crime Threat Assessment. Technical Report, European Cybercrime Center (2019). https://www.europol.europa.eu/activities-services/main-reports/internet-organised-crime-threat-assessment-iocta-2019
17. Good practice guide forensic readiness. UK National Technical Authority for Information Assurance (2016)
18. GovCERT.ch: Technical Report About the Espionage Case at Ruag. GovCERT.ch (2016). https://www.govcert.admin.ch/blog/22/technical-report-about-the-ruag-espionage-case
19. Grispos, G., Glisson, W., Storer, T.: Enhancing security incident response follow-up efforts with lightweight agile retrospectives. Digit. Investig. **22**, 62–73 (2017)
20. Johnston, A., Reust, J.: Network intrusion investigation preparation and challenges. Digit. Investig. **3**(3), 118–126 (2006)
21. Kovacs, E.: Hackers Behind Triton ICS Malware Hit Additional Critical Infrastructure Facility, SecurityWeek (2019). https://www.securityweek.com/triton-hackers-focus-maintaining-access-compromised-systems-fireeye
22. Lee, R.: The Hunter Strikes Back: The SANS 2017 Threat Hunting Survey. SANS (2017)
23. Malin, C., Casey, E., Aquilina, J.: Malware Forensics: Investigating and Analyzing Malicious Code. Syngress Press (2008)
24. MISP: Open Source Threat Intelligence Platform & Open Standards For Threat Information Sharing. Malware Information Sharing Platform (2019). https://www.misp-project.org/index.html
25. Nikkel, B.: Practical Forensic Imaging. No Starch Press, San Francisco (2016)
26. NIST: Draft NIST roadmap for improving critical infrastructure cybersecurity version 1.1. National Institute of Standards and Technology (2017). https://www.nist.gov/sites/default/files/documents/2017/12/05/draft_roadmap-version-1-1.pdf
27. NIST: Framework for Improving Critical Infrastructure Cybersecurity. National Institute of Standards and Technology (2018). https://nvlpubs.nist.gov/nistpubs/CSWP/NIST.CSWP.04162018.pdf
28. Pollitt, M., Casey, E., Jaquet-Chiffelle, D.O., Gladyshev, P.: A framework for harmonizing forensic science practices and digital/multimedia evidence. Technical Report, The Organization of Scientific Area Committees for Forensic Science (2018)
29. Ribaux, O., Walsh, S., Margot, P.: The contribution of forensic science to crime analysis and investigation: Forensic intelligence. Forensic Sci. Int. **156**(2), 171–181 (2006)
30. Roberts, S., Brown, R.: Intelligence-Driven Incident Response: Outwitting the Adversary. O'Reilly Media, Waltham (2017)
31. Sherstobitoff, R., Malhotra, A.: Operation sharpshooter. Techical Report, McAffee (2018). https://www.mcafee.com/enterprise/en-us/assets/reports/rp-operation-sharpshooter.pdf
32. Strom, B., Applebaum, A., Miller, D., Nickels, K., Pennington, A., Thomas, C.: MITRE ATT&CK: Design and Philosophy, MITRE Product MP18030 (2019). Project No.: 01ADM105-PI. https://www.mitre.org/sites/default/files/publications/pr-18-0944-11-mitre-attack-design-and-philosophy.pdf
33. SWGDE: Swgde digital multimedia evidence glossary. SWGDE (2016). https://www.swgde.org/documents/CurrentDocuments/SWGDEDigitalandMultimediaEvidenceGlossary
34. Zhang, E.A.: Indictment: Conspiracy to Damage Protected Computers. U.D.C.S.D (2018). https://www.justice.gov/opa/press-release/file/1106491/download

Defending Critical Infrastructure: Insights from Recommender Systems

Sébastien Gillard

1 Introduction

Critical infrastructures constitute cyber-physical systems composed of spatially distributed elements. Within this architecture, physical and electric elements communicate with control elements by information flows [6, 7]. This architecture is inherently vulnerable [2]. In the absence of encryption, or in the case of compromised encryption, an attacker may manipulate this information flow such that any particular element operates outside the parameters required for safe operations.

A critical infrastructure operator must therefore guarantee that any information transmitted between elements is correct and unaltered by outside interference [1, 8]. The operator therefore faces a double task: First, the information flow must be monitored continuously to identify deviations from the steady-state, second, if an attack has occurred, an appropriate response must be found which neutralizes the corrupted information flow and returns it to its steady-state.

In a world of zero-day vulnerabilities, timely responses to this problem are hard to identify. Operators face significant information asymmetry; they can only imperfectly predict which attacks will likely occur where and when. Generating accurate predictions is the harder the more complex the system is. Moreover,

Electronic Supplementary Material The online version of this article (https://doi.org/10.1007/978-3-030-41826-7_12) contains supplementary material, which is available to authorized users.

S. Gillard (✉)
Military Academy at the Swiss Federal Institute of Technology Zurich, Birmensdorf, Switzerland
e-mail: sebastien.gillard@milak.ethz.ch

M. M. Keupp (ed.), *The Security of Critical Infrastructures*, International Series in Operations Research & Management Science 288,
https://doi.org/10.1007/978-3-030-41826-7_12

operators only have limited information about the attackers and their behavior, such that the evaluation of each attack is associated with significant transaction cost. In the absence of perfect technological knowledge about the attack, they face the problem of choosing a particular response without knowing whether or not it will prove to be effective.

Past research has argued that isolating the system against any potential attack is prohibitively expensive, and therefore it recommends resilience as the weapon of choice [4]. While I do not dispute the validity of this argument, I propose an alternative view that uses insights from recommender systems. On the basis of this research, I outline how an autonomous decision support system that actively defends critical infrastructure could be developed.

Users face significant information asymmetry and evaluation cost as they attempt to pick, from a very large population, few items that fit their preferences best (e.g., movies or songs). Recommender systems provide decision support by predicting likely future choices given users' past interests, purchase behavior, and evaluations of items picked to date. Moreover, collaborative filtering is used to recommend items that have been picked by users whose preferences are similar to those of the focal user. Analytically, the user-item relationship is modeled as a bipartite network [9].

I propose that this method can be productively transferred to critical infrastructure protection. Defenders are imperfectly informed about the population of attacks, yet they must choose a particular response from many available responses. Hence, they are faced with essentially the same setting: imperfect information about the population, high search costs to evaluate alternatives, and uncertainty about whether or not the chosen response will prove itself. In a world of zero-day vulnerability, the defender lacks the time to evaluate each potential response, but instead requires an immediate recommendation concerning which response to deploy, even in the absence of perfect information about the attack. In the following section, a recommender system that lives up to this challenge is proposed.

2 Defense Strategy

Consider a critical infrastructure whose steady-state information flow can be described by a parametric function $f(x; \overrightarrow{p_0})$ which stores the values of the parameters required for operation in the vector $\overrightarrow{p_0}$. This steady-state is now attacked by an attack $a_i(x)$.

The operator attempts to defend the steady-state against this attack (or to restore this state) by deploying the response $r_k(x)$. The attack $a_i(x)$, for $i \in \{1, \cdots, A\}$, is a subset of all possible attacks against $f(x; \overrightarrow{p_0})$. The attack corrupts the steady-state information flow by altering one or more of the parameter values stored in $\overrightarrow{p_0}$. For a specific information value $p_{0,j}$, with $j \in \{1, \cdots, P\}$, the attack can be formally described by:

$$f(x; (p_{0,1}, p_{0,2}, \cdots, \widetilde{p_{0,j}}, \cdots, p_{0,P})) = a_i(f(x; \overrightarrow{p_0})) = f(x; \widetilde{\overrightarrow{p_{0,j}}})$$

This notation highlights that value $p_{0,j} = \widetilde{p_{0,j}}$ has been corrupted by the attack $a_i(x)$, and therefore the vector $\overrightarrow{p_0}$ is replaced by $\widetilde{\overrightarrow{p_{0,j}}}$. While this particular notation exemplifies the corruption of a single information value, an attack may target several values simultaneously.

Once the operator notes this corruption, a response $r_k(x)$, with $k \in \{1, \ldots, K\}$ is deployed to counter the attack $a_i(x)$, and to restore the steady-state information flow $f(x; \overrightarrow{p_0})$. This response must target the manipulated information value and apply measures that neutralize the corrupted values, formally:

$$\begin{aligned} f(x; \overrightarrow{p_0}) &= r_k(a_i(f(x; \overrightarrow{p_0}))) \\ &= r_k(f(x; \widetilde{\overrightarrow{p_{0,j}}})) \end{aligned}$$

An ideal neutralization is obtained if the response $r_k(x)$ is the reciprocal function of $a_i(x)$. Hence, the following relations are obtained:

$$\begin{aligned} r_k(x) &= a_i^{-1}(x) \\ a_i(p_j) &= r_k^{-1}(p_j) \\ r_k(r_k^{-1}(x)) &= r_k^{-1}(r_k(x)) = x \\ a_i(a_i^{-1}(x)) &= a_i^{-1}(a_i(x)) = x \end{aligned}$$

With this information, a resource matrix M of the dimensions $K \times A$, can be populated. It comprises all responses $r_k(x)$ to all attacks $a_i(x)$ which can corrupt $f(x; \overrightarrow{p_0})$. In other words, the elements $(m_{ki})_{k\in\{1,\cdots,K\},\, i\in\{1,\cdots,A\}}$ of M describe all possible combinations of attacks and subsequent responses. Populating M implies evaluating each of these combinations as follows:

$$r_k(a_i(x)) = r_k(a_i(f(x; \overrightarrow{p_0})) = r_k(f(x; \widetilde{\overrightarrow{p_{0,j}}}) = f(x; \overrightarrow{p_f})$$

This notation now connects the steady-state vector $\overrightarrow{p_0}$, the corrupted vector after the attack $\widetilde{\overrightarrow{p_{0,j}}}$ and the restored vector $\overrightarrow{p_f}$ after the response has been deployed. If the attack has been completely neutralized, there is no difference between the steady-state and the restored vector, else, some residual effect of the attack remains.

An element of M is retained if it can effectively mitigate or neutralize the impact of the attack, else, it is eliminated from the matrix. Effectiveness is measured by comparing differences (noted here by the symbol $\mathfrak{D}$) before and after applying the

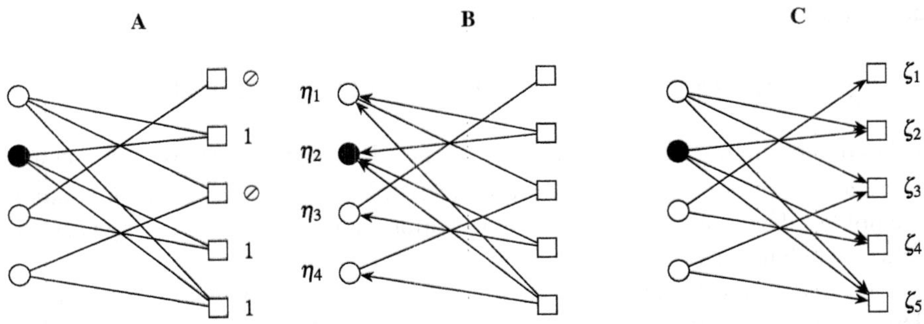

Fig. 1 Bipartite attacker-defender relations. The circles represent the attacks, the squares the replies and the black circle the targeted attack

response, formally[1]:

$$m_{ki} = \begin{cases} \oslash & \text{if } \mathfrak{D}(p_{f,j}, p_{0,j}) \geq \mathfrak{D}(\widetilde{p_{0,j}}, p_{0,j}) \\ 1 & \text{otherwise} \end{cases} \tag{1}$$

The information stored in M can now be used by a probabilistic spreading algorithm that calculates the recommendation matrix N [10]. Figure 1 illustrates this algorithm. It presents an example of a bipartite attacker-defender relationship with four attacks (circles), five responses (squares), and a focal attack (black circle). For the focal attack 2, responses 1 and 3 are ineffective, whereas in the past responses 2, 4, and 5 have been used. The operator now observes another instance of attack 2 (black circle) and must decide how to prioritize the five possible responses (i.e., which response to recommend first, which second, etc.).

The first step of this algorithm, as visualized by Panel A in Fig. 1, is to record the number of times κ_k that each response $r_k(x)$ was deployed to counter $a_i(x)$, i.e. the sum of all entries of 1 in the k-th line of matrix M. Using the data from Fig. 1 yields:

$$\kappa_1 = 1 \quad \kappa_2 = 2 \quad \kappa_3 = 2 \quad \kappa_4 = 2 \quad \kappa_5 = 3$$

For example, response 3 was deployed twice, and response 5 three times. The second step of the algorithm, as visualized by Panel B in Fig. 1, is to calculate weights for each response, using the count data obtained in the previous step. Assuming the links of the bipartite attacker-defender relationship are unweighted, a uniform distribution

[1]The following analysis focuses on one discrete corruption of an information value at a time. Condition (1) would have to be adapted by introducing weights if more than one information value is corrupted at a time.

can be calculated as follows:

$$\eta_1 = \frac{1}{\kappa_2} + \frac{1}{\kappa_3} + \frac{1}{\kappa_5} = \frac{1}{2} + \frac{1}{2} + \frac{1}{3} = \frac{4}{3}$$

$$\eta_2 = \frac{1}{\kappa_2} + \frac{1}{\kappa_4} + \frac{1}{\kappa_5} = \frac{4}{3}$$

$$\eta_3 = \frac{1}{\kappa_1} + \frac{1}{\kappa_4} = \frac{4}{3}$$

$$\eta_4 = \frac{1}{\kappa_3} + \frac{1}{\kappa_5} = \frac{5}{6}$$

The third and final step, as visualized by Panel C in Fig. 1, is to evaluate the effectiveness of the response by calculating:

$$\Omega(r_k(x), a_i(x)) \equiv \Omega(\overrightarrow{p_0}, \widetilde{\overrightarrow{p_0}}, \overrightarrow{p_f}) = 1 - \sum_{j=1}^{P} \frac{\mathfrak{D}(p_{f,j}, p_{0,j})}{\mathfrak{D}(\widetilde{p_{0,j}}, p_{0,j})} \tag{2}$$

If $\Omega(r_k(x), a_i(x)) = 1$, the effect of $a_i(x)$ has been completely neutralized by $r_k(x)$. For $0 < \Omega(r_k(x), a_i(x)) < 1$, neutralization is incomplete and the less effective the closer this score is to zero. Finally, both terms can be combined to calculate the recommendation scores as follows:

$$\zeta_2 = \eta_1 \cdot \Omega(r_2(x), a_1(x)) + \eta_2 \cdot \Omega(r_2(x), a_2(x))$$

$$\zeta_4 = \eta_2 \cdot \Omega(r_4(x), a_2(x)) + \eta_3 \cdot \Omega(r_4(x), a_3(x))$$

$$\zeta_5 = \eta_1 \cdot \Omega(r_5(x), a_1(x)) + \eta_2 \cdot \Omega(r_5(x), a_2(x)) + \eta_4 \cdot \Omega(r_5(x), a_4(x))$$

Since these values are scalar, they can be ranked to establish a preference order. Applying this algorithm to all attacks $a_i(x)$, a $K \times A$ recommendation matrix N is obtained. The critical infrastructure operator now has a full decision support system at hand that recommends an optimal response for each possible attack.

After these responses have been deployed, their performance can be measured. The critical infrastructure operator can compare the values of the original steady-state vector $\overrightarrow{p_0}$ with the restored vector $\overrightarrow{p_f}$. Any difference between these vectors suggests the attack still has a residual effect, implying the response was partially or completely ineffective. In this case, further response is required. This difference can be formally calculated by

$$\sum_{j=1}^{P} \mathfrak{D}(p_{f,j}, p_{0,j})$$

As long as this difference is not zero, an iterative deployment of responses is necessary unless the attack has been fully neutralized or impact of the attack is tolerable. After each round of attack and response, the recommendation matrix N is recalculated to reflect the novel information obtained during the latest round.

3 Illustration

Consider a variable x that captures the information flow required to operate a critical infrastructure. This flow can be specified and parameterized by a function f which, in this example, uses a $\sin(x)$ specification:

$$f(x; (A, \omega, \varphi, B)) = A \cdot \sin(\omega \cdot x + \varphi) + B, \tag{3}$$

The parameters of this function are described by the vector $\vec{p} = (A, \omega, \varphi, B)$, where A is the amplitude, $\omega = \frac{2\pi}{T}$ is the angular function of the period T, φ is the phase shift and B the intercept. The respective values of these parameters specify the properties of $f(x; \vec{p})$. The steady-state properties $f(x; \vec{p_0})$ of the system are defined by the following parameterization:

$$A_0 = 1, \qquad \omega_0 = 1, \qquad \varphi_0 = 0, \qquad B_0 = 0$$

Entering these values in (3) gives:

$$\begin{aligned} f(x; (A_0, \omega_0, \varphi_0, B_0)) &= A_0 \cdot \sin(\omega_0 \cdot x + \varphi_0) + B_0 \\ &= f(x; \vec{p_0}) = \sin(x) \end{aligned}$$

Figure 2 plots the function for $x \in [-4\pi; 4\pi]$. Any attack on the critical infrastructure would now seek to alter this information flow, e.g. by introducing malicious code, manipulating operations, etc. As a result, the information flow is corrupted and now deviates from its steady-state. This deviation can be captured by altering the parameter values. For the purpose of this illustration, it is assumed that only one parameter of $\vec{p}$ varies at a time.

Moreover, it is assumed that these parameters can only take one of the discrete values defined by the set $\mathfrak{P} = \{-2, -1, 0, 1, 2\}$, from which one can already exclude the respective default values $A, \omega \in \mathfrak{A} = \mathfrak{P} \setminus \{1\}$ and $\varphi, B \in \mathfrak{B} = \mathfrak{P} \setminus \{0\}$. Thus, each of the four parameters can take on four distinct discrete values, and hence there are 16 possibilities to alter the steady-state information flow. Each of these is interpreted as a potential attack. The set of attacks that attempt to alter A and ω is given by:

$$\begin{aligned} a_{A=-2}(x) &= a_{\omega=-2}(x) = -2 \cdot x \\ a_{A=-1}(x) &= a_{\omega=-1}(x) = -x \\ a_{A=0}(x) &= a_{\omega=0}(x) = 0 \\ a_{A=2}(x) &= a_{\omega=2}(x) = 2 \cdot x \end{aligned} \tag{4}$$

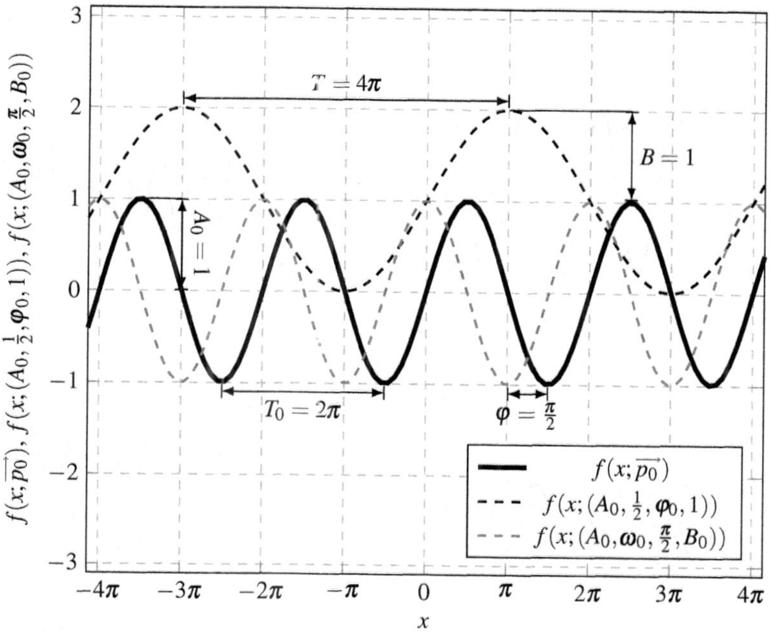

Fig. 2 Representation of the steady-state information flow $f(x; \overrightarrow{p_0})$ and the variations $f(x; (A_0, \frac{1}{2}, \varphi_0, 1))$ and $f(x; (A_0, \omega_0, \frac{\pi}{2}, B_0))$

By the same token, the set of attacks that attempt to manipulate φ and B is given by:

$$\begin{aligned} a_{\varphi=-2}(x) &= a_{B=-2}(x) = x + (-2) = x - 2 \\ a_{\varphi=-1}(x) &= a_{B=-1}(x) = x + (-1) = x - 1 \\ a_{\varphi=1}(x) &= a_{B=1}(x) = x + 1 \\ a_{\varphi=2}(x) &= a_{B=2}(x) = x + 2 \end{aligned} \tag{5}$$

Equations (4) and (5) now give the full catalogue of threats $\vec{a} = (a_{A=-2}, \cdots, a_{A=2}, a_{\omega=-2}, \cdots, a_{\omega=2}, a_{\varphi=-2}, \cdots, a_{\varphi=2}, a_{B=-2}, \cdots, a_{B=2})$. Figure 3 plots the original and the manipulated information flows.

The operator of the critical infrastructure now attempts to counter these attacks by responding, i.e. by introducing countermeasures that attempt to restore the steady-state information flow. Exploiting the fact that an optimal response $r_k(x)$ can be obtained from the reciprocal function of the attack $a_i(x)$, responses that attempt to restore A and ω to their original values are given by:

$$\begin{aligned} r_{A=-2}(x) &= r_{\omega=-2}(x) = -\frac{1}{2} \cdot x \\ r_{A=-1}(x) &= r_{\omega=-1}(x) = -1 \cdot x \end{aligned}$$

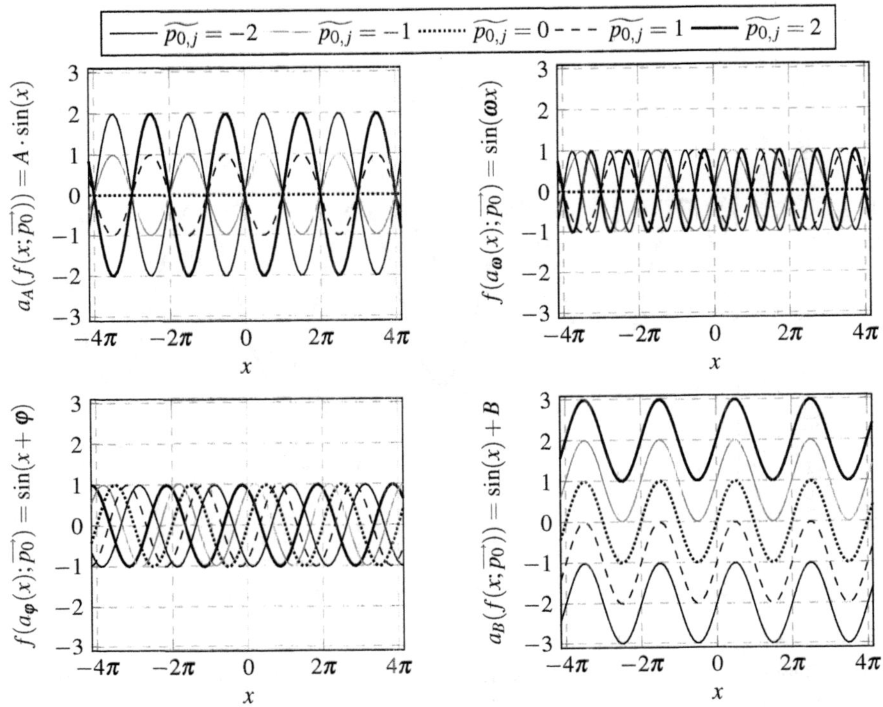

Fig. 3 Attack landscape for all elements of $\vec{a}$

$$r_{A=2}(x) = r_{\omega=2}(x) = \frac{1}{2} \cdot x$$

$$r_{A=0}(x) = r_{\omega=0}(x) = -\frac{1}{0} \cdot x = \emptyset$$

Note that for $A = \omega = 0$, the response is not defined, and hence any such response would never be recommended. This implies that no response against these attacks can be specified, such that they are indefensible in the short run. The responses $r_{A=-2}(x)$ and $r_{\omega=2}(x)$ illustrate how the respective attack is neutralized:

$$\begin{aligned} r_{A=-2}(a_{A=-2}(f(x;\overrightarrow{p_0}))) &= -\frac{1}{2} \cdot -2 \cdot \sin(x) = \sin(x) \\ &= f(x;\overrightarrow{p_0}) \end{aligned}$$

and

$$f(a_{\omega=2}(r_{\omega=2}(x)); \overrightarrow{p_0}) = \sin(2 \cdot (\frac{1}{2} \cdot x)) = \sin(x)$$
$$= f(x; \overrightarrow{p_0})$$

These responses are effective since they restore the steady-state $f(x; \overrightarrow{p_0})$. Analogously, for the parameters φ and B, the respective responses are:

$$r_{\varphi=-2}(x) = r_{B=-2}(x) = x - (-2) = x + 2$$
$$r_{\varphi=-1}(x) = r_{B=-1}(x) = x - (-1) = x + 1$$
$$r_{\varphi=1}(x) = r_{B=1}(x) = x - 1$$
$$r_{\varphi=2}(x) = r_{B=2}(x) = x - 2$$

These responses also neutralize the attack effectively. For example, $r_{\varphi=-2}(x)$ and $r_{B=2}(x)$ restore the steady-state information flow:

$$f(a_{\varphi=-2}(r_{\varphi=2}(x)); \overrightarrow{p_0}) = \sin((x + 2) - 2) = \sin(x)$$
$$= f(x; \overrightarrow{p_0})$$

and

$$r_{B=2}(a_{B=2}(f(x; \overrightarrow{p_0}))) = (\sin(x) + 2) - 2 = \sin(x)$$
$$= f(x; \overrightarrow{p_0})$$

Since there is no defense against $a_{A=0}$ and $a_{\omega=0}$, the response vector $\vec{r}$ comprises 14 responses $\vec{r} = (r_{A=-2}, \cdots, r_{A=2}, r_{\omega=-2}, \cdots, r_{\omega=2}, r_{\varphi=-2}, \cdots, r_{\varphi=2}, r_{B=-2}, \cdots, r_{B=2})$. By arranging $\vec{c}$ and $\vec{r}$ in matrix form, one obtains the information matrix M that contains all possible combinations of attacks and responses. The raw dimension of 14×16 elements in this matrix can be reduced as only the subset of effective responses should be considered.

The raw matrix $M = (m_{ki})_{k\in\{1,\cdots,14\}, i\in\{1,\cdots,16\}}$ is therefore reduced to four distinct blocks, one for each parameter of $\vec{p}$. These blocks are populated with effective replies by adapting (1) as follows:

$$m_{ki} = \begin{cases} \oslash \text{ if } \mid p_{fj} - p_{0,j} \mid > \mid \widetilde{p_{0,j}} - p_{0,j} \mid \\ 1 \text{ otherwise} \end{cases}$$

Applying this rule yields:

$$\begin{array}{c} \text{Attack } a_A \\ \begin{array}{cccc} -2 & -1 & 0 & 2 \end{array} = A \end{array} \qquad \begin{array}{c} \text{Attack } a_\omega \\ \begin{array}{cccc} -2 & -1 & 0 & 2 \end{array} = \omega \end{array}$$

$$M_A = \begin{bmatrix} 1 & 1 & \oslash & \oslash \\ 1 & 1 & \oslash & \oslash \\ 1 & 1 & \oslash & 1 \end{bmatrix} \begin{matrix} -2 \\ -1 \\ 2 \end{matrix} \ \text{Reply } r_A \qquad M_\omega = \begin{bmatrix} 1 & 1 & \oslash & \oslash \\ 1 & 1 & \oslash & \oslash \\ 1 & 1 & \oslash & 1 \end{bmatrix} \begin{matrix} -2 \\ -1 \\ 2 \end{matrix} \ \text{Reply } r_\omega$$

$$\begin{array}{c} \text{Attack } a_\varphi \\ \begin{array}{cccc} -2 & -1 & 0 & 2 \end{array} = \varphi \end{array} \qquad \begin{array}{c} \text{Attack } a_B \\ \begin{array}{cccc} -2 & -1 & 0 & 2 \end{array} = B \end{array}$$

$$M_\varphi = \begin{bmatrix} 1 & \oslash & \oslash & \oslash \\ 1 & 1 & \oslash & \oslash \\ \oslash & \oslash & 1 & 1 \\ \oslash & \oslash & \oslash & 1 \end{bmatrix} \begin{matrix} -2 \\ -1 \\ -1 \\ 2 \end{matrix} \ \text{Reply } r_\varphi \qquad M_B = \begin{bmatrix} 1 & \oslash & \oslash & \oslash \\ 1 & 1 & \oslash & \oslash \\ \oslash & \oslash & 1 & 1 \\ \oslash & \oslash & \oslash & 1 \end{bmatrix} \begin{matrix} -2 \\ -1 \\ -1 \\ 2 \end{matrix} \ \text{Reply } r_B$$

Coupling these blocks yields the final resource matrix M that assigns all possible replies to all possible attacks:

$$\begin{array}{c} \text{Attack } a \\ M = \begin{bmatrix} M_{A \in \mathfrak{A}} & \oslash & \oslash & \oslash \\ \oslash & M_{\omega \in \mathfrak{A}} & \oslash & \oslash \\ \oslash & \oslash & M_{\varphi \in \mathfrak{B}} & \oslash \\ \oslash & \oslash & \oslash & M_{B \in \mathfrak{B}} \end{bmatrix} \ \text{Reply } r \end{array}$$

Collaborative filtering can now be applied as illustrated in Fig. 1 (panel C), using (2) to manipulate each element as follows:

$$\Omega(r_k(x), a_i(x)) = 1 - \frac{|\ p_{f,j} - p_{0,j}\ |}{|\ \widetilde{p_{0,j}} - p_{0,j}\ |}$$

Applying this process for each possible attack $a_i(x)$ yields the recommendation matrix N whose elements constitute the recommendation scores:

$$\begin{array}{c} \text{Attack } a_A \\ \begin{array}{cccc} -2 & -1 & 0 & 2 \end{array} = A \end{array} \qquad \begin{array}{c} \text{Attack } a_\omega \\ \begin{array}{cccc} -2 & -1 & 0 & 2 \end{array} = \omega \end{array}$$

$$N_A = \begin{bmatrix} 1 & 3/4 & \oslash & \oslash \\ 2/3 & 1 & \oslash & \oslash \\ 1/3 & 1/4 & \oslash & 1 \end{bmatrix} \begin{matrix} -2 \\ -1 \\ 2 \end{matrix} \ \text{Reply } r_A \qquad N_\omega = \begin{bmatrix} 1 & 3/4 & \oslash & \oslash \\ 2/3 & 1 & \oslash & \oslash \\ 1/3 & 1/4 & \oslash & 1 \end{bmatrix} \begin{matrix} -2 \\ -1 \\ 2 \end{matrix} \ \text{Reply } r_\omega$$

$$
\begin{array}{cc}
 & \text{Attack } a_\varphi \\
 & \begin{array}{ccccc} -2 & -1 & 0 & 2 & = \varphi \end{array} \\
N_\varphi = & \left[\begin{array}{cccc} 1 & \oslash & \oslash & \oslash \\ 1/2 & 1 & \oslash & \oslash \\ \oslash & \oslash & 1 & 1/2 \\ \oslash & \oslash & \oslash & 1 \end{array}\right] \begin{array}{c} -2 \\ -1 \\ -1 \\ 2 \end{array} \ \text{Reply } r_\varphi
\end{array}
\qquad
\begin{array}{cc}
 & \text{Attack } a_B \\
 & \begin{array}{ccccc} -2 & -1 & 0 & 2 & = B \end{array} \\
N_B = & \left[\begin{array}{cccc} 1 & \oslash & \oslash & \oslash \\ 1/2 & 1 & \oslash & \oslash \\ \oslash & \oslash & 1 & 1/2 \\ \oslash & \oslash & 0 & 1 \end{array}\right] \begin{array}{c} -2 \\ -1 \\ -1 \\ 2 \end{array} \ \text{Reply } r_B
\end{array}
$$

Sorting these scores to identify the best response $r_k(x)$ to attack $a_i(x)$ yields the final recommendation matrix N:

$$
\begin{array}{cc}
 & \text{Attack } a \\
N = & \left[\begin{array}{cccc} N_{A\in\mathfrak{A}} & \oslash & \oslash & \oslash \\ \oslash & N_{\omega\in\mathfrak{A}} & \oslash & \oslash \\ \oslash & \oslash & N_{\varphi\in\mathfrak{B}} & \oslash \\ \oslash & \oslash & \oslash & N_{B\in\mathfrak{B}} \end{array}\right] \ \text{Reply } r
\end{array}
$$

The critical infrastructure operator can now deploy this defense mechanism by a two-step evaluation. In the first step, the operator checks if the sum

$$\sum_{j=1}^{4}(p_{f,j} - p_{0,j})$$

equals zero. If so, then there is no difference between the steady-state information stored in $\overrightarrow{p_0}$ and the information stored in $\overrightarrow{p_f}$, that is, the information has not been altered. If the sum is not zero, the information has been manipulated, i.e., an attack has occurred. The operator can assess the impact of the attack by calculating, for each element stored in $\overrightarrow{p_0}$, the difference of

$$(p_{f,j} - p_{0,j})$$

If this difference is equal to zero for the respective parameter, the information is unaltered, and there is no need for action. In all other cases, the information was altered, i.e. an attack has occurred. For example, assume that $p_{0,2} = -2$, implying that an intruder has corrupted the steady-state information $\overrightarrow{p_0}$ to $\overrightarrow{\widetilde{p_{0,\omega}}} = (A_0, -2, \varphi_0, B_0)$. As a result, the original function $\sin(x)$ is corrupted to:

$$
\begin{aligned}
f(a_{\omega=-2}(x); \overrightarrow{p_0}) &= \sin(-2 \cdot x) \\
&= f(x; (A_0, -2, \varphi_0, B_0))
\end{aligned}
$$

Table 1 Response performances

Attacks ρ	Method	Solving time t_s (s)	Residual σ	Penalty $\mathfrak{H}$
100	MPR	$(1.062 \pm 0.004) \times 10^{-4}$	0	$(9.97 \pm 0.21) \times 10^{-2}$
100	RVR	$(1.162 \pm 0.006) \times 10^{-4}$	$(1.37 \pm 0.03) \times 10^{-1}$	$(9.99 \pm 0.21) \times 10^{-2}$
100	LRR	$(1.311 \pm 0.007) \times 10^{-4}$	$(2.75 \pm 0.04) \times 10^{-1}$	$(9.86 \pm 0.21) \times 10^{-2}$
1000	MPR	$(1.056 \pm 0.004) \times 10^{-4}$	0	$(9.98 \pm 0.21) \times 10^{-2}$
1000	RVR	$(1.149 \pm 0.006) \times 10^{-4}$	$(1.37 \pm 0.03) \times 10^{-1}$	$(9.98 \pm 0.21) \times 10^{-2}$
1000	LRR	$(1.319 \pm 0.007) \times 10^{-4}$	$(2.74 \pm 0.04) \times 10^{-1}$	$(10.03 \pm 0.21) \times 10^{-2}$
10,000	MPR	$(1.032 \pm 0.004) \times 10^{-4}$	0	$(10.00 \pm 0.21) \times 10^{-2}$
10,000	RVR	$(1.127 \pm 0.006) \times 10^{-4}$	$(1.38 \pm 0.03) \times 10^{-1}$	$(10.01 \pm 0.21) \times 10^{-2}$
10,000	LRR	$(1.294 \pm 0.007) \times 10^{-4}$	$(2.75 \pm 0.04) \times 10^{-1}$	$(9.99 \pm 0.21) \times 10^{-2}$

The operator can now consult the recommendation matrix N. For this particular attack, the response is $r_{\omega=-2}(x)$:

$$
\begin{aligned}
f(r_{\omega=-2}(x); (A_0, -2, \varphi_0, B_0)) &= \sin(-2 \cdot -\frac{1}{2} \cdot x) = \sin(x) \\
&= f(x; \overrightarrow{p_0})
\end{aligned}
$$

Finally, the operator can verify if the value of ω corresponds to its steady-state level; if not, the response can be applied iteratively.

4 Evaluation

The performance of the proposed defense system is evaluated by simulating three attack scenarios that comprise 100, 1000, and 10,000 attacks. Each of these three simulations is repeated 1000 times, and the results from each single simulation in each scenario are averaged.

In these interactions, responses given by the approach developed here are termed Most Preferred Response (MPR). These responses are compared to two alternative approaches, namely the random choice of a valid response from the resource matrix M (termed RVR), and the conscious choice of the response with the lowest rating in the recommendation matrix N (termed LRR).

These three response options are evaluated by the sum of residuals:

$$
\sigma = \sum_{h=1}^{5} \sum_{v=1}^{\rho} \mid p_{f,v}^{h} - p_{0,v}^{h} \mid
$$

where ρ captures each attack and $h \leq 5$ is a counter of how many times the defender has attempted to neutralize the attack.

If the information flow is still compromised after five attempts, or if no response to an attack can be given (i.e. the case of $A = \omega = 0$), a value of 1 is added a to a penalty variable $\mathfrak{H}$.

Table 1 documents the results of this evaluation. The proposed response method MPR yields the best defense performance. While some attacks cannot be defended against, implying some penalties, those attacks that can be defended are completely neutralized, as no residual remain. By comparison, both alternative response methods perform clearly worse. Since relatively few responses are specified in this particular illustration, RVR and MPR values differ little, but this difference can be expected to grow as the numerical magnitudes of both attack and response possibilities grow. Finally, LRR performs worst, implying that the effectiveness of responses can be reliably ordered by computing recommendation scores.

5 Conclusion

In contrast to approaches that emphasize resilience, the defense proposed here improves over time as operators witness attacks. Since after each round of attacks, data are recorded and the recommendation matrix is recalculated, the precision of the recommendation score improves, such that more effective responses are developed over time. Even if there is no immediate response to a novel type of attack, the recorded attack data can still be used for forensic analysis and thus inform the development of future responses for novel attack scenarios. Moreover, the defense proposed here is essentially iterative; the performance of any response can be measured, and the response can be deployed repeatedly until no residuals remain. Critical infrastructure defense therefore becomes the more effective the more often the system is attacked. Over time, a repository of effective responses is obtained, and effective responses from this repository can be recommended at short notice.

A significant advantage of recommender systems is that recommendation accuracy is independent of user demographics. The system need not consider any personal information since users reveal their preferences by picking and rating items. This fact implies that any recommender system can generalize recommendations for many users without loss of accuracy. The defense strategy proposed here is independent of particular system architectures or operators, and therefore it can be tailored to the idiosyncrasies of any specific system. Implementing such a system probably requires greater investments than approaches that rely on passive resilience, but these investments are rewarded by greater response effectiveness.

The strategy proposed here discusses a static case only, but it can be extended to more dynamic environments. First, the model can be dynamized by introducing temporal variables [5]. Thus, the model can continuously monitor attacks over time and decide autonomously when to deploy responses. Second, the model could consider a case where a single attacker targets several parameters at the same time, or a case where several agents attack simultaneously.

Effective recommender systems operate autonomously and do not require human intervention. Therefore, the system proposed here should be automated [3]. As the complexity of the attacker-defender interaction grows with the number of attackers and the introduction of temporal variables, the system should be able to learn autonomously and improve its own operating parameters. This type of machine learning will pave the way towards an automated defense of critical infrastructure and, ultimately, the development of artificial intelligence that only requires human intervention for performance measurement and code updates.

References

1. Briesemeister, L., Cheung, S., Lindqvist, U., Valdes, A.: Detection, correlation, and visualization of attacks against critical infrastructure systems. In: 2010 Eighth International Conference on Privacy, Security and Trust, pp. 15–22. IEEE, Piscataway (2010)
2. Brown, G.G., Carlyle, W.M., Salmeron, J., Wood, K.: Analyzing the vulnerability of critical infrastructure to attack and planning defenses. In: Emerging Theory, Methods, and Applications, pp. 102–123. Informs, Aurora (2005)
3. Cazorla, L., Alcaraz, C., Lopez, J.: Towards automatic critical infrastructure protection through machine learning. In: International Workshop on Critical Information Infrastructures Security, pp. 197–203. Springer, Berlin (2013)
4. Gordon, L.A., Loeb, M.P., Lucyshyn, W., Zhou, L.: The impact of information sharing on cybersecurity underinvestment: a real options perspective. J. Account. Public Policy **34**(5), 509–519 (2015)
5. Maglaras, L.A., Kim, K.H., Janicke, H., Ferrag, M.A., Rallis, S., Fragkou, P., Maglaras, A., Cruz, T.J.: Cyber security of critical infrastructures. Ict Expr. **4**(1), 42–45 (2018)
6. Mo, Y., Kim, T.H.J., Brancik, K., Dickinson, D., Lee, H., Perrig, A., Sinopoli, B.: Cyber–physical security of a smart grid infrastructure. Proc. IEEE **100**(1), 195–209 (2011)
7. Rinaldi, S.M., Peerenboom, J.P., Kelly, T.K.: Identifying, understanding, and analyzing critical infrastructure interdependencies. IEEE Control. Syst. Mag. **21**(6), 11–25 (2001)
8. Scarfone, K., Mell, P.: Guide to intrusion detection and prevention systems (idps). Technical Report, National Institute of Standards and Technology (2012)
9. Yu, F., Zeng, A., Gillard, S., Medo, M.: Network-based recommendation algorithms: a review. CoRR **abs/1511.06252** (2015). http://arxiv.org/abs/1511.06252
10. Zhou, T., Ren, J., Medo, M., Zhang, Y.C.: Bipartite network projection and personal recommendation. Phys. Rev. E **76**(4), 046115 (2007)

MIX
Papier aus verantwortungsvollen Quellen
Paper from responsible sources
FSC® C105338

Printed by Books on Demand, Germany